MULTICULTURAL
COU

DATE DUE

2/16/13			

Demco, Inc. 38-293

MULTICULTURAL COUNSELING

Perspectives from Counselors as Clients of Color

ARETHA FAYE MARBLEY

Routledge
Taylor & Francis Group
New York   London

Routledge
Taylor & Francis Group
270 Madison Avenue
New York, NY 10016

Routledge
Taylor & Francis Group
27 Church Road
Hove, East Sussex BN3 2FA

Printed in the United States of America on acid-free paper
10 9 8 7 6 5 4 3 2 1

International Standard Book Number: 978-0-415-95686-4 (Paperback)

Library of Congress Cataloging-in-Publication Data

Marbley, Aretha Faye.
   Multicultural counseling : perspectives from counselors as clients of color /
Aretha Faye Marbley.
      p. cm.
   Includes bibliographical references and index.
   ISBN 978-0-415-95686-4 (pbk. : alk. paper) 1. Cross-cultural
   counseling. 2. Psychiatry, Transcultural. 3. Minorities--Counseling of.
   4. Minorities--Mental health. 5. Minorities--Mental health services. I. Title.

BF636.7.C76M37 2010
158'.3089--dc22
                                                                    2010031853

Visit the Taylor & Francis Web site at
http://www.taylorandfrancis.com

and the Routledge Web site at
http://www.routledgementalhealth.com

My Two Best Friends

Donna Reynolds
12/4/1955–10/1/1996

Clinton Daylie
10/28/56–2/16/2002

My First Granddaughter

Ryann Michelle Dawson
Born 8/25/2008

Thanks, Donna and Clint. Though you did not live to see this happen, it is because of both of you that our vision shall live on. To my beautiful angel, Ryann Michelle, who has just arrived, I shall one day pass the baton to you to carry that vision of social justice and healing beyond and into the generations to come.

Contents

Preface
Treading on Sacred Ground

They are coming to bare their souls before you. That's sacred ground they are treading.

—Mai Li

My hand trembled slightly as I turned the doorknob and entered the room. With major trepidation after many days, perhaps weeks, of agonizing as to whether I should see a psychologist, I had finally gotten the nerve and courage to visit the student counseling center. Before college, the only thing that I knew about psychologists (I am not sure if I even knew the word psychologist) was that they helped crazy people. No one in my family had ever seen a mental health professional, unless you include my eldest sister, who, in 1968 at age 24, was confined to a mentally ill ward in Cook County Hospital on the west side of Chicago with a diagnosis of paranoid schizophrenia, and Mama (my Aunt Johnnie), who, 40 years earlier in 1928, from ages 20 to 24, was confined to what was then referred to as a lunatic asylum with a diagnosis of crazy.

To my knowledge, neither of them received therapy per se; my sister had extensive and massive shock treatments, and my mama was caged and treated like a wild animal and watered down with hoses for more than 4 years. Yet, unbelievably, here I stood frozen, a junior (a premed–psych major, in fact) at a prestigious research institution with several psychology courses under my belt, fearful to enter the office of a psychologist.

An old White man (looking back, he was probably about 41) stood up from behind a black reclining chair, took a cigar out of his mouth with his right hand, motioned with his left hand for me to take a seat to his right, and introduced himself as Dr. Schmidt. He then eased back down and slowly reclined back into his cushiony chair, put the cigar back in his mouth, and folded his hands behind his neck.

Strangely, he did not ask for my name or what brought me to counseling, just sat staring at me with steel-blue eyes. I waited for what seemed like 5 minutes before giving him my name. We sat another 5 minutes in silence. Slowly and shakily, I began spitting out information about my background, possibly to explain why I was there and partly to cover up my nervousness. As words rushed out, and I spilled my guts and told family secrets to a complete stranger, he said nothing, not a damn thing. He never even acknowledged that I was there, nor that I was human.

Exactly 50 minutes later, he stood up and said, "Your time is up." I stood up at once, feeling invisible and broken up inside from this inhuman experience; thanked him; and left hastily out of the door that I entered—never to return. Following this encounter, it would be more than 25 years before I would formally step foot into a White male therapist's (or anyone's) office for counseling.

Traditionally, the lack of success that people of color have experienced with counseling services has been accredited to factors such as inaccessibility, ethnicity and race differences, and Eurocentric epistemologies and axiology. Through counselors of color giving their points of view as clients, this book proffers an understanding of the engagement of clients of color in counseling services in the words of the clients of color themselves.

Regardless of the origin of their cultural stories, the essential point is that, with respect to language, delivery of characterization, and plot, as therapists, these individuals of color quickly made the stories their own and through them revealed much about themselves, their clients, their world, and their clients' world. My hope is that this book will equip mental health professionals with ways they can use stories as a creative process to help clients and counselors make breakthroughs in counseling. It is also my hope that the nature of their shared reality can be communicated to and understood by others in the context of the cultural traditions of the storyteller's people.

Through the storytelling (from multiple ethnic, racial, and gendered worldviews) of males and females from each of the four major U.S. groups of color (African American, American Indian, Asian and Asian American, and Hispanic/Latino), students will gain more insights into the failure of counseling services to provide people of color with more effective counseling services.

Accentuating the experiences of counselors of color in their roles as clients and counselors provides a greater understanding of the perceptions that people of color have of therapeutic services (including the counseling process, theory, and outcome) that have not previously been developed. Materials from this text may be used in the mental health profession and other interested fields to gain better insight into factors that hinder the success of people of color with counseling services as well as to facilitate an understanding of how to provide effective counseling services for people of color.

The book's focus is well suited for college-level counseling courses, and it may be a useful supplementary book for other courses in mental health such as psychology, marriage and family therapy, and social work. When possible and appropriate, the theoretical basis for grounding the chapters is shown. To that end, other mental health professionals will find it useful in their work with people of color. This book is also a supplementary textbook for multicultural counseling courses. In addition, it will be useful as a supplementary guide for other graduate-level courses addressing issues of access and the success of mental health services for people of color, diversity and multiculturalism, and multiple marginality. Efforts were made to make this book more useful and readable, capturing the richness of the diverse cultures of the individuals in this book.

Last, the experiences of the people in this book cross disciplines, including those of higher education, women's studies, sociology, and human sciences. Educators and practitioners working in an array of academic, health, and mental health areas will benefit from the discussions of initiatives geared to meet the comprehensive mental health needs of people of color.

Multicultural Counseling: Perspectives From Counselors as Clients of Color began with my dissertation and continues with my passion for social justice and critical social justice womanist and activist scholarship around the experiences of women and people of color in education and mental health. This book is a vehicle through which to hear their voices.

ORGANIZATION OF CHAPTERS

The reader will find an extensive array of topics, activities, and resources focusing on the disability experience. The book is divided into three major sections. The first section, "Counternarratives," contains chapters covering critical concepts and issues in counseling for people of color using firsthand accounts from real individuals. I begin Chapter 1 with the purpose and rationale for studying the experience that people of color have with mental health services. It zeroes in on research related to people of color and their experience with counseling and psychotherapeutic services. It emphasizes the importance of understanding counseling experiences that influence the decisions of people of color to terminate counseling early, report negative counseling outcomes, or not use counseling services.

Chapter 2 provides the background information highlighting the origin of the initial research study, its design and analysis, data on participants in the study, and the questions framing the research. For example, the individuals in this book are practicing licensed professional counselors (LPCs) or licensed marriage and family therapists (LMFTs). In the second section, Cultural Stores, Chapters 3 through 7 provide an overview of the literature on (respectively) African American, Asian and Asian American, Hispanic/Latino, Native American, and gender (men and women of color) historical experiences in mental health, followed by a discussion of the counselors' experiences as they relate to each of the emerging themes. Each of these chapters concludes with implications and recommendations for counseling and psychotherapy with that group.

In the third section, The Art of Forgiveness, Chapter 8 provides follow-up information for the participants 12 years after the original study. It revisits seven of the eight participants, then compares and contrasts their later responses to their earlier ones. Using a modified and abbreviated version of the original qualitative instrument, the participants respond to the original questions and incorporate their subsequent experiences as counselors and clients with mental health care. Last, Chapter 8 provides recommendations for transforming counseling to satisfy the needs of people of color.

Chapter 9 focuses on social justice efforts for women and people of color. This is a coauthored chapter (with graduate students) on social justice initiatives for women and each of the groups of color in the areas of education, politics, health, and mental health. It culminates with a call for the mental health field to take responsibility and perhaps consider making a public apology for its role in the historical and systematic injustices that women and people of color have suffered in mental health.

Chapter 10 concludes with the implications of practice, theory, and methods for the profession and future research; global recommendations for the mental health field; and higher education programs that are geared toward preparing clinicians and educators to address the mental health needs of individuals who are racially marginalized. This chapter also has a discussion of the impact of discrimination (racism, sexism, and bias) in academic and training programs and its relative influence on the matriculation into mental health experiences for people of color.

Acknowledgments

The image of my Great-Great-Grandma Evelina—a slave woman of the 18th century, treading onward through the wilderness of oppression and pain, with an unwavering faith in God and love for her family and a belief in the goodness of humanity—juxtaposed against that of Barack Obama, the first African American president of the United States, has been a source of inspiration. At the same time, both of them are a reminder of how far we have come as African American people and how much farther we have to go.

I am truly humbled by the unselfish sacrifices that so many have made so that I would have this opportunity to reach this level of achievement. Therefore, I begin by thanking my sources of inspiration, my African ancestors; without them, I would not be physically, nor spiritually, nor intellectually what I am today.

I thank Dr. Alice Denham for her sharp editorial eye, her knack for finding just the right words, her unlimited generosity, and, most of all, her sheer bravery to not only edit my work but also enter my world and walk with me on journeys unknown even to me. I would like to thank my dissertation team (though they advised me many years ago), Drs. Larry Burlew, Catherine Roland, the late Nudie Williams, and Nancy Haas, for their patience, guidance, support, and expertise as I completed the original qualitative study. Thanks also to my coauthors, Rachelle, Greg, ShaRhonda, and Julie.

I would also like to thank my participants, Joshua, Shawn, Mai Li, Wai, Angelica, Alexias, Lioma, and Woodro, for making me feel welcome throughout the study. As doctoral students, in many phases, even though they were in the midst of comprehensive exams, internships, finals, and defenses, and later as professionals in the midst of tenure, promotion, publishing, and grant seeking, they created time to talk and meet with me for hours. By opening themselves both personally and professionally (and reopening themselves 12 years later), their generous sharing made rich contributions to this book and has resulted in lifetime bonds and friendships.

Last but not least, I would like to thank the Almighty, and my family and friends (though many they are), for their love and support. A special thanks to my three mothers, Mae Helen, Sareor, and Johnnie, for my life, my spirit, and my soul. Thanks to my sisters and best friends, Juanita and Brenda, and all three sets of siblings: Ruth, the late Levi, Cornelius, James Jr., Norvella, and Carrie; Carol, the late Felecia, Cynthia, and Kim; and Larry (sister-in-law Barbara), the late Lou V., and Jaster. Thanks also to my other family: Bobbie and Cloteel (who are not only cousins but also sisters and friends); my nephews; my nieces, especially my fellow writer in residence, Loukisha Marbley; my cousins; and my aunts for a lifetime of inspiration. Your many phone calls, e-mails, letters, greeting cards, hugs, and kisses helped sustain me.

Thanks to my loving children, daughter ShaRhonda and son-in-law Brian; and to Courtney and Dominique (Cynthia) for their tolerance as I completed this book. Special thanks to my best friend, Dr. Fred Bonner II, a professor at Texas A&M University, and to my soul mate, Eddie Dixon, a teller of untold stories.

Thanks, Mama, for lending me your eyes, your special gift to love, and your glimpse of eternal life. Although you have transcended on, your love of life and people will live on through me and through so many others that I have shared it with, that they have shared it with, and so on, and so on. You were right: "Where there's a will, there's a way."

To the many women and people of color, young and old, who struggle every day for survival, I validate you and your experiences, and I salute you!

Section *I*

Counternarratives

1

From Hills and Molehills
All Across America

*T*he counseling field is struggling to find ways to metamorphose counseling to meet the needs of individuals who have been historically and currently marginalized—not only in the United States generally but also within its mental health systems. Research on the marginalization of people of color in mental health translating into a lack of success with counseling services has been attributed to variables such as inaccessibility, ethnicity and race differences, acculturation, racial identity, and Eurocentric epistemologies and axiology.

Dr. Martin Luther King's (1968) plea to let freedom ring "[f]rom the prodigious hilltops of New Hampshire, the mighty mountains of New York, the heightening Alleghenies of Pennsylvania, the snowcapped Rockies of Colorado, the curvaceous slopes of California and the hills and molehills of Mississippi" (p. 156) was a plea for liberty, that is, respect, equity, justice, and equal rights for people of all creeds, colors, and religions all across the United States. It was a gut-wrenching cry against the massive injustices committed against the descendants of the African people. But more importantly for those groups historically under bondage, it was not a plea for liberation but, rather, a demand for freedom.

For the past 300 years or more, anecdotes of massive injustices (like the following, captured by Carnes, 1995) have resonated from the hilltops, mountains, curvaceous slopes, and hills and molehills all across the United States. In the 1830s, forced from their homeland, Cherokee people walked into exile on the Trail of Tears; in 1842, a North Carolina slave girl escaped a nightmare and followed her dream to freedom; in 1885, Chinese laborers were attacked in Wyoming; in 1890, the U.S. government's campaign to subdue American Indians culminated in a massacre on the plains; in 1913, a Northern Jew became a scapegoat for Southerners' fears; in 1917, Mexican Americans endured a reign of terror by the Texas Rangers; in 1923, White Floridians wiped an African American community off the map; in 1942, a young Japanese American pondered the meaning of freedom behind barbed wire. Moreover, even today we have witnessed hate crimes such as the decapitation and dragging death of James Byrd Jr., an African American man, in 1998; and, as late as February 2006, the bombings of five Black churches (and four predominantly White churches) in Alabama (Dornin, Mattingly, Phelan, & Walsh, 2006). These stories of injustice, hatred, and intolerance are all real to people of color.

Additionally, contemporary and historical accounts of intolerance in the United States are found in folklore, novels, literature, movies, government documents, art galleries, museums, and so forth. They clearly reveal the United States' racist attitudes, biases, fears, and intolerance for differences. Carnes (1995) stated that even before the European settlers set foot on U.S. soil, they were corrupted with wild stories about the *savages* who resided there.

Unfortunately, the Gettysburg Address, Declaration of Independence, Bill of Rights, and preamble to the U.S. Constitution addressed and outlined the principles of democracy and the concepts of equality, justice, and freedom for all American people, but did not translate into actual rights for many of them. Sadly, marginalized groups such as women, people of color, people with disabilities, and lesbian, gay, bisexual, transgender, transsexual, queer, questioning, intersex, and allied (GLBTQIA) populations in the United States have yet to fully enjoy the promised freedom, justice, and equality put forth in these profound historical documents. To marginalized groups, the idea of equality and independence declared in 1776 still belongs to White, able-bodied, heterosexual men.

This chapter provides an overview of the historical treatment of people of color and the effects of environmental oppressors, such as racism and discrimination, followed by detailed accounts of the experiences of clients of color with counseling services. Counselors who hope to work with clients of color must start with a conceptually grounded framework that includes an understanding of the sociopolitical history of multiple oppressions that form the cultural context for their clients' presenting problems. It also covers how the mental health field in general and the counseling and psychotherapy areas in particular are microcosms of the United States' biases, specifically in their delivery of services to racially marginalized people.

Thus, first and foremost, this overview becomes a testament to the existence of several disparities affecting mental health care for people of color compared with White Americans. These disparities include the following: People of color (a) have less access to available mental health services, (b) are less likely to receive needed mental health services, (c) continually receive a poorer quality of mental health care in treatment, and (d) are underrepresented in nonpathological mental health research. The recognition of these disparities through the voices of people of color brings to the forefront information that can be seriously addressed and remedied. I offer guidance on future courses of action to eliminate these disparities and to ensure equality in access, utilization, and outcomes of mental health care.

This chapter is uniquely concerned with the perceptions of African Americans, Asians and Asian Americans, Hispanic Americans, and Native Americans regarding their experiences of counseling services. It also seeks to ask and answer questions relating to those factors identified in the mental health literature that may impact the success of clients of color in counseling, such as how the levels of education, racial identity, acculturation, and multicultural competencies and skills of professional counselors (specifically, counselors of color) influenced their professional roles in working with culturally diverse students, supervisees, and clients.

COUNSELING AND PSYCHOTHERAPY: MICROCOSMS OF AMERICAN RACISM

At the turn of the 21st century, 10 years into the new millennium, the counseling field continues its struggle to minimize mental health disparities and provide adequate mental health services for clients of color. This inadequacy is manifested in people of color underusing and having perceived dissatisfaction with counseling services. From multicultural-counseling research, inequities in mental health counseling services for clients of color have been attributed to factors such as clinicians being multiculturally incompetent; accessibility, ethnicity, and race differences; different acculturation of clients of color; the racial identity of both clients and clinicians; and counselors' Eurocentric epistemologies and axiology.

To further legitimize the mental health condition of people of color, the *Surgeon General's Report* (U.S. Department of Health and Human Services [USDHHS], 1999) was the first mental health report to acknowledge that all Americans, specifically people of color, do not share equally in the hope for recovery from mental illnesses. The report concluded, based on research, that groups of color do not have equal access to mental health care and receive poorer quality mental health services than the dominant group, and mental health care that is based on science is inadequate. This means that mental health care should also be based on relationships, respect, and cultural differences.

Epistemological racism can be defined as the current range of research epistemologies—positivism, and postmodernisms and poststructuralisms—that arise out of the social history and culture of the dominant race (Scheurich & Young, 1997). These epistemologies logically reflect and reinforce some social history and racial groups while excluding the epistemologies of other races and cultures; this has negative results for people of color in general and clients of color in particular. Guralnik (1976) referred to *racism* as any program or practice in which one race dominates; embedded in that definition is the notion of power. Starting with the modernist era, "European colonial and territorial expansion was typically undertaken under the rationale of the supremacy of White civilization, along with other rationales, such as those about economics and religion" (Scheurich & Young, 1997, p. 7). White folk have unquestionably dominated Western civilization for hundreds of years. Consequently, when one group dominates for centuries (as European Americans have), the ways of the dominant group become so deeply embedded that they typically are seen as the status quo or appropriate norms rather than as historically evolved social constructions. Fortunately, in the new millennium, we now have a richer vocabulary of words to describe the broader range of racism. For example, Derald Wing Sue's (2007) research has expanded on *postmodern racism* in counseling.

Further, the institutionalized cultural biases deeply implanted in our educational system and its epistemologies reflect the racism deeply ingrained in the United States' fabric, making academe and mental health (its derivative) mirror images of

American values and biases. In academe, the entrance of culturally diverse groups led to what Graff (1992) referred to as *culture wars*. Ironically, on one hand, the ivory tower stands with open arms, seemingly "welcoming diversity and innovation" (Graff, 1992, p. 6). On the other hand, however, academe occupies itself with minimizing, hiding, or ignoring race, class, gender, and nationality conflicts.

Consistently, in the mental health field, research reporting on the mental health problems of people of color reflects the social movements in the United States, and thus stands in part as a social microcosm of its biases. These biases are discussed in most of the earlier empirical research that focused on African Americans (e.g., Parham & Helms, 1981; Usher, 1989).

As further evidence of racial bias, many educators, social scientists, psychologists, and counselors subscribe to textbooks, theories, measurement tools and instruments, and research findings based almost entirely on a worldview and assumptions specific to a Euro-American culture. Earlier studies focused on race preference as a predictive variable in cross-cultural counseling studies. These studies are inconclusive in that the race factor may be a good or a single predictor of the active participation, continuation, or successful outcomes of clients of color in counseling.

Reasonably, then, one might argue that mental health practitioners have been trained in this unicultural perspective and practice. The counseling profession has perpetuated a uniperspective, the societal phenomenon of racism called *Eurocentrism*, which therefore exists as a reflection of historical injustices.

CONTEMPORARY EUROCENTRIC AND MULTICULTURAL THEORIES OF COUNSELING AND TRAINING

I believe that it is important for me to adapt myself and my style, and what I do, to the uniqueness of that person, whether it is a person; whether it is a system—a family; depending on what their culture is, what their situation is, what their needs are. So, I find myself maybe being more directive and providing more structure, if that's what the situation requires. Or I may be more of a sounding board if that's what the person needs.

Eclectic in the approach itself or in the techniques, but from a humanistic, existential kind of basic philosophy, health oriented and goal oriented, based on the goodness. I'm very system oriented, almost in terms of not looking at the individual, not that the individual is not here. But taking into account not just the family, but the whole system, society, the whole institution, and taking that into account, both in understanding the person and trying to help the person.

—Angelica

From a multicultural perspective, inadequately prepared mental health practitioners and researchers may account for some of the concerns related to clients of color. This inadequacy in clinicians' preparedness to work with a multicultural clientele may be linked to the current Eurocentric theoretical frameworks used for training counselors. The fact that these Eurocentric theories do not adequately explain, predict, describe, or provide useful interventions to culturally diverse clientele could be contributing factors to the ineffectiveness of counseling outcomes with clients of color.

In the last 20 years, much has been discussed and written on preparing educators and counselors to work in a diverse and pluralistic society, a movement away from training programs based on Eurocentric models. According to D'Andrea and Daniels (1997), three events influenced this movement: (a) the dramatically changing demographic makeup of the United States (a change into a majority of non-White citizens); (b) the failure of our educational and mental health delivery systems to adequately address the needs of people coming from different cultural backgrounds; and (c) the need to dismantle environmental barriers that impede individuals' ability to realize their human potential, such as racism and ethnocentric thinking. Yet, according to Ponterotto, Casas, Suzuki, and Alexander (2010), little guidance and leadership existed in how to deal effectively with multicultural issues more comprehensively and systematically. In short, many counselor education programs fell short in the training of skilled, competent multicultural counselors, most noticeably in the areas of counseling and supervision. Though little has changed, we are making major strides in that direction.

Moreover, multiculturalism is a growing influence in the entire mental health profession, and the counseling profession emerged as one of the precursors and frontrunners in the multicultural movement. For example, the American Counseling Association (ACA) was one of the first to establish a division dedicated to multicultural issues of culture, ethnicity, and race. Over the years, ACA also has published several books specifically addressing culture and race, and ACA frequently sponsors themes of diversity-responsive counseling at national, state, and regional conferences. In addition, there are several instruments available to assess multicultural competence for both counselors and counselor-training programs. In 1994, the Council for the Accreditation of Counseling and Related Educational Programs (CACREP) adopted multicultural standards that are required of all counselor preparation programs that apply for its accreditation. Last, the Association for Counselor Education and Supervision (ACES) responded to the multicultural standards and their implications for training and practice. However, the multicultural movement is by no means complete and is perhaps only in its infancy.

Mental Health, Race, and Ethnicity

The counseling would have to be unique. It would have to be molded or, um, what's the word I'm looking for—to that particular case. Fitted. Tailored to that particular case or that person.

—Alexias

Good mental health is fundamental to the prosperity of not only individuals but also societies, communities, and nations. It is vital for overall well-being, good health, wellness, and fitness as manifested in a person's ability to be productive and have functional relationships, resilient self-esteem, and healthy coping skills. In short, good mental health is essential to productivity in every arena of human life, including the functioning of a healthy society and its institutions such as families, schools, and communities.

The prevalence of mental illness and mental disorders such as depression, schizophrenia, and bipolar disorder is found globally and has similar rates for ethnic and racial groups, yet there are major mental health disparities and inequities for people of color as compared to Whites. This is especially evident among vulnerable groups such as those who are homeless, incarcerated, in protective care, and institutionalized, all of whom have a high need for mental health care. In these groups, not surprisingly, people of color are disproportionately represented.

In fact, the surgeon general's report titled *Mental Health: Culture, Race, and Ethnicity—a Supplement to Mental Health: Report of the Surgeon General* (USDHHS, 2001) revealed that issues of racial, ethnic, and cultural inequities and disparities exist in the availability, utilization, and quality of mental health services. These documented disparities in mental health care for people of color provide a solid rationale for the need to advance the field's knowledge and research, and find effective strategies and techniques for meeting the mental health needs of groups of color.

People of color, like the communities of color, are plagued with an abundance of social and psychological problems but are usually not as responsive to contemporary interventions when compared to mainstream clients. Simply put, despite the multitude of visible ills plaguing communities of color, people of color are not utilizing counseling services as often as Whites–European Americans.

A Theoretical, Conceptual, and Hypothetical Framework

Rogler, Malgady, and Rodriguez's (1989) research framework is used as a theoretical research lens to sort through the overwhelming amount of (and fragmented) multicultural literature on people of color and provide a coherent, useful framework to understand the migration of people of color through the mental health terrain. This framework, in theory, like the study of the individuals in this book, is interested in the successive experiences of clients of color, beginning with the emergence of the mental health problem and ending with the posttreatment period. The framework does not assume the success of the person's help-seeking effort in allaying the emotional problem that prompted the effort, and it does not predict where the effort will terminate. In this regard, the framework allows for research aimed at societal and historical forces to be included. As a consequence, this model emerges as an excellent theoretical framework for attempting to understand the phenomena of underutilization, premature termination, and reports of negative outcomes as they relate to the complexity of experiences of people of color with mental health services.

The conceptual framework organizes clinical service mental health research on people of color according to a hypothetical temporal sequence composed of five phases. Although the conceptual framework consists of five phases, this study concentrates on the four phases that are most pertinent to the study: phase 1, emergence of mental distress; phase 2, help-seeking behaviors; phase 3, evaluation of mental health; and phase 4, psychotherapeutic services. It briefly touches on phase 5, posttreatment adjustment, as it relates to people of color and their relationship to counseling and psychotherapeutic services.

Phase 1 traces the *emergence of the distribution of mental health problems* among people of color; mental distress created by the migration, relocation, and forced immigration of groups in the United States; and the stress process resulting from their experiences as ethnically and racially marginalized people. It covers the minority experience, intragroup differences as they relate to racial identity, multiple perspectives, and the history of the treatment of people of color, as well as the continuation of environmental oppressors.

Phase 2 covers *help-seeking behaviors*. It centers on how clients of color use and experience counseling services, and it investigates factors involved in underutilization and in alternative resources such as natural support networks. Phase 3 is concerned with the *evaluation of mental health*. It looks at acculturation (related to intragroup differences) and cultural bias in mental health measurements and assessment. It also examines factors influencing the mental health diagnosis of people of color in counseling interviews.

Phase 4, *psychotherapeutic services*, focuses on the literature related to clinical practice and the effectiveness of attempts to render therapeutic modalities culturally sensitive. It discusses factors involved in premature termination and failure to show positive outcomes, culturally sensitive therapeutic treatment for people of color, and counselor training and preparation. Phase 5, *posttreatment adjustments*, focuses on (a) the reintegration of the client into the family and the community, and (b) the posttreatment adjustment and the adequacy of services provided. It includes factors involved in successful or positive outcomes.

Next, the literature reviewed has been impacted by and is inseparable from sociohistorical, economic, and political factors, on top of environmental oppressors such as sexism, racial and cultural biases, prejudice, discrimination, and Eurocentric and ethnocentric thinking. Thus, this chapter will explicate contemporary Eurocentric and multicultural theories of counseling and training, and how the former contribute to perpetuating the discrimination.

Conversely, mental health literature related to racial identity, acculturation, and multicultural perspectives and competencies is introduced to help students understand the massive differences that exist with the groups of color and to aid in eliminating the stereotyping, thus providing effective counseling for people of color.

Underutilization, Premature Termination, and Ineffectiveness of Counseling Services

Within the complex processes of immigration and acculturation, fast growth is taking place in the United States' communities of color that ignited a multicultural movement and as a result will forever change the face of our nation. Despite the impact of the multicultural movement as the fourth force in counseling and psychotherapy and the progress that has been made in the field, racial and ethnic disparities continue. This means that despite the many standards and competencies set forth for working with culturally diverse populations, and even with the major push for counseling services and psychotherapeutic interventions that are culturally responsive and sensitive, the field is still unsuccessful in attracting, retaining, and providing effective services for people of color.

RACIAL IDENTITY, ACCULTURATION, AND MULTICULTURAL PERSPECTIVES AND COMPETENCIES

We are also very diverse people. Though there are very distinct differences, we all accept each other by tribe. There are certain commonalties that have the federal government treating us all essentially the same because they were dealing with indigenous people.

—Woodro

There are more differences than similarities. For the most part, we don't look at the differences in research; we try to lump everybody—all African Americans together, and Native Americans together—and deal with it that way, instead of looking at Cherokees, Chickasaws, Choctaws.

—Lioma

Research has shown that there are more differences found within each ethnic or racial group than are found solely between them (Herring, 1996; Rogler et al., 1989; Sue, Ivey, & Pedersen, 1996). Thus, acculturation, diverse or multiple experiences, and racial identity are tools that can be used to identify the massive differences within each group of color. These tools are interrelated with how people view themselves, how they view others, and how they perceive how others view them; the process of shedding societal racism and oppression; developing a nonracist, multicultural perspective; and levels of acculturation. Level of acculturation and stage of racial identity development are related to such factors as client dropout rate and attitude toward the counselor. For example, Sue and Sue (1990) found that for Hispanic Americans, the level of acculturation may influence the type of problems, the way problems are interpreted, the counseling process, and the goals in counseling.

Earlier empirical research examined factors such as acculturation, racial identity (Helms, 1995; Parham & Helms, 1981), and multicultural perspectives (Ivey, Ivey, & Simek-Morgan, 1993; Pedersen, 1997; Sue, Arredondo, & McDavis, 1992) as a method of surveying intragroup differences found within groups of color.

The Entrance of Multiculturalism

Pedersen (1991) described multiculturalism as the fourth force in counseling and psychotherapy, that is, one that was powerful enough to ignite a movement. In a more provocative manner, Solomon and Solomon (1993) spoke of multiculturalism as "[t]he most important, the most stimulating and, at the same time, the silliest movement that has touched the university in years" (p. 184). Regardless of its importance, stimulation, or silliness, at the turn of the 21st century, the multicultural movement has infiltrated nearly every academic discipline and major field, meeting resistance while provoking controversy and debate, and has rooted itself firmly in the fabric of the academy.

Multiculturalism, along with Sue and others' (1992) multicultural-counseling competencies and standards, has challenged not only ACA and the American Psychological Association (APA) but also nearly every academic discipline and professional field of study to rethink their ethical guidelines, training programs, and Eurocentric paradigms. Thus, for nearly a half century, researchers in mental health have attempted to generate ideas concerning the lack of success with people of color.

The Euro-American establishment continues despite the fact that the majority of the people in the world are non-European, non-American, and non-Western. These unchallenged worldviews and theoretical assumptions help to continue the practices of racism and of ethnocentric attitudes, fears, and intolerance for a mere acceptance of differences. For instance, assumptions that African Americans and other ethnically different groups are intellectually inferior, based on work by European researchers such as Herrnstein and Murray (1994), undermine and negate the arguments and findings of most scholars of color as to the reasons why most people of color are not scoring higher on standardized tests.

Despite multicultural reform initiatives, such as extensive diversity training in most master's and doctoral counseling programs, published multicultural competency standards, mandatory diversity courses, and a code of ethics that recognizes and infuses diversity by embracing a cross-cultural approach, people of color are still not faring well in counseling, although there have been some clear improvements. Despite having diversity training and the awareness, knowledge, and skills to work with diverse groups, many clinicians are still ill equipped to meet the needs of clients of color. Consequently, counselor educators and scholars are relentlessly searching for therapeutic models, techniques, and frameworks that take care of the needs of people of color.

THE DISTRIBUTION OF MENTAL HEALTH PROBLEMS AMONG PEOPLE OF COLOR

This perpetuation of the notion of intellectual, social, and economic inferiority based on Eurocentric axiology and epistemologies makes a real understanding of the distribution of mental health problems among people of color at worst skewed and at best inconclusive. A more factual understanding of the manifestation of mental health problems as applied to folk of color appears to be sandwiched somewhere between an oppressive historical and contemporary reality and the racism and epistemological racism evident in the research and clinical practice that sustain the counseling profession.

Mental Distress Created by the Migration, Relocation, and Forced Immigration Experiences

For nearly 3 centuries, Black and White issues have dominated U.S. culture, and over the years they have expanded to include the experiences of other groups of color. These issues have been accompanied by race issues, including oppression, racism, and discrimination, and have spread into all corners of both academe and the mental health professions. Much research has been conducted on the mental distress and damaging economical, social, and psychological effects of the migration experience on Hispanics and Asians; the effects of relocation and its continuing saga against American Indians; and the forced immigration—and 300 years of slavery—of African Americans.

The Minority Experience and the Stress Process: A Historical Perspective on Mental Health

Although there are historical differences in the logistics of the abuse levied against these racial and ethnic groups, the commonalties of their oppressions have linked them in what could be referred to as a "minority experience" of living in the United States. For most groups of color, these environmental oppressors, combined with vast cultural differences and a distinct psychological reality, are yet to be adequately addressed in mental health research and clinical practice.

The firsthand experiences of people of color with U.S. racism, prejudice, discrimination, and multiple other injustices are widespread and continue to be felt strongly. Traces of centuries of vicious mistreatment levied against Native Americans, Asians, Hispanics, African Americans, and others linger all across the United States and all across this world. These experiences are visible not only in the research but also in art galleries, museums, folklore, and novels such as Harper Lee's (1960) *To Kill a Mockingbird*, Crow Dog and Erdoes's (1990) *Lakota Woman*, and Dews's (1995) *This Fine Place So Far From Home*. Other examples of this widespread mistreatment and betrayal of people of color have been mentioned in this chapter in Carnes's (1995) stories of great historical injustices and hatred mounted against people of color living in the United States (e.g., the African American community wiped off the map by White Floridians in 1923).

Environmental Oppressors in Mental Health

Until about the last 20 years, differences in cultural values and worldviews have been virtually ignored or omitted in the research, literature, and theories that support clinical practice in the area of counseling and psychotherapy. It has taken the projection of a future demographic shift in the racial makeup of the United States to change the focus to the importance of counselors being prepared for a pluralistic society.

Not surprisingly, racial issues such as bigotry, racism, and discrimination have remained prevalent in the mental health field. Historically, academe has approached conflict as quietly and passively as possible, and counseling programs housed within universities are no different. Nevertheless, in the counseling field, some researchers and educators have taken the positive stance that counselor education programs genuinely value diversity. Like academe, these authors seem rather too quickly to glide over the conflict that accompanies diversity: The conflict that multicultural issues bring clashes with the innate status quo posture. Counseling programs simply have bypassed addressing the conflict and processing the issues surrounding cultural diversity and have gone straight for the solutions—the strategies.

If racism is evident in programs or practices where one race dominates, as in the counseling profession, then one might reasonably argue that this profession in some ways perpetuates this social supremacy. This domination of theories, research, and clinical practice based on a Eurocentric orientation has resulted in what is now being referred to as *cultural encapsulation*. Recently, researchers in the field of multicultural counseling and psychotherapy have concentrated on such variables as racial identity development, acculturation, and multicultural perspectives in order to explain the enormous intragroup differences found within ethnic and racial groups.

Intragroup Differences: Racial Identity and Multiple Perspectives

Some of the problems hindering progress with diverse groups may have resulted from the pendulum swinging away from individual differences and toward group similarities. This swing has often resulted in misinterpretation and overgeneralization. Thus, recent research has focused on the phenomenon of intragroup differences existing within all ethnic and racial groups. The enormous differences existing within the various ethnic and racial groups residing in the United States make generalizing and theorizing based on racial or ethnic group affiliation complex, difficult, and seemingly impossible.

Racial and Ethnic Identity Development

In 2000, for the first time, the U.S. Census Bureau allowed for multiple racial categories. Historically, it has been the dominant culture (usually via the Census Bureau) that has maliciously and haphazardly created labels for people of color. First, for people of color, names have significance and thus are emotionally charged. Next, historically, those imposed labels have been hurtful, harmful, denigrating, and destructive to their racial uplifting. For example, for African Americans, there are distinct differences among the imposed labels of the *N word*, *Negro*, and *Colored* in contrast to *Black*, *Afro-American*, *people of color*, and *African American*. Similarly, Native American Indians feel strongly and differently about the terms *Indian*, *Native American*, and *American Indian*, as do Hispanics and Latinos for the terms *Hispanic* and *Latino(a)*.

Theorists and researchers in the counseling field began to look at racial identity development as one means of explaining the differences found in these studies as well as the massive differences found within each racial and ethnic group in counseling encounters (Cross, 1987, 1991; Helms, 1985, 1989, 1990). Studies of racial identity, though distinct from but interrelated and linked to race, began to gain momentum in the counseling literature.

According to Greeley, Garcia, Kessler, and Gilchrest (1992), a starting place for this assessment of racial consciousness is with instruments created to assess stages of racial identity development. Helms (1990), in contrast, considered racial consciousness and racial identity interrelated but distinct. She claimed that racial consciousness pertains to the awareness that (socialization due to) racial-group membership can influence one's intrapsychic dynamics as well as interpersonal relationships, whereas racial identity is concerned with the quality of that awareness or the various forms in which awareness can occur, that is, identity resolution. (Helms, 1990, p. 7)

Nevertheless, there is awareness that some measure of cultural, ethnic, or racial identity is essential for most counseling situations.

Race is defined as culture that is biologically determined or in genetically discrete groups. People tend to categorize themselves into race categories based on physical and visible characteristics such as skin color, hair texture, nose shape, and eye color. Research shows that race accounts for a small percentage of the differences that exist among ethnic and racial groups (Long & Kittles, 2003; Witherspoon et al., 2007). That is to say, racial differences between these groups are small—a lot smaller than variations within the groups themselves. In other words, genetically speaking, race does not exist in modern humans, even though more recent studies have shown that self-identified race matches respondents' genetic background (Boerwinkle, Schork, & Risch, 2005; Rosenberg, Pritchard, Weber, Cann, & Kidd, 2002). This means that the concept of race as defined by physical features or intellectual abilities is not valid from a biological perspective; therefore, physical traits reflect phenotype and do not provide information on genes.

Some notable scholars (Asante, 2003; Billingsley, 1993; Staples, 1984), including earlier intellectuals such as James Baldwin and W. E. B. Dubois, have believed that the concept of race was created by opportunist White European and American elites, and has been used to deny property, power, and status to non-White groups for more than 4 centuries. In other words, race is a psychological, socially constructed (and even federally legislated), unneeded term that has been imported into mental health from a racist society.

In distinguishing race from racial identity, Helms (1990) defined *racial identity* as referring to a "sense of group or collective identity based on one's perception that he or she shares a common racial heritage with a particular racial group" (p. 3). In addition, "racial identity refers to the quality or manner of one's identification with the respective racial groups" (Helms, 1990, p. 5).

Although some identity models appear to use *race* and *ethnicity* synonymously, Helms further distinguished race and ethnicity using Casas's (1984) definition of ethnicity "as a group classification of individuals who share a unique social and cultural heritage (customs, language, religion, and so on) passed on from one generation to another" (p. 4). In reality, members of different racial groups could share the same ethnic group, and, likewise, members from different ethnic groups need not share the same racial group.

Identity work is one way to become more self-aware. This is an important assessment tool for counselors working in a multicultural environment to aid in understanding some of within-group differences. Rollock, Westman, and Johnson (1992) felt that White professionals who do not increase their cultural knowledge have propensities toward overpathologizing and, by their refusal to take on other roles to deal with practical problems, tend to undermine therapeutic effectiveness.

Finally, because of the massive intragroup differences, including different generations, the process of self-labeling is not without confusion, internal controversy, or difference of opinions. Nevertheless, I have made every effort in categorizing groups of color to be respectful of each group's right to self-identify, and to provide a rationale for the terms I used to identify each group of color in this book.

Help-Seeking Behavior

There are two aspects relevant to phase 2, *help-seeking behavior*: (a) the extent to which people of color, in relation to their needs, underutilize mental health services; and (b) the interrelationships among the factors that explain underutilization. This section examines research on factors involved in underutilization, including alternative help-seeking behavior, such as the use of indigenous or natural support systems.

Factors Involved in Utilization

The underutilization of mental health services by people of color is well documented, and it is a complex, multitiered, macrolevel problem. For example, when clinical settings provide services that are bilingual, bicultural, and in ethnic neighborhoods, people of color tend to use the services more. Earlier studies have examined underutilization as it relates to variables such as preference for a counselor, credibility, racial identity, and alternative resources.

Alternative Resources: Indigenous Support Systems

Sue, Ivey, and Pedersen (1996) proposed that multicultural counseling and therapy (MCT) theory acknowledges traditional healings and advocates the integration of those helping traditions indigenous in non-Western, non-European cultures. Corollary 5C of the MCT theory states, "Though the Western meaning of counseling developed from a Euro-American academic setting in the 20th century, counseling has been available historically whenever individuals have helped other individuals with personal problems" (Sue et al., 1996, p. 21). For most groups of color, both contemporary and traditional indigenous systems exist as viable healing and helping networks in their communities.

Indigenous support systems refer to those sources of help that occur naturally within the traditions of many non-European, non-Western cultures. Historically, these natural support systems predated Western civilization, serving as a source of help for solving personal, spiritual, and vocational problems. Past studies of natural support or indigenous models have described healing practices in Asian, Native American, African, and Hispanic cultures (Idowu, 1992; Kakar, 1982; Lee, 1996; Lin; 1983; Makinde, 1974; Vontress, 1991). For example, in Mexico and Mexican American communities, traditional healers (*curanderos* and *curanderas*) use herbalism, chants, music, and massages to alleviate mental and physical suffering;

and in certain tribes of West Africa, herbalists or healers use spiritual forces to eliminate physical and mental health problems. Billingsley (1968) wrote,

> The Negro community includes within itself a number of institutions which may also be viewed as subsystems. Chief among these are: schools, churches, taverns, newspapers, neighborhood associations, lodges, fraternities, social clubs, age and sex peer groups, recreation associations, and small businesses, including particularly, barber shops, beauty parlors, restaurants, pool halls, funeral societies, and various organized systems of hustling. (p. 24)

Acculturation

Acculturation is another variable that has been linked to the underuse of counseling services by clients of color. Acculturation entails "the complex process whereby the behaviors and attitudes of the immigrant change toward those of the host society as a result of exposure to the latter's cultural system" (Rogler et al., 1989, p. 5). Further, the acculturative problems associated with immigration, relocation, and forced immigration are thought to be multiple and stress inducing. The problematic issues surrounding acculturation embody the negative effects of being exposed to racism, discrimination, and prejudice, and they result from the psychological and interpersonal changes associated with people of color adjusting to the host society; a stripping, stealing, or abandonment of one's cultural identity and values in a hostile society; the acquiring of prestige, status, and economic goods that go along with having arrived; and the strain of having to separate from one's referent group or family.

Factors Influencing the Diagnosis of People of Color in a Counseling Interview

Some of the factors involved in the misdiagnosis of clients of color are related in part to culturally insensitive and biased instruments. Recently, multicultural research has focused on other factors, such as researcher biases, epistemologies, and axiology. Professionals of color working with a White clientele in a counseling situation, who are ignorant of cultural knowledge, also risk therapeutic ineffectiveness. Last, in the areas of measurement and assessment, Sedlacek (1994) identified five diversity issues plaguing the field of counseling: (a) what groups should be included, and what terms should be applied to those groups; (b) the development of a single instrument or measure that would be valid for all; (c) studies and research that were not designed for culturally different people; (d) the importance of missing or incomplete data, and how the lack of those data may bias the sample and invalidate the instruments and the procedures; and (e) a shortage of well-trained professionals working in this area.

Psychotherapeutic Services

Psychotherapeutic services (phase 4) address two research issues related to the appropriateness and effectiveness of mental health treatment services provided to people of color. The issues addressed in this phase are drawn from research on the relation-ship between therapy and culture defined in the literature and how it relates to cul-turally sensitive treatments for people of color. This phase addresses (a) emic (culture specific) or etic (universal) approaches to counseling; (b) contemporary approaches; and (c) the development of culturally appropriate therapeutic interventions.

Culture can be defined as the "totality of manners, customs, and values of a given society, inclusive of its socioeconomic system, political structures, science, religion, education, art, and entertainment" (Wolma, 1989, p. 80). Because ethnic differences embody a broader class of variables than do culture, Sue and Zane (1987) argued that ethnicity should not be used as a substitute for culture. Further, according to Sue and Zane (1987), ethnicity is more directly related to the thera-peutic relationship and indirectly related to the therapeutic process. Other stud-ies (Sue & Zane, 1990; Bryson & Cody, 1973; Burrell & Rayder, 1971) looking at ethnic and racial differences have indicated that variables such as the counselor's credibility, expertise, and attractiveness were more important than racial and cul-tural variables.

Multiple Perspectives

Urgency for the inclusion of a multicultural perspective is foremost in our pro-fession and long overdue. Although awareness of and responsiveness to cultural diversity are needs that reach far beyond the areas of education and counseling, multiculturalism has shaken and rocked the cornerstones of counseling and psy-chotherapy. Multiculturalism has emerged as the fourth force in counseling and psychotherapy, sparking a multicultural-counseling movement.

Multicultural counseling is loosely defined as any counseling relationship in which the client and the counselor belong to different cultural groups, hold dif-ferent assumptions about social reality, and hold different worldviews (Das, 1995). Vontress (1988) defined multicultural counseling as "counseling in which the coun-selor and the client are culturally different because of socialization acquired in distinct cultural, subculture, racioethnic, or socioeconomic environments" (p. 74). In a similar vein, Pedersen (1988) described multicultural counseling as a situation in which two or more people with different ways of perceiving their social environ-ment are brought together in a helping relationship. With a slightly different view-point, Axelson (1993) described multicultural counseling as the "interface between counselor and client that takes personal dynamics of the counselor and client into consideration alongside the emerging, changing, and/or static configurations that might be identified in the cultures of the counselor and client" (p. 13).

Posttreatment–Adjustment

Phase 5, the *posttreatment–adjustment* phase, begins after the client terminates therapy. Posttreatment–adjustment explores the posttreatment–adjustment issues of clients of color. Certainly, most of the research presented touched on factors inad-vertently or directly affecting posttreatment–adjustment and the adequacy of ser-vices provided as they relate to reintegrating people of color into their families and communities. For example, the changing ethnic profile of the United States, with its changes in immigration and migration patterns and changes in ethnic group population characteristics, has had a snowball effect on every aspect of the interactions of people of color with counseling services.

In summary, empirical studies adequately support the assertion that people of color are not faring well in counseling. Factors such as racial identity, the training and development of counselors and clients, culturally insensitive theories and counselors, the level of acculturation of clients of color, counselors' lack of multicultural training, culturally biased assessments, and a lack of trust on the part of clients of color add a lot of weight to whether clients of color underuse, prematurely terminate, and have negative outcomes with counseling services.

2

An Amalgam of Cultural Stories

It's 2:15 a.m. Sunday morning, and I sit here at my computer analyzing my data and grappling with my feelings and thoughts about my chosen profession.

One of the final questions I had asked each of the participants was to use a word or phrase that would capture what they felt about counseling.

Sitting here reflecting, I began to hear each of their distinct voices one by one. All eight of their male and female voices—the African Americans, American Indians, Hispanics and Latinos, and Asians begin to chime in such unison and humanness—with a sort of collective consciousness, capturing the essence of what we do as counselors. Rather than marginality, inequities, social injustice, racism, oppression, and discrimination, their words ring out with messages of growth, renewal, compassion, collaboration, spirituality, conviction, faith, and hope.

One by one, their words (which capture what counseling means to them) resonated in my mind: "Ambivalence, because that's my idea of counseling in real life; how it's taught and how it's practiced"; "A relationship between two people: I have to look at it that way"; "It reminds me of a caterpillar that turns into a butterfly"; "Unique, because everyone, every case, every individual is unique in his or her own way"; "Like smoke—it starts from the outside and you breathe it in and it totally covers you to purify you"; "It's like a pilgrim's journey and this person has invited me to walk with him for the short stretch, and for that short period of time our paths intersect. The Bible says, 'In a multitude of counselors, there is safety'"; and "The word is hope. Yes, that's it: I feel hopeful."

As I close my entry for the night, I reflect on those messages, culturally significant yet such profound and humanly connected messages that profess a belief in our profession and its future. These individuals in their roles as healers found growth, renewal, respect, faith, and hope in the counseling relationship. Because of the revelation and discovery in their journeys, when I think about the future of people of color in counseling, I feel hopeful. Yes, that's it; I feel hopeful.

In an effort to further bridge that gap in the literature on the experiences of people of color in mental health, this book was undertaken with multiple purposes in mind. First, the voices of the individuals in this book bring clarity to the existing multicultural theoretical and empirical research in regard to the encounters of people of color with mental health services. Next, it provides firsthand insight into the experiences of people of color with counseling services that best illuminate why most people of color tend to underutilize, prematurely discontinue, or report unsuccessful outcomes in counseling. Through the experiences, stories, and testimonials of the nine individuals in this book (the eight study participants, and a ninth participant who was in the follow-up study), some of the factors that contribute to or hinder clients of color using counseling services are discovered.

To set the stage for the remainder of the book, this chapter provides background information on a previous study I conducted that looked at people of color and their experiences with mental health services. The next four chapters focus specifically on this study—chronicling and explicating the experiences of African Americans, Asians and Asian Americans, American Indians, and Hispanics and Latinos, respectively.

Without providing a pedantic and exhaustive discussion of the research methods used in this investigation, this chapter will provide a cursory overview of the participants, the settings, findings related to the research questions in the initial study, and other salient aspects of the study's design. Based on the participants' experiences as both clients and counselors, Chapters 3, 4, 5, 6, 7, and 8 specifically address their experiences, whereas Chapter 9 will take a closer look at social justice issues for these groups and Chapter 10 provides critical recommendations and conclusions.

AN INSIDER'S PERSPECTIVE

Although my experiences and those of the individuals in the case studies are not meant to be representative of all people of color, they do, however, echo those of so many others who look, act, and think like us—me and these individuals of color. So, as a result of my experiences and the experiences of the individuals interviewed, this book was intended to provide inside conversations about mental health services with clients of color who understand the counseling language as well as the stories, voices, and utterances of clients of color who have not been fully heard.

The study participants are seasoned counselors with a shared professional identity, and the use of technical language was instrumental and fundamental to the establishment of a shared context of understanding among them and other clients of color. As such, not only did they have the experience and perception of clients, but also, by their status as practitioners, educators, supervisors, and students of counseling (being on this side of the tracks, so to speak), they had the concepts, rich language, and inside knowledge of the counseling profession that clients who are not mental health professionals (those on the other side of the tracks) may have lacked. Care was taken to ensure that the interpretation and analysis of their language and nonverbal behaviors are culturally appropriate and grounded in their cultural frameworks.

The voices of these counselor-clients provide inside perspectives from professional counselors who have experienced the marginality, inequities, and silencing of people of color in mental health. As a result of their status, experiences, and knowledge, they provide insider insight into the low retention rate among, underuse by, and lack of success with clients of color in counseling that heretofore has been lacking. By listening to the voices of these counselors of color as clients who are more likely to have a greater understanding of the therapeutic process, counseling theory, and counseling outcomes, the mental health profession gains better insight in distinguishing the professional biases of counselors who seek therapy versus the naïveté and different expectations of regular clients.

THE INITIAL STUDY

A Phenomenological Approach

In the advancement of multicultural education and training, qualitative studies become vehicles to better understand the nature of these traditions, worldviews, and support systems. These studies can conceivably better serve and retain people of color in counseling. Including the perceptions of clients of color regarding their experiences adds depth that number crunching in quantitative research cannot. Briefly, this multiple-case-studies approach was designed from a phenomenological theoretical orientation in order to fully understand their unique personal and professional experiences and perceptions of counseling, counselors, and counseling outcomes.

The four case studies consisted of four males and four females who self-identified as members of one of the four major ethnic U.S. groups of color—African American, Asian or Asian American, Hispanic or Latino, and American Indian—with the understanding that there are members of other racial groups residing in the United States who also identify as non-White. Eight individuals participated in my initial research study: Joshua, Shawn, Wai, Mai Li, Woodro, Lioma, Angelica, and Alexias. Yuchen (an Asian female) was added during the 12th year follow-up phase in Chapter 8. At the onset of the study, each of these individuals chose a pseudonym of personal or ethnic significance to them, and these pseudonyms are used throughout the book.

They were licensed professional counselors (LPCs) and doctoral students enrolled in counselor education and marriage and family therapy programs in the south-central region of the United States (Texas, Arkansas, Oklahoma, Tennessee, and New Mexico) who had shunned, dropped out of, or experienced what they perceived to be unsuccessful counseling as clients. The females ranged in age from 26 to 42, with a mean age of 36.5; the men ranged in age from 40 to 50, with a mean age of 45.

The initial study was conducted in five parts: (a) a standard open-ended interview, (b) informal conversational interviews, (c) interactive follow-up interviews, (d) the administration of Racial Identity Attitude Scales, and (e) a debriefing and interpretation of the instruments. In-depth, open-ended interviews; direct observation; and collection and examination of written documents were the qualitative data collection methods used. In conjunction with personal interviews and observations, written documents and data that consisted of detailed descriptions of their activities, actions, and feelings and the full range of interpersonal interactions were collected.

As part of the study, each person self-administered one or more of three racial identity instruments that best described their race—the White Racial Identity Attitude Scale (WRIAS), Black Racial Identity Attitude Scale (BRIAS), and/or People of Color Racial Identity Attitude Scale (POCRIAS)—and were later debriefed. They maintained a journal about any comments, feelings, or reactions related to any parts of the study. Telephone, electronic, and in-person follow-up interactive interviews were conducted throughout the data collection phase and periodically during the 12 years between the original and follow-up segments of the study. Secondary sources consisted of personal accounts (i.e., diaries, journals, and personal notes) and clinical documents.

Last, each of them provided documents that indicated the number or percentage of clients of color they had seen. They shared any of their old journals, diaries, or materials that provided significant information regarding their experiences with counseling services but that did not violate their clients' confidentiality. Detailed descriptions of each of the individuals are included in the subsequent chapters.

Findings

Three major themes emerged as important factors with people of color in their use of, retention in, and success with counseling services: *bias, credibility,* and *culture. Bias* is used to describe experiences of discrimination or prejudice due to gender, race or ethnicity, or socioeconomic status. Regarding *credibility, increased minority representation* in counseling is used to convey the strong affective component of clients of color having individuals who are culturally, ethnically, and racially like them, individuals whom they trust to understand them. *Culture* includes *culture-centered networks* and *interventions, homegrown representation,* and *cultural knowledge.*

Bias   Bias, in terms of gender, socioeconomic conditions, and race and culture, affected the counselors of color in their experiences and perceptions of counseling. First, gender preference was an important consideration for their roles as clients. Second, socioeconomic bias was an important factor in determining their utilization of counseling services. Participants' perceptions of socioeconomic factors were divided in terms of cost (e.g., the inability of clients of color to pay for counseling services) and counseling as a middle- and upper-class phenomenon. Consequently, traditional, less acculturated, economically marginal clients of color are shunning counseling.

Credibility   They viewed dialoguing with the client through language and conversation as a chance to build up trust and construct a safe environment for the client. In short, they believed that clients of color often need more time to make the necessary language and cultural translations, make sure the environment is safe, and avoid being misunderstood. And, last, they advocated for more minority representation in counseling. Some of them felt strongly that it was a necessity for the specific groups of color to do work with their specific groups.

Culture   From their views, culture involves (a) traditional counseling and clients' support systems coming together within partnership, (b) divine intervention, and (c) tailor making something. They all felt that it was essential to have sensitivity to the client culture, to respect the massive intragroup differences existing within their individual cultures, and not to generalize cultural information. They also felt that it was key to have a collaborative approach with indigenous systems and that counselors working in a multicultural situation have to be creative in finding ways that are acceptable and compatible with traditional cultures. In other words, each ethnic group has its own culture with traditions, indigenous systems, nuances, and mores, and a unique history and sense of spirituality. Thus, counselors must honor those differences by using theories, techniques, and strategies that are consistent with the cultural background of their clients.

Racial Identity, Level of Acculturation, and Level of Multicultural Competency

In order to address the cultural differences present within each case study, the participants identified their ethnic group as being separate from their racial group. Further, in order to understand some of the within-group differences of each case study, each person was assessed for level of acculturation, stage of racial identity development, and multiple perspectives via his or her multicultural awareness and knowledge. According to the scores on the instruments, all eight were in the Internalization stage of racial identity development. Last, although they were acculturated to the majority culture and embraced many aspects of the dominant culture, all of them maintained strong ties to and affiliations with their ethnic group.

Are people more alike than different? Contrary to Lioma and Woodro's focus on differences (as evident by their words quoted in Chapter 1, section on Racial Identity, Acculturation, and Multicultural Perspectives and Competencies), I held the belief that people are more alike than different. At the end of the initial interviews, I discovered that we were saying the same thing. However, as an African American, for me being different meant discrimination. In contrast to Lioma and Woodro, in the American Indian world likeness is understood, but differences are celebrated.

Storytelling

I guess I like people's stories and talking about life. I like to understand behavior or why things happen.

—Angelica

I wrestled with how to endow Joshua, Shawn, Wai, Mai Li, Woodro, Lioma, Angelica, and Alexias's experiences within their cultural contexts with meaning, that is, how to share these individuals' perceptions and experiences with mental health services and professionals in a way that would be factual, grounded, and reflective of the color and richness of their gendered, racial, ethnic, and cultural backgrounds. I wanted to adopt a brave and intriguing metaphor with a cultural, spiritual persona and, most importantly, one that crosses and transcends cultural barriers.

According to Eisner (1991), a metaphor can be a powerful tool to aid the researcher in examining actions with a renewed sense of curiosity. The cultural story, which as of late has been used in family therapy, is the metaphor used to refer to the process of being allowed to tell personal stories in such a way that they encompass social constructions of ethnicity, the life cycle, class, and race and are within the context of society's stories (McGill, 1992). In fact, these participants indicated in their interviews that they have a sense of curiosity about people and their stories.

As I reflected on how they shared their lived experiences and how I listened, I remembered the art of storytelling that was so much a part of my growing up and a tradition and ritual in the African American community. I remembered sitting next to each of these individuals, totally and personally enthralled by what they were telling me and how that conjured up old memories of me sitting across from old folks, reliving the vivid memories of their past lives and adventures. It was then that it hit me: "Yes, that's it, storytelling—the perfect metaphor for their cultural stories!"

Cultural Stories and the Art of Storytelling

I, like other scholars of color, have written out of a need to be heard. Likewise, I, like other scholars of color, write out of the need to be understood or just express my feelings about situations and issues.

—Aretha

Rubin and Rubin's (1995) approach to qualitative research stresses *relativism* as an opportunity to learn about, understand, and get more insight into other people's worldviews as legitimate to them as yours is to you. Likewise, not respecting the worth or legitimacy of someone else's views is a barrier to communicating across cultural boundaries. In an effort to recognize the legitimacy of people of color, the counseling literature for the last 40 years has become less culturally encapsulated and progressively more inclusive of differences in cultural values and worldviews. Along with the inclusion of groups of color is an emergence of conceptually grounded frameworks that include an understanding of sociopolitical, economic, historical, and societal ramifications, as well as multiple oppressions that shape the cultural milieu for clients of color and their presenting problems.

Storytelling in its most simplistic form is simply telling others of or about something. The telling of old stories especially has multiple purposes and meanings. These were personal stories that challenged young minds and ignited their imaginations while tapping into their inner wisdom. In a cultural context, however, storytelling is dynamic, vibrant, and the sharing of many rich stories. Storytelling is grounded in the cultural traditions of people of color, and is often orally passed down through generations to teach the customs of their culture and to preserve memories and thoughts of it. In those stories were symbolic and hidden messages such as parables with morals or lessons to be learned. Whether the story is real (verifiable) or not, it tends to be heartfelt and what we refer to in the counseling field as *phenomenological*.

For these individuals and me, our storytelling is as much a communal experience as it is a spiritual one. It is a reliving of the vivid memories of our past lives and lived experiences (both inside and outside of counseling) and those of our clients of color. For instance, Mai Li and Joshua shared that they enjoyed hearing their clients' stories. Mai Li stated, "When I see a person, I'm curious about where he comes from or she comes from, his parents and the intergenerational stuff that he or she carries." According to Joshua, "When I used to do group therapy, I would employ a lot of singing, a lot of role-playing, a lot of storytelling."

For all of these cultures, telling stories was the traditional way of learning, transmitting culture, engendering hope, and passing on legend, but most importantly it was a primary means of educating their young. As an example, African slaves were stripped of all their possessions, but slave owners could not take away their stories. Slaves used their vivid imaginations to tell stories of hope and faith. Animals were often heroes and sheroes in African folktales. These stories were passed through generations to preserve the history, culture, and faith of African people. In another example, Woodro, the American Indian participant in the study, shares the following childhood experience:

> We were raised with particular stories that my grandmother shared with us when we were little. The beliefs of the Cherokees, the little people that are part of our mythology, some of the animal stories, and the books you will see in print, such as the book over there by Mooney, *The Myths and Legends of the Cherokee People*. I heard these things before they were ever in print.

I Feel Hopeful   That was me, the 19-year-old me in the scenario in the Preface, whose hand trembled as I turned the doorknob to enter the office of a White male psychologist. That is, I was the one who left hastily out of the door following an inhuman experience—never to return. For me, this counseling encounter was huge, an infested sore looming over my professional identity for decades.

Having been robbed of potentially successful counseling experiences, I often wonder how I can effectively help diverse clients and students and prevent them from having similar negative and ineffective experiences. For this reason, like Mahatma Gandhi, I believed, "We must become the change we want to see in the world" (Gandhi, n.d.). I also believe, as Dr. Martin Luther King Jr. (1964) said,

> I am not yet discouraged about the future. Granted that the easygoing optimism of yesterday is impossible. Granted that we face a world crisis which often leaves us standing amid the surging murmur of life's restless sea. But every crisis has both its dangers and its opportunities. Each can spell either salvation or doom. In a dark, confused world the spirit of God may yet reign supreme. (para. 39)

As the researcher and author of this book, I am an African American female, a counselor educator, and a faculty member who has and continues to be on both sides of the fence of counseling, that is, as a counselor and client both present and past. As an African American woman, I have also experienced racial prejudice and cultural bias in both academe and academic workplaces. As a counselor of color, I realize the necessity and importance for people of color to have their experiences of racial and cultural biases validated in a counseling encounter.

As a client, various times I shunned or discontinued counseling before fully actualizing or accomplishing my goal. In 1984, nearly 10 years later, while pursuing my master's program in counseling, I tried to unravel what had happened in that therapeutic relationship between me and the White male therapist. After completing my Theories course, I concluded that his aloofness was due perhaps to his psychoanalytical theoretical approach to counseling. Yet, during the clinical experience of my master's program, I felt more of the same aloofness from faculty supervisors.

Although my doctoral program was more integrated with a multicultural perspective, my earlier master's-level counselor education preparation and training primarily consisted of contemporary Euro-American styles of psychotherapy. In fact, I had multiple negative and unsuccessful encounters with counseling services. Very few of the White therapists whom I've known have shown a genuine understanding of my problems or helped me to deal with them successfully. Nor has the majority of my training as a counselor prepared me to work with people who are culturally like me. As a result, as a client, even today, I have not always developed trust, or felt acceptance or an understanding of my cultural orientation, with therapists.

Perhaps this is due in part to LPCs, counselor educators, and counselor education programs themselves that have not done the personal multicultural counseling work necessary for making the personal transformation that Ivey, Ivey, and Simek-Morgan (1993) referred to as a *call to consciousness* in order to be effective with clients of color.

Reflecting back on my first experience as an African American client in 1977, I sometimes feel cheated and robbed of an effective, healthy, and helpful counseling experience—a missed opportunity to utilize my chosen profession as a vehicle to process my own issues. Now, as a multicultural educator and activist who uses critical race theory and multicultural counseling and psychotherapy (MCT) as theoretical lenses to reflect on earlier counseling experience, I know that I was cheated and I know that the White male clinical psychologist was not just a psychologist but also a racist.

Yet, regardless of that experience and other experiences of racism and discrimination in mental health, I remain hopeful, and I believe firmly in the healing power of counseling. I feel altogether confident that the counseling field, armed with more knowledge from clients of color regarding their perceptions of counseling experiences, can sequester the element of hope and function to empower African American people and other diverse groups.

At the same time, although they are committed and headed in that direction, I firmly believe that the field of counseling and psychotherapy, including its professional associations and accreditation bodies, has neither fully realized the importance nor completed the necessary steps to fully embrace cultural diversity in order to adequately prepare counselors to work effectively with a culturally diverse clientele. When this happens, perhaps another dream can be attained: All Americans will have equal access to mental health services with an equal chance of success.

With much effort, I have made it a pivotal point—perhaps a catalyst for me—to become intimately involved in this multicultural movement in counseling and psychotherapy. I am back to tell my cultural story and those of others who share with me cultural similarities, minority statuses, and, sadly, similar harmful stories of their experiences before and while seeking help. I am back to add my voice and my experience to the dialogue and become a change agent in my profession in an effort to transform how people of color are faring with mental health services. As a consequence of eternal hopefulness, this is a textbook that is based on real lives.

Respect them. If you don't have that kind of learning of that culture, if you are open enough and respectful, you can still be a very good multicultural kind of a counselor.

—Wai

People of color rarely experience counseling as being safe. Institutional racism is prevalent in the mental health field. From the literature on multicultural counseling and psychotherapy and Sue, Ivey, and Pedersen's (1996) MCT theory, several themes and assumptions emerge as theoretical tenets to explain the dismal state of mental health for people of color. Historical factors impact race relations and tend to determine the degree to which, and the quality of how, different culturally diverse groups may interact with each other. For example, because African Americans' interactions with European Americans have been historically and affectively different from American Indians' interactions with European Americans, the dynamics and power issues inherent and based on the historical relationships between ethnic and racially different groups may play out differently in counseling. As such, this should be duly noted and addressed in cultural competency standards and training.

Next, in order to achieve more success and make more progress with people of color in counseling, it is imperative to have more culturally, ethnically, and racially diverse counselor educators teaching, researchers conducting research and developing theory, counselors practicing counseling and psychotherapy, test developers creating culturally appropriate instruments, and supervisors providing supervision and training with that sensitivity in mind. More often than not, people are more similar than different, especially in their human needs for safety, acceptance, unconditional regard, and respect for their dignity, worth, and cultural differences. As a result, the element of trust plays a critical role in cross-cultural dyads. Finally, the voices of clients, especially those who have been traditionally marginalized in our society, should be heard, and they should be empowered to speak for themselves in all mental health arenas—counseling sessions, research, textbooks, and the like.

CONCLUSION

Each of the three emergent themes (and their subthemes), in tandem with Rogler, Malgady, and Rodriguez's (1989) theoretical research framework, and grounded in Sue et al.'s (1996) MCT theory, will serve as one set of lenses to fully understand the impact that ineffective counseling services have on the mental health experiences and help-seeking behaviors for these individuals. From both cultural and gendered worldviews, these frameworks are important in exploring some of the factors that clients of color themselves see as contributing to the high attrition rate in counseling services by their ethnic and racial groups.

Additionally, two different contexts will be considered, with their experiences as clients and their experiences as counselors working with clients of color serving as the backdrops for discussion. In this manner, the emergent themes serve as crosspieces for the four chapters that focus specifically on the four major U.S. groups of color through the experiences of these men and women of color. With some of them, I have developed lifelong relationships (personally and professionally); with others, I have touched bases once or twice during the 12 years between the original and follow-up studies; and with still others, I have not corresponded at all. More information about these individuals will be shared in subsequent chapters.

The following four chapters identify the critical themes in each case study participant's successful or unsuccessful experience with mental health services. The identified themes (and subthemes) include the following: (a) *bias* (gender, socio-economic, and racial-ethnic), (b) *credibility* (empowerment of the client, sharing and bonding in the client–counselor relationship, and essential qualities), and (c) *culture* (cultural knowledge, dialoguing, culture-centered networks and interventions, and minority representation).

In addition, there are wonderful stories about counseling from eight individuals to read and listen to. Each story, in a different way, relates how each group and each individual within his or her group view mental health services from a cultural perspective. They tell of what is happening now and then, and what has hidden meaning in the characters, words, places, and experiences of them and their clients. There are subtle messages and hidden meanings in the identities, characters, words, places, spaces, and experiences they share. Just like the story-telling of the past, their stories are respected, kept intact, and told the same way by me, the storyteller-author, as they were told to me. In that manner, I present with great curiosity their cultural stories combined with the study's empirical findings on the perceptions that clients of color have of factors and variables that may hinder or contribute to their utilization of, retention in, and success with counseling services.

Section II

Cultural Stories

3

The Black or African American Client's Story
The Souls of Black Folk

I noticed that with you. When you first called, you were very academic, very intelligent. You started out with all the buzz words of our chosen profession. But when we began to really talk, you reverted back into the local colloquialism. [He laughs.]

—Joshua

This chapter provides an overview of the literature on African Americans' experiences in mental health followed by a discussion of African American study participants' experiences as they relate to the emergent themes. Using these participants' experiences as a center point, the chapter will highlight the intragroup differences existing among Black Americans, provide discussion on counseling relationships that African Americans view as successful based on the personal and professional experiences of the African American participants, and discuss how the factors addressed in the first two chapters (bias, culture, and credibility) directly relate to African Americans. The chapter concludes with implications and recommendations for counseling and psychotherapy with African Americans.

Embedded in the stories in this chapter on African Americans, like DuBois's (1903/1996) book *The Souls of Black Folk*, is a compelling storyline of African American life that includes the struggles and the triumphs, and the human abuse clashing with their spiritual strength. Like African Americans themselves, some of their stories are complex, tragic, and profoundly paradoxical, but they are accurate stories of the lives of Black people in the United States. The stories in this chapter, like those in *The Souls of Black Folks*, are prophetic, inspirational, and timeless. Shawn's and Joshua's stories capture the issues relevant to African American people just as poignantly today as Dubois's book captured them more than 100 years ago. Or have the issues of the 19th and 20th centuries merely remained unchanged?

AFRICA: THE ANCESTRAL HOME OF ALL HUMANS

I believe that civilization did start in Africa. I believe that is where the beginning is, in Africa, because of the whole slavery thing, not just the ones brought over to America, [but] even the Egyptian slaves. I associated them with people who are my skin color, knowing that just because you are my skin color that doesn't make you African American per se, but still all of that is a piece. And the American piece is because of the United States. That is how I associated those two together.

—Shawn

Every human being alive today, regardless of race, ethnicity, culture, and national-ity, originated from the womb of the Black Eve of sub-Saharan Africa. In stronger words, human evolution began on the continent of Africa in the *hood*. Although most scholars (Fagundes et al., 2007; Grine et al., 2007) have by now agreed on this, the African origin of anatomically modern humans remains one of the most curious stories of all and the focus of much heated debate.

In fact, paleoresearchers (Barham, 2001; Bickerton, 2003; Chase & Dibble, 1990; Manica, Amos, Balloux, & Hanihara, 2007; McBrearty & Brooks, 2000; McDougall, Brown, & Fleagle, 2005; Watts, 2002; White et al., 2003; Wurz, le Roux, Gardner, & Deacon, 2003) from multiple disciplines (zoology, anthropology, genet-ics, climatology, archaeology, and linguistics) have surprisingly concluded with consensus that, ancestrally, modern human beings are descendants of an African Adam and African Eve. According to Manica and others, as modern humans, we all trace the root of our genealogical tree to the same forefather and foremother, who probably lived in South-Eastern Africa.

Furthermore, some anthropologists (Grine et al., 2007) believe that the contem-porary human race could share common ancestry with a being in Africa who lived about 120,000 to 220,000 years ago. Geneticists (e.g., Wells, 2002), through the analysis of DNA from people in all regions of the world, concluded that all humans alive today descended from a single man who lived in Africa around 60,000 years ago. In addition, today there is general agreement that *Homo erectus*, the precursor to modern humans, evolved in Africa and gradually expanded to Eurasia beginning about 1.7 million years ago. Last, Manica and associates (2007) combined their genetic data with new measurements of a large sample of skulls to show definitively that today's humans originated from a single area in sub-Saharan Africa.

This story of Africa as the ancestral home of all humans is a precursor to the story of the African Diaspora. It is one that traces the African Diaspora beyond the slavery era, back to those who inhabited Africa millennia ago. Most importantly, knowing that all modern humans are kinfolk is the ideal segue into any discussion on racially and ethnically different groups and a great introduction to the African Diaspora.

THE AFRICAN EXPERIENCE IN AMERICA

I remember going to the Majestic Hotel, and I don't mind saying that on camera, in Hot Springs, Arkansas. They had just built a new part of it, and the place where we stayed looked like the old part of it. And I remem-bered going down to the swimming pool with my friend, my best friend, and the pool was full of White people.

I remember sticking my big toe in to test the water, and all those people jumped out the pool except for an old, White couple from Germany. I never will forget that. Everybody else jumped out. This was in 1970. It was a great cultural shock for me then.

—Joshua

The African Diaspora

Although Black America is not a monolith, the tracing of modern humans may be a bit problematic and even more controversial than tracing the African Diaspora. The story of how Africans were captured in slavery to be scattered all over the world, were stripped of their way of life (language, traditions, families, and dignity), and yet managed to rise is a documented, undisputable fact, though perhaps no less heated, or controversial, or debated in the research. As historical milestones in the sojourn of Africans in America, both slavery and emancipation are precursors to and set the tone and stage for African Americans' experiences and perceptions of mental health services.

To some Black Americans, as to some European Americans, discrimination, like slavery and lynching, is not real. Thus, the African Diaspora offers a few possible and plausible explanations for the different opinions, experiences, perceptions, and feelings voiced about the Black experience in the United States and those issues germane to the Black community.

For nearly 4 centuries, an estimated 10 to 20 million African slaves were transported to North America and the Caribbean Islands in the Atlantic slave trade (Johnson, 1990). As a result of this African Diaspora, the racial and ethnic identities of people of African descent, especially African Americans, include Hispanic and Latino, Native American, and European ancestry. Katz (1986) asserted that more than 90% of African Americans have American Indian ancestry.

As a consequence of the sexual exploitation of African women during slavery, most African Americans have European ancestry (Mannix & Cowley, 1962). Others of African descent share with African Americans eternal ties to the motherland, but their religions and ethnic and national identities vary greatly. They are Christians, Muslims, Jews, Catholics, and Buddhists. They are citizens (or descended from citizens) of countries such as Jamaica, Haiti, Brazil, the Virgin Islands, Mexico, Puerto Rico, Central America, Canada, and those throughout Europe, Asia, and Australia, and they include native-born Africans, Afro-Europeans, and Afro-French (Cross, 1991). For some, these ethnic national identities (e.g., Afro-Caribbean or Afro-Hispanic) are as far as they wish to go back.

The storytelling of the African Diaspora centers on the amazing resiliency of African people and their culture despite their scattering throughout the world and the horrific experience of forced migration and slavery, followed by the decades of marginalization that preceded and followed the civil rights movement of the 1960s. Thus, any in-depth understanding of African Americans is based on an understanding of African American history and culture beginning with slavery and the years of being exposed to the most persistent and violent forms of individual, institutional, and societal discrimination.

Even more amazing, whether resulting from the constant reestablishment of African traditions during the continuous transporting of slaves during the Middle Passage (the journey from Africa to the Americas by slave ship) or resulting from culture that was simply passed down through the generations, elements of African culture can be found wherever people of African descent reside in the world—whether as a result of slavery or the Diaspora, aspects of culture such as language, music, food, folklore, and the art of storytelling have endured.

Resulting from this legacy of hundreds of years of American slavery, African Americans have trod through a wilderness of lynching, Jim Crow laws, racism, poverty, disenfranchisement, racial profiling, and discrimination of all kinds. Yet, despite the numerous obstacles and attacks that society has mounted against them since slavery, African Americans have been resilient and creative in finding ways to survive, retain some of their African values and structure, and use acculturation, assimilation (when needed), and wholesomeness that contribute to American society. This creativity, resiliency, knack for survival, and wholesomeness are evident in the African American case study presented in this chapter, and should be highlighted in the literature on African Americans.

For African Americans, relics of African customs have remained and are quite evident in contemporary African American culture, such as their resilient belief that "it takes a village" to raise a child. In fact, the term *African American* is an ethnic term symbolizing a culture that is shared between people who live in the United States and those who reside in Africa. Ideally, the term *African American* is a move to centralize and solidify persons of African descent and their U.S.-born ancestors toward cultural, sociopolitical, and economic ties to and centeredness with Africa (Harper, 1994).

People of African Descent

> I'm surrounded by my family, the place where I attend worship services, any kind of social gathering, and the people are usually people who look and sound like me.
>
> —Shawn

Throughout much of U.S. history, African Americans have been by far the largest of the groups of color in the United States. In more recent years, due to declining Black birth rates and increases in immigration, other groups of color (e.g., Hispanics and Latinos) have risen in size comparable to the African American population. According to projections by the U.S. Census Bureau (2008b), in 2010 African Americans numbered 41.1 million, or roughly 13.5% of the nation.

A profile of African Americans reveals that they are living longer than before, but not as long as European Americans; nor are they as healthy. The number of African American families is increasing, but with more being maintained by women who are at or below the poverty level. Although there are better high school completion rates than ever before, there are still vast racial achievement gaps in levels of educational performance, educational attainment, college enrollment, and college graduation rates between Blacks and Whites. This brief statistical profile of African Americans is not meant to represent them from a deficit angle, but rather to highlight that tremendous racial disparities still exist for African American people and provide a partial explanation of the social ills that exist in the African American community.

First, let me pause and define the use of the terms *Black*, *Black American*, and *African American* in this book and discuss how those terms may explain some of the differences that exist within the Black community. *Black* is a color category ostensibly referring to skin color, even though Blacks range in color from passing as White to dark or "deep chocolate"—the latter similar in color and traditions to coastal East Africans. This means that color is not about the individuals' skin color but, rather, the relationship among the lighter and darker races, as opposed to dark- or light-skinned people.

Historically, in the United States, racial labeling decreed that people having any amount of Black ancestry could never identify as White. This strict government identification can be traced back to slavery and to the "one-drop (of Black blood, or ancestry) rule" that prevented any person of African ancestry (however small or invisible that ancestry was) from being considered White. During this era a Black person could, however, have some other non-White racial identity such as American Indian and Hispanic.

The term *Black Americans* is used for any Blacks who are American, whether by birth or naturalization and regardless of their ancestry, nationality, language, culture, or traditions.

The term *African American*, in contrast, refers to those Black Americans who are the descendants of slaves. They came to colonial America and, later, the United States in shackles by way of the Middle Passage, as opposed to those Blacks and other groups of color whose relatives and ancestors were immigrants who voluntarily came to the United States on airplanes or boats (legally or illegally), that is, of their own volition.

Thus, this diversity of Black Americans, particularly the different experiences found in their ancestral lineages, illustrates the variety found within the Black experience and provides one reason for Black Americans' diverse and sometimes contradictory perceptions and experiences of being Black. This, in and of itself, results in broad implications for the emergence of mental health in the Black community and for developing mental health strategies to effectively address Black and African American mental health needs.

Next, and logically, just as there are White folk in the United States whose ancestors were not slaveholders, there are Blacks and Black Americans whose ancestors were not slaves. In other words, there are Black Americans whose ancestors came from other countries and continents and whose heritage is not buried in the viciousness of slavery. As a result, they will not have worn the heavy burden of generations filled with discrimination and violence that followed U.S. slavery. Likewise, there are Black Americans (native or immigrant) who ancestors were not slaves, and who have not overtly experienced racism, discrimination, or prejudice; yet they are, like African Americans, the recipients of the American institutions of oppression, inequality, social injustice, and hate crimes—more byproducts of U.S. slavery.

Similarly, there are European Americans whose ancestors did not own slaves; who were not racist, prejudiced, or actively discriminatory against people of color;

and yet who struggle with believing they are privileged. Nevertheless, White people in the United States, regardless of their ancestry and lack of prejudice and racism, do benefit from and enjoy the social, political, cultural, and financial advantages of being White—another direct derivative of U.S. slavery.

AN AFROCENTRIC WORLDVIEW
IN MENTAL HEALTH SERVICES

God allows me to be a better family member, which allows me to be a better neighbor, which allows me to be a better person.

—Joshua

African American values and cultural orientation are based on the collective thought and unity of their people. *Harambee* is a Swahili word that signifies the village concept of coming together relationally. This commonly held value expresses facing life not alone but pulling together, and recognizing the power of one but also the power of many; that is, pulling together eases the burden one might face. *Consubstantiation*, a theological doctrine that everything in the universe is connected as a part of a whole, is another commonly held belief among people of African descent.

In the African American community, there is a constant interplay among systems and among subsystems (Billingsley, 1968). That means that the focus in the African American community is on cooperation and group cohesiveness. For African Americans, the cliché "The whole is greater than the sum of its parts" and the biblical scripture "A house divided amongst itself will not stand" capture the essence of their Afrocentrism. Further, the interactions are circular rather than linear, and when one part is not functioning properly, the other parts are adversely affected.

Thus, from a cultural perspective, a healthy way—one that is consistent with the notions of the village, *Harambee*, and consubstantiation—of viewing the African American family should begin with the notion of *Afrocentrism*. Afrocentrism promotes the strength perspective of African people as centered, located, oriented, and grounded as opposed to weaker, pathological portrayals in earlier research. As a result, according to Asante (2003), Afrocentrism is meant to convey the profound need for African people to be relocated historically, economically, socially, politically, and philosophically.

According to Bell, Bouie, and Baldwin (1990), the fundamental principles underlying the African American worldview are "oneness with nature" and "survival of the group." The principle of *oneness with nature* asserts that all elements in the universe (human, animals, inanimate objects, and natural phenomena) are interconnected; that is, humanity, nature, and the self are conceptualized as the same phenomenon.

The principle of *survival of the group* prioritizes the survival of the corporate whole (the community), which includes all Black people, rather than the individual or some segment of the community apart from the corporate whole. Cultural values consistent with the basic principles of the African American worldview are interdependence, cooperation, unity, mutual responsibility, and reconciliation.

With such a violent, traumatic, and abusive history, it should be no surprise that African American people to a great extent need mental health services. Yet, it has taken far too long for the mental health profession to realize the need for an Afrocentric approach that connects the blight and shackles of slavery to the mental health of African American people. For example, African American females' (girls and women) personal-historical context of sexual assault should be considered when exploring their physical and sexual abuse cognitions and experiences.

Consequently, an Afrocentric worldview is one that could augment any therapy with African American clients (Caldwell & White, 2001; Parham, 2002; Parham & Caldwell, 2006; Parham, White, & Ajamu, 2000). In fact, African American scholars from multiple academic disciplines have argued the need for an Afrocentric worldview for not only the mental health profile of African Americans but also criminal justice, medical, educational, and political profiles. Ultimately, Asante (2003) believed that an Afrocentric worldview will not always correct the miseducation of African American students, but for all students from preschool to college, it is beneficial to all regardless of race, color, ethnicity, ancestry, and country of origin. All in all, the concepts of Afrocentrism, "it takes a village," and *Harambee* have been major forces in the survival of African Americans. Thus, from cultural systemic lenses, Afrocentrism (Asante, 2003) appears to be an appropriate framework for understanding traditional African American life and for viewing this African American case study.

"IN A MULTITUDE OF COUNSELORS, THERE IS SAFETY"

Yes, counseling works. Counseling works for everyone. The Bible says, it's a scripture, "In a multitude of counselors, there is safety."

—Joshua

Well, for one I was a little ambivalent about going into counseling. So that was a little bit of the talking, but there's a piece of me that said, "You don't talk to people outside of your family about things that are just going on with you, not necessarily other family members. That's something that you just keep within the family."

—Shawn

African Americans' historical experiences as victims of sexual abuse, physical violence, and psychological trauma, with intergenerational trauma and the unending effects of a history of slavery, racism, and sexism, should be considered in the diagnosis and treatment of abuse and trauma. Yet African Americans, like their other brothers and sisters of color, underutilize, drop out of, and are not effectively helped by counseling services.

Research indicates that premature termination rates for African American clients are related in part to the clients' trust level. Although ascribed status as defined by Sue and Zane (1987) is important for achieving credibility, Poston, Craine, and Atkinson's (1991) study suggested that the ascribed status of being in the counselor role may not offset the mistrust that some African Americans have of Whites in general.

You don't necessarily know these things are right, but because you've been taught a certain way, you seem to believe in them without challenging certain beliefs. I am interested in challenging some of those beliefs because if I don't know anyone else, it is important for me to know myself and to check my attitudes and beliefs about different things.

—Shawn

The Psychological Distress of Racism and Sexism

I remember my first cultural shock was really in the 10th grade. I was president of the drama club. We went to Hot Springs, Arkansas, at the end of the year. And when we got over there, we had already booked and paid our fees and everything. And the people at the hotel saw that we were Black, and they went up on their fees, so that we didn't have enough money to pay for it. So I called back to the White principal and told him that they wouldn't allow us to stay, because they went up on the fees. He told me, "Don't you come back. I want you to stay, and I'll pay the rest of it. Whatever they charge, I'll pay for it."

—Joshua

I grew up in the South, and the discrimination still goes on and things like that. It is not so much in your face, but it is the subtle things. It's hard to change when you are accustomed to doing things a certain way and believing things a certain way, believing what your grandparents or whatever passed down.

—Shawn

The oppressive and abusive experiences in African American male and female lives suggest that racism and sexism may have unique and interactive links to psychological distress. Therefore, understanding the historical cultural values and experiences of people of African descent as a means of developing appropriate counseling interventions is another powerful tool that can and should be used when counseling African Americans.

As opposed to White women, African American women, with multiple identities accompanied by multiple constraints, have historically been victims of oppression, marginality, poverty, and discrimination (Vasquez & Magraw, 2005) relating to their minority statuses of being Black, female, and poor. As a result of those statuses, the African American woman is often a victim of the exponential effect of being all three. As a female, she, along with her White sisters and others sisters of color, has increased likelihood of being poor as compared to men, and there is much evidence that poverty and economic inequality are linked to depression in women.

The mental, physical, moral, scholarly, and intellectual attacks on African American men have been cruel, vicious, and mentally inhuman. Both society and the academic literature have mercilessly perpetuated negative stereotypic images and descriptions of African American men, painting a dismal picture of Black men in general. The African American man has been characterized as being the absent parent, angry, violent, irresponsible, animalistic, irresponsible, a stud, a criminal, and an endangered species. Again, any work in counseling African American men must begin with a context of a lifetime of abuse and discrimination and a model that empowers them rather than rendering them invisible.

CASE 1: THE AFRICAN AMERICAN STORY: JOSHUA AND SHAWN

This case study comprises the cultural stories of two African American counselors (one male and one female) who as clients have shunned, had successful and unsuccessful encounters with, and had negative and positive outcomes of counseling services. The large intragroup differences within the African American ethnic group make generalizing and theorizing based on the ethnic theme of these two individuals complex and, in fact, impossible. To illustrate the within-group differences, the African American client, the first case study presented, consists of the perspectives of two African Americans who are different in gender, upbringing, and age, but have had somewhat similar experiences with counseling services.

Yehoshua (Joshua)

We need that Paul figure … we need that Barnabas figure … we need the Timothy. And we need a Joshua.

—Joshua

Yehoshua is the Hebrew name for *Joshua*, Moses' successor. Joshua is a biblical figure in the Old Testament who was a brave, fierce, intelligent, and charismatic leader, and at the same time a loyal, obedient, and quiet servant. As such, Joshua was singled out by God to complete Moses' mission of successfully leading the Hebrew slaves out of Egypt (the land of bondage) into the Promised Land.

At the time of this study, Joshua, a 42-year-old African American male, was pastoring an African American, inner-city Church of God in Christ (COGIC) located in a large Southern city. Shawn, an African American female, is a 28-year-old from the same city, working as a graduate assistant in her counseling department, Each of these individuals is described in detail, and their level of acculturation, stage of racial identity, and multiple intragroup perspectives are discussed.

Pastor Joshua speaks and moves very gingerly and quietly, which sort of betrays his intimidating, well-over-six-feet, 200-plus-pound frame. He moves gently through his space, but with a sense of dignity, authority, and just a fleeting hint of power. His words and soft voice are laced with much ethnic, racial, and cultural pride, as well as self-confidence, self-esteem, self-efficacy, and self-identity.

Joshua chose his pen name from the biblical figure Joshua. As a pastor, he teaches his congregation that we need several people in our lives. We need a Paul figure, who is that counselor and mentor for us. We need that Barnabas figure, who was a friend of Paul, and can tell him his faults and pull his coattails. We need a Timothy, who Paul helped to bring up, and who needs nurturing and having values imparted to him. And, he later added with a laugh, we need a Joshua.

Joshua is married, and his past occupations include being a correctional officer, a police officer, and a Federal Bureau of Investigation (FBI) recruit. He has a bachelor of arts (BA) degree in criminal justice and a master of science (MS) in rehabilitation counseling, and is currently pursuing an doctorate of education

(EdD) in counseling and education. His current professional memberships are the American Counseling Association (ACA), Tennessee Counseling Association (TCA), and COGIC. As a client, he has participated in a range of counseling encounters, including group and individual counseling but primarily pastoral counseling.

Acculturation   When I asked Joshua to describe his relationship to the African American community, he replied,

> I love it. I'm glad I'm a part of it. I believe that I've been privileged and blessed to be a part of it. I am so much a part of it that I'm in the process of buying or building a house, or one of the two, and I refuse to buy or build in an area outside of where my people live.

Discussing the role that language plays in his culture, he continued,

> It is very, very important. When I first began to pastor and teach, then I had to consciously revert back or refrain from using certain words that I took for granted that everyone used. When I left the professional setting and just began to pastor, my language changed. Sometimes it is hard to balance the two.

Multiple Perspectives   Joshua's exposure to people who are racially, ethnically, and culturally different from him is vast. He has traveled and attended workshops throughout this country. Nevertheless, he reflects that going to high school was where he really became more exposed to people from other racial backgrounds and got his first dose of racism. Growing up in the South, Joshua was surrounded by racism, yet he was taught not to be racist. In fact, some of the greater positive impact during his childhood came from White people. He remembers his 11th-grade English teacher, who not only challenged him but also helped him explore himself.

It was during this conversational topic that Joshua reclined back into his chair, rested his chin on his hands, looked upward and to the right, paused for a moment, and recollected the harsh realities of the culture shock, racism, and abuse that came along with exposure to the White race at such a young, tender, and impressionable age. For instance, Joshua again recalled that painful high school incident where he and his classmates were stuck in another city because the hotel increased the housing fees when they saw they were Black.

In spite of the few moments of pain from dredging up those memories, Joshua's spiritedness returned and he continued his sharing. He had fond memories of his English teacher, a White woman, who through her constant encouragement validated him and his minority experience, empowered him as an African American man, and positively and profoundly impacted his entire life. He shared,

> I was coming into myself; I was reading Black poetry, really finding out who I was as a person, as an African American. I was becoming very militant, and she encouraged that. I was on the newspaper staff, and she was the sponsor, and she encouraged us to explore ourselves and our identity. I remember one time we had old antiquated books, and in our literature book, it stated

that Europe was the cradle of civilization, and she turned to me and said, "Do not believe everything you read; everybody knows that Africa was the cradle of civilization."

Joshua, reflecting on his training and what he called his "brainwashing," concluded that the way he was educated in school and taught White history was like the education of almost all African American people. He felt strongly that "being an African American, we have been taught about the other cultures." This, coupled with his experiences as an African American male in a White racist society, qualified him to be above average in multicultural awareness and knowledge. In fact, when I asked Joshua to rate himself in multicultural or cross-cultural counseling on a scale from 1 to 10, with 1 being low, he replied with a wide smile, "Honey, when I think of my lifelong exposure and acclimation to the White folk, I give myself a 10." He later added with seriousness, "Like I told you, I was raised to be multicultural. I give myself a 10."

Joshua's document delineating the racial and ethnic breakdown of his counseling clientele by percentage showed 70% African American, 29% European American, and 1% other.

Racial Identity   Joshua's score placed him in stage 5 of racial identity development. According to Helms (1984), in stage 5, internalization, the individual achieves a sense of inner peace or acceptance of self. This acceptance of self or inner peace allows the person to respect other races and worldviews.

Shawn

My July 3, 1997, journal entry reads,

> This day has been one of the days that you sort of want to forget. Though I was able to complete two of my interviews, Murphy had been *acting*. Yes, Murphy's Law had interrupted the morning events, and the fact that Shawn (my second scheduled interviewee) and I played phone tag for a couple of hours didn't make it any better. Shawn approached me and introduced herself with a very soft "Hello" and shook my hand warmly. She was a medium tall, cocoa-brown, slender woman who moved softly with very slow, deliberate, controlled steps. I knew instinctually that it was Shawn (even though she looked nothing like I had imagined her to look). The softness and warmth of both her voice and handshake were a sort of betrayal of the womanish strength that was so evident in her approach, her appearance, and her presence.
>
> This regal young woman approached me with an air of African dignity, which is like an African queen. She wore a pastel-green dress with a fitted bodice that flared at the hips. Long, thick, French braids that hung down below her neck bounced in and off her face as she came closer. I noticed, when she looked directly into my eyes, a pair of soft, rounded eyeglass frames. A refreshing combination of elegance, professionalism, realness, and African American culture was evident. So much so, that in spite of my fatigued and manic/depressive state, I found myself relaxing and looking forward to the interview.

Shawn, the youngest of the participants, is the only one who is single. She is engaged to a doctoral student in the counseling psychology program at her university. She has a BA in psychology and an MA in counseling, and is currently pursuing her PhD in counseling. She describes her theoretical orientation as follows: "I am a little Rogerian, depending on the client, of course. I am a little Adlerian, family constellation and things like that, like how people relate to each other. And a little systemic." She is in the process of joining ACA.

Acculturation   Shawn is a 28-year-old African American female who affirms a very strong kinship with the African American community. When asked what connects her to this community, she responded by saying simply, "My church, my family, and my neighborhood are African American."

Racial Identity   Shawn self-administered the Black Racial Identity Attitude Scale (BRIAS) and obtained a high score in stage 5, the internalization stage.

Multiple Perspectives   According to Shawn, she has always been around people who are racially different, mainly, she said, "Caucasians and a handful of Hispanics, at least, as far as the school setting and things like that." In addition, while attending college in St. Louis, she lived in an apartment complex alongside a lot of Mexican Americans and Caucasians. In her document on the racial and ethnic breakdown of her counseling clientele by percentage, the racial breakdown was 20% Caucasian and 80% African American.

To ascertain Shawn's perceptions of her multicultural awareness, knowledge, or skills, I asked Shawn to rate herself on a scale from 1 to 10 in the area of multicultural or cross-cultural counseling. She replied very conservatively, "I think there's a lot out there that I don't know. But, just for myself, I would like to be a little more educated. Okay, I would give myself a 5."

AFRICAN AMERICAN CLIENTS: EMERGENT THEMES

Biases

Gender   With both Joshua and Shawn, preference to seek counsel from females and female counselors is consistent with African American culture and traditions, in particular the nurturing, supportive role that African American mothers and grandmothers have played. Historical and contemporary gender roles in the African American community are discussed further in Chapter 8.

Socioeconomics   The need for financial support has always been prevalent in the African American family, including middle-class families. African American families have historically lagged behind White families in annual income. According to McAdoo (1981), an income gap exists between Black and White families regardless of family composition, but the gap was narrowest for married-couple families with working wives (p. 137). The literature indicates that higher socioeconomic status is generally associated with larger support networks that comprise both family and friends. Both Joshua and Shawn work in African American communities, and believe that socioeconomics (status or finance) can be an important variable in African American clients' decision of whether or not to opt for counseling.

> The African American culture, [and] I suspect [this] is the same truth of other cultures, is kind of layered by the socioeconomic status of the people. People of a higher economic status are more willing to receive counseling. In the lower socioeconomic status, it's usually being forced upon them.

In addition to her African American clients, Shawn, as an African American student with little money, has firsthand knowledge that socioeconomics can be a major barrier to going to counseling:

> I was very satisfied in hindsight; I am glad that I used the free service. Regarding my clients, many have expressed that if the insurance won't pay, their child wouldn't be able to attend. Most are poor and receiving some type of assistance.

Ethnic, Racial, and Cultural   For Joshua and Shawn, like most African Americans, being bombarded with real-life experiences of racial biases is an every-day occurrence. With these experiences of racism, prejudice, and discrimination comes a paranoia or inability to trust Whites.

Joshua commented, "Professionally, and in the ministry, I have had to break down racial lines."

Shawn commented, "The counselor that I had was Caucasian, and I was thinking, 'Is she going to understand me?'"

In Summary

According to Sandhu and Brown (1996), bias in the form of prejudice is so pervasive and persistent in pluralistic societies that it affects a wide range of variables such as surnames, gender, ethnicity, and race. This section has uncovered the many perceptions of bias and their influences on participants' successful or unsuccessful experiences, and on their decisions about whether to participate, continue, or discontinue in counseling. These are responses to one of the underlying questions targeting the African American participants' perceptions of what factors are involved in the counseling experiences they considered successful, including active utilization, completeness of counseling, and achieving positive outcomes.

For the African American participants, biases ranged from gender preference, to the restrictive nature of living in poverty and being economically marginalized, to the day-to-day and real-life experiences of racial biases, racism, prejudice, and discrimination. African American counselors' exposure to negative environmental and social stressors, like other counselors of color, may have diminished credibility, that is, the value of the therapeutic relationship. That reality for so many African American clients has created paranoia toward and mistrust of White people that often trickles down into therapeutic relationships. Many times in a cross-cultural counseling situation, clients must first struggle through the issue of trust before any "real" counseling can begin. That means, as Yu and Gregg (1993) stated, "The presence of a culturally different person in a counseling group has more implications than a mere difference in birthplace or ethnic origin" (p. 87).

CREDIBILITY

With this theme, participants' comments reflect their perspectives as clients and as counselors. Credibility, as discussed by Sue and Zane (1987), is directly "related to the much discussed notions of expectancy, trust, faith, and effectiveness in therapy" (p. 40). The participants discussed three areas related to this notion of credibility: (a) empowerment, (b) bonding, and (c) essential qualities.

Counselor Perspective

Empowerment   Empowerment, according to McWhirter (1994), means that powerless people are made aware of the debilitating power dynamics in their lives and are helped to regain and exercise control. Joshua and Shawn, more humanistic in their comments, implied that all clients have the innate potential to self-empower, and the job of counselors is to help them discover or tap this sometimes dormant potential. What Joshua considered successful is "allowing that person to come into balance and bring about closure of an event or an incident in their lives." Shawn, on the other hand, felt that

> [o]nce they find that answer inside, they will be able to use whatever they've learn[ed] about themselves inside to be able to function outside. It works for those who want it to work and for whoever is willing to give it a try and willing to take a look at themselves, and change if necessary.

Bonding With the Client   Concurrent with empowerment is a sense of bonding with the client. This is illustrated in the following statements. Joshua, as a counselor facilitating a veterans' rap group, reflected on the message he tries to convey to other Vietnam veteran group members: "Me telling you that I'm not perfect, and you're not the worst individual in the world with the things that you are going through, I have been through"; and Shawn evaluated her feedback to her clients as follows: "Instilling some type of hope. Allowing them the opportunity to do some inward looking and time to trust. I let the client tell me about him or her and just go from there."

Essential Qualities   For these African American clients, the most important step involves a more personal approach to communicating with the client, such as Joshua's statement that counselors should "bring a person to a state of balance and closure of an incident in their lives," and Shawn's thought that counselors should "always be willing and open to listen to the client." Yet, this does not seem to negate the need for skill and expertise. Joshua stated, "Training and education can go a long way in helping bring about a lot of enlightenment. By the same token, experience is great."

Client's Perspective

Empowerment   McWhirter's (1994) theme of empowerment as aiding clients in regaining and exercising control by focusing on clients' internal strengths continued in Joshua's and Shawn's client perspectives on empowerment.

Joshua commented,

> The way a man thinks in his heart, so is he; I had to go through a long transition just to get to this point. It really helped me to come into focus, into balance with what was going on in my life at that time. And knowing that what I was going through wasn't an isolated thing, it helped, very much so.

Shawn commented that because counseling was a safe place for her to speak openly and freely, she was able to do some self-reflecting: "I was willing to go back, go back and continue looking at things."

Sharing and Bonding   Joshua found counselor self-disclosure to be helpful and bonding: "He shared with us his experiences about going through the same thing that we were going through. Knowing that what I was going through wasn't an isolated thing helped." Similarly, Shawn was able to explore some personal issues because of the counselor's sharing. "I was able to look at some of the things going on within myself and to talk freely and openly about them, not feeling like I would be judged. She was real genuine with me and open."

Essential Qualities   Several studies investigating race in conjunction with other variables have suggested that race in and of itself is not a stable predictor of a client's preference for a counselor (Atkinson, Furlong, & Poston, 1986; Cimbolic, 1972; Parham & Helms, 1981). Rather, variables such as the counselor's skill level, expertise, and experience are more salient factors.

In their own therapy, Joshua and Shawn believed that most of the credit for the success of the sessions was due to the skill of the counselor. Joshua stated, "Even though it was an informal group session, it was a successful one and a powerful one because the facilitator was able to bring us to a closure." Shawn stated, "As counseling went on, I realized that I was willing to take a chance because there was nothing in that first session to make me think that this woman wasn't competent, not capable of doing counseling."

In Summary

Certainly, the African American participants' educational training to a degree has influenced their professional roles, at least in terms of skill building and professional experience. However, their graduate training did very little to formally prepare them for working with ethnically, racially, and culturally diverse clients. Joshua felt that the purpose of the formal training that he received from his graduate studies was to expose him to the cultural shock of the academic environment. He stated, "Very much so, having to deal with these differences. The whole experience has been an experience." Most of the training has come from initiatives taken by them, such as attending workshops, doing research on culturally diverse groups, and getting involved in different cultures.

In the perceptions of these African American participants, the concept of *credibility* in the effectiveness in therapy, evidenced through empowerment, sharing, bonding, and essential qualities, was shared. In their roles as counselors and clients, the themes of internal strengths, a sense of balance, and self-disclosure emerged. They discovered credibility with the help of competent, skilled counselors and a willingness and strength to look inside. With the counselors' self-disclosure, genuineness, and nonjudgmental stance, they could take the risk and learn to trust mental health professionals.

CULTURE

Along with the awareness that mental health delivery systems in the United States are not adequately meeting the needs of persons coming from different cultural, ethnic, racial, and socioeconomic backgrounds, there is the challenge to develop effective methods for reducing attrition and premature termination once African Americans have actually entered treatment. In the counseling and psychotherapy literature, several factors have been identified and several strategies proposed to address these issues. Multicultural counseling and psychotherapy research recognizes that the key components of multicultural competence include the development of awareness, knowledge, and skill with respect to ethnically and racially different groups. In the forefront of culturally sensitive or responsive counseling is knowledge of a client's culture.

Cultural Knowledge

On the BRIAS, both African American participants' scores placed them in the internalization stage of racial identity development. According to Helms (1990), the main motif of the internalization stage is "the Internalization of a positive personally relevant Black identity" (p. 28). Helms further described persons in the internalization stage as able to find value in people who are culturally different and as no longer needing to judge people by their cultural, racial, or ethnic group memberships. Similarly, as persons in the internalization stage, the African American participants were able to practice comfortably with people from different cultures. Their advice for counselors working in cross-cultural or multicultural situations is that, minimally, some insight is needed when counseling culturally different clients. Likewise, they caution that counselors have to take precautions not to overgeneralize this cultural knowledge and unthinkingly apply it to every client without regard to individual differences existing in that culture.

Joshua commented, "To deal with people from different ethnic backgrounds, you need to have at least some sort of insight into where they come from and how to deal with them." Shawn commented, "To me, there is a cultural piece that is involved, and not that every person will be exactly like what we read about in the multicultural book, but just that awareness gives us information about the client."

Dialoguing

As counselors, the African American participants were able to connect with the African American clients who spoke and understood their language. Shawn said simply, "The people in my community, my church or whatever, we just have an understanding about words or language." According to Joshua, he identified and communicated with his people by speaking their language, and when he spoke to them with his educated, bourgeois male language, they would come to him and say, "Pastor, you're using those fifty cent words."

Culture-Centered Networks and Interventions

Because of the large numbers of African Americans who tend to shun counseling and the fact that counseling is viewed negatively in the African American community, the African American participants felt that there was a need for and a method of integrating natural support systems in counseling. Joshua explained,

> Many will go to the pastor rather than to a psychiatrist, which is viewed as negative. Bring in the family, the church, and other support systems. Counseling is chosen in the African American community when these two support systems come together and agree you need counseling.

Shawn explained,

> Some counseling is seen in a negative light, and people are not willing to be open to that. Explore something different, the family, the church, just not being heard by the counselor. First ask the clients if they would be willing to have a family member participate with them.

HOMEGROWN REPRESENTATION

Several researchers, such as Atkinson, Morten, and Sue (2003) and Sue and Sue (2007), have stated that increased minority representation in counseling and psychotherapy is critical to the establishment of a multicultural program. The African American participants have also witnessed personally and professionally how the lack of minority representation in all areas of counseling has adversely affected African Americans' participation in counseling, and therefore they have become advocates for a leadership that reflects the ethnic and racial breakdown of its clientele.

Joshua commented, "There are only a few African American agency supervisors who are in counseling, and those African Americans are assisting instead of being in training where they can impart this information."

Shawn commented,

> We are a minority as far as numbers and things like that. It just keeps it real to me, like reality to me. I do want to focus on minorities and minority programs. I do want to do that, and I think that more people are starting to accept counseling in a way.

IN SUMMARY

One of the guiding research questions in this study is "What are the racial identity stages of development, the level of acculturation, and the level of multicultural competencies and skills of the ethnic and racial counselor educators in training, and how do they perceive and view these factors?" Neither participant self-described as fully acculturated to the majority culture; rather, they were more bicultural. They both reported very deep ties to the African American community. For example, Shawn said that she was immersed in her family, her church, and social events with people who were like her. Similarly, Joshua said, in describing his relationship to his community, that he felt blessed and privileged to be a part of his community and to build his home there.

Under the theme of culture, overall, the African American participants' knowledge and sensitivity were important to the client culture, but not just to lump everyone from that cultural background together. They believed that using African American language improved the quality of their relationship with African American clients. In terms of assessing the role that indigenous systems played in working through life events rather than using counseling services, these participants found that a collaborative approach with the natural support systems in the African American community works well with African American clients. In terms of professional roles, they advocated an increase in African American representation, believing that it could have a positive effect on the entire field of counseling and psychotherapy.

4

The Asian and Asian American Client's Story
The Myth of the Model Minority

I realized that as we discussed, and as I talked about racial injustices I experienced, I felt the pain of the racial tensions and oppressions. Issues of race are difficult to talk about. It easily becomes emotionally charged. I am thinking of some of the class discussions we have had in my classes, both as a student and as an instructor.

—Mai Li

Actually, I travel in Canada, I witnessed those Chinese immigrants there. There's some things that I don't really admire about their lifestyle over there. For those immigrants that just migrate over there, they are very afraid of being laid off. They are very insecure, they are afraid of everything, even though they have their college degrees. Most of them got their degrees from Hong Kong, maybe that's another reason why they are afraid. They don't even feel good to go out and seek help or services. Maybe, the language is the thing. I learned from an Australian friend, who is a Chinese who migrated there. For the services to the immigrants, some of the Chinese don't join, but she knows that they have the need, but somehow they don't feel good to join with those Europeans.

—Wai

MIXING APPLES AND ORANGES: THE MASSIVE DIFFERENCES EXISTING AMONG ASIANS

Say, for example, if I talked about my relationship with my wife, my children, or some of the cultural issues. It takes more time for me to really trust you or that you will understand. But if you were of the same culture (unless you are stupid or ignorant), I will trust you more, if the two of you are of the same training or background.

—Wai

Just different cultures. That's how God made us. It reminds me of the song (she sings), "Red and Yellow, Black and White, we are precious in his sight. Jesus loves the little children of the world." That's just the way I celebrate life.

—Mai Li

*I*n statistics, perhaps, there remains an element of truth in the cliché "There are liars, damned liars, and statisticians." At a glance, research shows that among the five major racial and ethnic groups in the United States, Asian Americans are the most successful (outperforming even Whites) as measured by having the highest college degree attainment and graduation rates, advanced degree attainment rates (professional or doctorates), median family income, overall employment rates, and employment rates in professional and high-skill occupations. In that vein, the media and scholars proclaim and showcase Asians as the *model minority* (Suzuki, 2002; Yu, 2006), even though Asians collectively represent a small percentage of the U.S. populace and are vastly different (e.g., Chinese, Japanese, Korean, Filipino, Vietnamese, Indian, Yemeni, Iraqi, Palestinian, and Saudi Arabian).

Granted, there are a disproportionate number of successful Asian Americans compared to the other ethnic and racial groups, but the statistics don't tell the complete story. Upon further investigation, this perception of the successful ethnic group is true for only a select few Asians. In stronger words, it is the proverbial lie; in less harsh words, it is a myth that does a grave disservice to Asian Americans and Asian immigrants (Lee, Vue, Seklecki, & Ma, 2007).

First, Asia is a continent—the world's largest continent, in fact, with the greatest population (60% of the world's total) and with about 37 countries and an additional 14 Arab nations. As such, Asians are not and cannot be considered a homogeneous group, but have massive intragroup differences. Thus, coming from countries with such different cultures, languages, and religions and vastly different traditions, value systems, and lifestyles, Asians are possibly the most heterogeneous of all the ethnic and racial groups.

Asians are poles apart in terms of country of origin (including those from the United States), regions (Arabia, Pacific Islands, South Asia, and East Asia), culture, traditions, languages, religions, history, sociopolitical experiences, and English proficiency. For example, most Pacific Islanders, similar to Native Americans and Mexican Americans, and unlike Asian Americans, are not immigrants but are descendants of the original inhabitants of land claimed by the United States. Although they share similar cultural traditions and ancestry with some Asian groups, Pacific Islanders share the forced relocation history of American Indians and Alaska Natives, whose lives drastically changed upon contact with earlier Europeans in the Americas.

Next, for some Asian immigrants (Japanese, Chinese, Filipinos, Koreans, Taiwanese, and Asian Indians), the select few who come to the United States are la crème de la crème, that is, they are the most educated, skilled, resourceful, and advantaged. In contrast, Asian immigrants from less wealthy countries (Vietnam, Cambodia, and Laos) are in dire poverty and highly disadvantaged with the lowest education attainment rates, lowest socioeconomic index (occupational prestige), and highest high school dropout rates, and they are the most mocked, victimized, and discriminated against.

Even with their impeccable credentials, Asians, like the other groups of color, have not escaped discrimination. For example, on one hand, as a group, certain Asian Americans have been highly successful (in obtaining a good education and job, and making a good living). But, on the other hand, that level of attainment is enjoyed by only a select few. In major urban cities (Los Angeles, San Francisco, Chicago, and New York), the poverty rate for Asians is nearly twice that of Whites.

A GLANCE AT ASIAN AMERICAN HISTORY, DEMOGRAPHICS, AND ISSUES

Maybe if I work hard and teach and survive, maybe not a job right away, if I join in the multicultural sessions (divisions of ACA), I would not be an outsider. But somehow, I still don't belong. I just don't feel I could really live the good life or that ideal life that I am looking for in this country. Maybe if I was born here, that would make a difference, but I migrated here; that is something different.

—Wai

Asians, like the Hispanic-Latino population, are a rapidly growing racial group in the United States. Similarly, the collective history shows that Asian Americans, like African Americans, Native Americans, and Hispanic/Latino Americans, have endured a barbaric history of intolerance, hatred, violence, and discrimination. Nonetheless, this great increase in the Asian population is closely tied to the abolishment of quotas based on national origin after the passage of the Immigration and Naturalization Act of 1965 that allowed Asians and immigrants from other developing non-European countries to be admitted to the United States (Edwards, 2001).

Prior to 1965, two federal immigration laws—the Immigration Act of 1917 and the Immigration Act of 1924—banned people from Asia and the Pacific Islands from entering the United States, in essence making immigration from Asia and surrounding areas illegal (Joshi, 2006). And even the passing of these two landmark pieces of federal legislation further demoralized Asians, relegating them to the bottom rung of American citizenry.

For example, in 1923, South Asian Americans' U.S. citizenship was snatched away by the U.S. Supreme Court in the case *United States v. Bhagat Singh Thind*. This followed closely on the heels of another Supreme Court decision to not allow a Japanese man to receive citizenship as a person of the White race (*Takao Ozawa v. United States*, 1922).

Although the Chinese (even predating Columbus) and Filipinos were among the first Asians to come to the United States, the common thread in Asian American history beginning in the 1500s and ending with anti-Arab discrimination following the attacks of September 11, 2001, has been one of abuse and discrimination. Their history includes forced labor, labor exploitation, lynching and hanging, segregation, victimization by anti-Asian movements (hate crimes), and Asians being unfairly jailed, stripped of their culture and civil rights, denied citizenship, labeled a threat to U.S. national security, and militarily and forcefully removed and relocated from their homes without warning or compensation.

COUNSELING ASIAN POPULATIONS

The Malaysian/Chinese culture is very Asian. Therapy, counseling is a no-no. They don't want you talking in public. It is a family affair, and we have family secrets and family members who know best. That determines what we do. Family will hold this conference consisting of themselves only, and it is a shame to talk to any one person outside the family.

—Mai Li

First, family. All my extended family members are there in Hong Kong, including my wife's extended family. Language. Food. I think familiarity. I feel more familiar with that culture, even though I have been here for 5 years. That is still closer to my heart.

—Wai

Unequivocally, historical events and circumstances shape the mental health profile of Asians, as they do with any racial and ethnic group, just as culture dynamics shape the expression and recognition of mental health problems. As such, counselors working with Asian clients should have an awareness of history in the United States and abroad of Asian clients combined with specific cultural knowledge and traditions. Therefore, an examination of the past history of Asian American clients is helpful in identifying the problem and developing a treatment plan.

Asians, compared to the other ethnic groups, have the lowest rates of utilization of counseling services (Gwynn et al., 2008). In terms of accessibility, Asian Americans' low access and utilization of counseling services can be traced to several factors such as cultural barriers, lack of money or health insurance, and language barriers, which include access to interpreters and bilingual therapists. Although the rates vary among Asian subgroups, lack of insurance coverage (ranging from a high of 34% for Korean Americans to 20% for Chinese American) is, as with many Americans, a problem. This is further convoluted by Asian immigrants who qualify but refuse to apply for Medicaid or Medicare for fear of being denied citizenship. Also, due to the small number of Asian mental health clinicians in general, a shortage of bilingual clinicians and interpreters who speak Asian clients' languages, and Asian clients' lack of proficiency in speaking English, a large number (nearly half) of the Asian American and Pacific Islander population has limited access to the mental health care system.

Culturally, keep in mind that as a group, Asians are a close-knit private people who are more likely to live in households consisting exclusively of relatives. Moreover, Asian cultures and religions discourage telling family problems to outsiders and openly displaying emotions. For that reason, family members are less likely to seek help outside of the family unit. Additionally, Asians' mental distress and problems are likely to be expressed physically as opposed to emotionally.

Counselors are encouraged to resist the urge to lump everybody together, and to instead become familiar with the individual subcultures, traditions, and experiences of Asian clients through their stories and the lens of their cultural group's unique history in the United States. This means that when working with Asian clients, counselors should be cognizant of the differences among the Asian cultures and allow Asian clients to self-identify their ethnic group and ethnic identity. Last, it is important to hear their emergent stories, not just the ones of the discrimination, abuse, and inequalities but also those of spirituality, resiliency, victory, and success.

LISTENING CLOSELY

Listen more. Don't assume that you know something. A client may say something like "I feel insecure." Now, insecure to you may mean something opposite of the insecurity of the client. Just be honest and listening, trying to understand where the client comes from. This person may be coming from a different world, not your world. Try to find out what this person means.

—Mai Li

Rooted in Mai Li and Wai's stories and experiences as Asian clients, and those of their people, are the triumphs of strong, determined people who rose to the top despite the odds. You can hear the silence of their struggles as immigrants, refugees, and American-born Asian citizens who triumph over oppression and discrimination on the path to making outstanding contributions to the economy, beginning with their work on the transcontinental railroad, mining in California, and on sugar plantations in Hawaii.

Thus, this chapter views the collective experiences of Asians within the context of their diverse cultures, history, and experiences in the United States, as heard in the stories of Mai Li's and Wai's own counseling and that of their Asian clients. From these stories, you will hear of their achievements way beyond IQ and other intelligence-related variables in fields such as science, medicine, technology, and education, as well as those made in sports, the military, and the arts—essentially, every arena of American life. If we listen closely, the stories of Mai Li, Wai, and other Asian clients tell us of the anguish that accompanied their collective experiences as Asians.

CASE 2: THE ASIAN STORY: MAI LI AND WAI

I have had lots of exposure to different people. Just growing up in a multicultural country, and then after I was done with my English education here, then I had to go and teach in Malaysia. Language-wise, I speak three different languages. Ben [her husband] and I stayed in Singapore for 5½ years where we had some theological training in pastoral work. It was in the discipleship center [that] we had our first theological training, and it was very multicultural. It was a community of about 30 students from all over the world. In addition, before I did my MA in theology [I did 4 years in a Moslem country], that was a whole introduction into the Moslem world and way of thinking.

—Mai Li

Both Wai and Mai Li were at the highest level of racial identity development, and in terms of ethnic identity were very grounded in their own culture and simultaneously acculturated to mainstream American society. Yet they are multicultural children of the world, having traveled broadly and speaking multiple languages. As a result, they are both comfortable with and skilled in working with diverse people regardless of race, ethnicity, age, gender, sexuality, or disability. Their clinical experience has crossed multiple boundaries, including oceans and countries. They had gathered up an array of clinical strategies and techniques, including indigenous healing, along the way. With their theological backgrounds, you hear the spiritual healing, love, forgiveness, buoyancy, nurturance, and transformation in their clinical work—it comes across even from the printed page.

Mai Li

Mai Li is a 41-year-old Malaysian Chinese female. She has a bachelor of science (BS) degree in biology and a master of arts (MA) degree in theology, and is currently a doctorate of education (EdD) candidate in marriage and family therapy. She is completing her second internship and works as a teaching assistant. She describes her specialties as gender and parenting, and holds membership in the Association for Marriage and Family Therapy (AMFT) and Texas Women in Higher Education (TWHE). She has certifications in counseling from Singapore and in education from Malaysia.

In English, Mai Li means *Mary*. The name Mary, like Joshua, has a biblical origin. Mai Li explains that Mary, the mother of Jesus, occupies an important cornerstone in her Christian faith (she grew up a Chinese Buddhist; later on, she converted to Christianity). The name *Mary* represents the virtues that Mai Li most admires, such as unwavering faith, strength, steadfast love, and compassion.

Acculturation   Mai Li is Malaysian Chinese, but because of ethnic diversity and lack of fluency in the Chinese language, she finds herself ostracized and on the outside of the Chinese community. She explained, "I want to be of the Chinese culture, but that was not my experience, my upbringing. I speak Chinese at the marketplace and a dialect of Chinese; with my mom, I speak Malay." In terms of being one of them, she says,

> Chinese see us as not genuine Chinese. They call us bananas. Chinese, Yellow on the outside, but White on inside. Because we don't speak Chinese as well as we do speak English. So I'm English speaking. If I lived in Malaysia, it would be Malaysian-English. Different from English and Malay. It's just a different flavor of English.

Though born in Malaysia of Chinese ancestry, Mai Li describes her referent group as English-speaking overseas Chinese Christian.

When I asked her to describe her relationships, including affiliations or ties that connect her to the English-speaking overseas Chinese Christian group, she replied,

> I live with them. The Malaysian, I'm immersed in the culture. The present church congregation is exclusive of this group of people, with a smattering of Indians, but basically more English-speaking Chinese. My own sisters and brothers are all I need. Also, the food we eat. My daughter dances sometimes. But it's really the food and language, the style of language. The jokes [she laughs].

Multiple Perspectives   As a young child growing up in Malaysia, she said that she was in school in a multicultural area right from the beginning, Her neighbors were all of different races, and as she put it, "I had bilingual friends for my neighbors. I had Indian people for my neighbors." She described that time in her life as "just happy and playing." As she grew older, Mai Li was saddened by the color differences that divided people. When asked with what referent group or racial, ethnic, or cultural group she identified, she responded, "English-speaking overseas Chinese. But, Chinese brought up in the Western worldview, basically. English-speaking, Western worldview. Christian is even better."

I asked Mai Li to describe her philosophy of counseling, including theoretical orientation and worldview. Of philosophy, she said, "I have deep respect for the healing of persons not only at the emotional level, but [also in] totality. We are spiritual beings. Dignity, honesty, respect—all of these things are words I'm very attuned to."

Of worldviews, she said,

> My task is to come alongside, to understand the worldview of that person and work with that worldview. It's not for me to enforce my values very strongly; like this is the way to go or this is the answer. I believe that the client has answers of his or her own. My task is to help him clarify or help her clarify what the issue is and for him or her [to] arrive at their own solution.

Of theoretical orientation, she said,

> I think of myself as a more intergenerational therapist. I use a genogram a lot. Very intergenerational. And it's very neat how things bring insight to many people as to why they are the way they are right now. I have the individual focus as well as the larger focus of the family and the generations. And then, patterns from generations to generations and the clients can see what it's like.

When asked to discuss the diversity and multiculturalism of her clientele, she answered, "I have Hispanic clients, and I have Asian clients. I have White American clients, I have African American clients. I have not had anyone who was lesbian, homosexual. I wouldn't have an issue with it."

Mai Li's document delineating the racial and ethnic breakdown of her clients by percentage was as follows: 20% Hispanic (mostly Mexican American), 70% Anglo or Caucasian, 5% Asian (mostly Filipino), and 5% African American.

Mai Li, like the other participants, was asked to rate her multicultural awareness, knowledge, and skills. Although Mai Li has had multiple-layered experiences with culturally different groups, it was her acculturation to American society that forced her to be less conservative in her rating of herself. Mai Li replied, "Here I've learned to be more appropriate in rating myself." On a scale from 1 to 10, in the area of diversity and multicultural counseling, she said, "I would think I would be pretty high. It would be between 8 or 9."

Racial Identity   Mai Li self-administered the People of Color Racial Identity Attitude Scale (POCRIAS) and obtained a high score in stage 5, the internalization stage.

Wai

Wai was very prompt and friendly, but seemed a little guarded during the initial part of the first meeting. He is a 40-year-old Chinese male. He has earned a BS in social work, a master of education (MEd) degree in counseling, and a master of divinity (MDiv) degree, and is currently pursuing an EdD in counselor education. In Hong Kong, where he worked as a counselor, licensure was not required. He considers his specialty area to be early childhood, and he is very profoundly influenced by play therapy. He maintained,

> The play therapy professor really inspired me, and I'm very loyal to person-centered therapy. Even though I've had only one class with him, and minimal contact as my co-chair, I still admire and respect him a lot. He made a very strong impact.

For Wai, play therapy was very empowering, and he applied it in his own life: "I try and I appreciate and really practice those things with my two girls." During the interview, Wai returned time and again to the influences of spirituality, play and Rogerian therapy, and Christianity, and how each of those influences played out in his counseling relationships (as client and counselor).

> I admire the professor who was counseling me at the beginning stage of my counseling study in Hong Kong seminary. He would seek a good counselor or some spiritual person to counsel him or provide him with a learning opportunity.

Wai's responses to the interview questions seemed genuine and spontaneous, yet initially he was a little reluctant to discuss the cultural piece. It was only after I asked him to tell me the word for *counseling* in Cantonese that he began to loosen up and talk about his culture and the impact of cultural influences on his experiences.

Acculturation   Wai described his referent group as "Cantonese Chinese Hong Kong," with some Christian background. Even though he had lived in the United States for 5 years, he still felt closer to his own cultural groups because of the affiliations and ties that connect him to his and his wife's families back in Hong Kong. Further, Wai said, "I eat the food and speak the language. When I speak English, I feel that there is a gap between my feeling and what I've experienced. When I speak my own tongue, I feel closer, more connected to my culture."

Racial Identity   Wai self-administered the POCRIAS and obtained a high score in stage 5, the internalization stage. According to Helms (1990), the internalization stage of the POCRIAS is an integration of positive own-group racial identification with the capacity to realistically appreciate positive aspects of Whites; in comparison, the autonomy stage of the White Racial Identity Attitude Scale (WRIAS) is racial humanism expressed from a positive White (nonracist) orientation.

Multiple Perspectives   Wai was not well versed in the multicultural literature, but he was conscious of, knowledgeable about, and responsive and sensitive to
multiculturalism and human diversity. I did a lot of reflecting during the interview,
and at the end of the interview, I did a summary. Wai seemed to appreciate the
summary. At the end of our initial interview, he commented to me, "I appreciate
this interview. I now realize that I'm more knowledgeable and sensitive to other
cultures than I had realized."

Wai's document delineating the racial and ethnic breakdown of his clients by
percentage was as follows: Clientele in Hong Kong consisted of 99% Asian (mostly
Cantonese Chinese) and 1% other, whereas his clientele in the United States consisted of 96% Anglo or Caucasian, 2% African American, and 2% other.

Wai, like Joshua, felt that his exposure to culturally diverse groups in the United
States gave him an above-average amount of knowledge in multicultural counseling. When asked to rate himself on a scale from 1 to 10, he gave himself a 10+ in
the area of cross-cultural counseling.

ASIAN CLIENTS: EMERGENT THEMES

Bias

Gender   Gender bias for both the Asian participants was based on feeling intimidated by counselors of the opposite gender. Wai, the Asian male, said he had no gender preference, but admitted feeling intimidated by female counselors. Mai Li felt
strongly about having a female counselor, and felt intimidated by male counselors.

Socioeconomics   Socioeconomic bias for the Asian clients is a complex mixture of clients experiencing financial strain and those clients from the lower socioeconomic strata being mistrustful of counseling and much more traditional in the
utilization of helping networks. Mai Li shared, "Minorities are more used to community living where their needs are met within the community. You don't have to
pay to talk to some stranger somewhere. The distrust of the counseling movement
is that it is middle class."

However, Wai felt that some pay is necessary regardless of clients' financial
situation to ward off abuse of free counseling services and to provide an incentive
to attend counseling sessions. Wai shared, "Some people in China and also here in
America are too poor to meet even the minimal scale. Some clients abuse the system; they don't have a commitment. Some charge is needed as a respect and as an
incentive." On the other hand, Mai Li, as a student, would not have had counseling
if it had cost money. She explained, "I got into the therapy because the first session
was free."

Ethnic, Racial, and Cultural   The Asian participants, as world travelers,
know firsthand the damage and pain of racial and ethnic discrimination and how
discrimination is even more potent in a counseling encounter. Mai Li shared a
telephone encounter with a potential Hispanic client:

I called her, and she heard my slight accent and my name, Ms. Wu. And she said, "Um, I don't know. How long have you been in this country?" Now, it's just my name and a slight accent. "Do you understand my culture, understand me?"

As people of color and international students, these Asian participants were adamant that counselors must be aware of their biases leaking into the counseling sessions. Wai explained, "In counseling, I need to be very sensitive to clients' differences and at the same time be very aware of my prejudices and not let those prejudices interfere in the counseling."

In Summary

For the Asian participants, the bias perceived has included gender, as experienced by the fear of or feeling of intimidation by counselors of the opposite gender; socioeconomics in the major role that finances play when clients decide whether or not to participate in counseling; and the awareness and sensitivity of how racial, ethnic, or cultural biases can interfere in counseling, and the adverse consequences of allowing this to happen.

Nelson and Holloway's (1990) study of gender and power involvement in supervision and Cooke and Kipnis's (1986) study seem to have some implications of support for Mai Li's discomfort or feeling of disempowerment with a male counselor. Nelson and Holloway found that supervisors were shown to reinforce their female trainees' powerful messages with low-power, encouraging messages significantly less often than they did with male trainees, and female trainees were shown to be significantly less likely than males to assume an expert role in response to supervisor low-power messages.

CREDIBILITY

Counselor's Perspective

Empowerment   Wai and Mai Li view empowerment within the confines of the therapeutic relationship. For example, Wai's theoretical orientation, philosophy, and way of life incorporate the client-centered approach. To illustrate, he took the principles of child-centered therapy and applied them to his own daughters. He said, as a result, "They seem more empowered. Just like the children do with me in play."

However, for Mai Li, humanistic philosophy is demonstrated in her understanding of the roles that the clients' inner potential and the counselor's genuineness and humility play in the clients' retention in counseling or counseling sessions. According to Mai Li, "If therapists can foster a sense of trust in their client, the client will carry on. Genuineness. Humility. Taking the client not back or in front, but alongside them."

Bonding With the Client   For the Asian participants, as counselors, credibility through bonding entailed a sort of egalitarian relationship with the client that involved mutual respect and sharing in the form of counselor self-disclo-sure. Speaking about his session with a gay male client, Wai, for example, said, "I shared some of my experiences or some of my fantasies about liking a man or a woman. I don't mind in that sense. Even though I'm a straight man with a wife, he appreciated the genuineness." However, for Mai Li, bonding took place more in the unconditional acceptance and the development of an egalitarian relationship. She said, "Unsuccessful therapy is when the client loses hope, is not validated as a person, is frustrated, [and] does not feel safe."

Essential Qualities   Both Wai and Mai Li felt that credibility in terms of necessary counselor qualities involved the counselors' skill and competence. Wai emphasized success as the importance of counselors being "insightful, able to stimulate, and give feedback, that is successful." Conversely, Mai Li stressed, "Competence in knowing what you are doing, coming across as confident in what you are doing, but not that you know all."

Client's Perspective

Empowerment   Wai and Mai Li, as clients, felt that credibility in counseling sessions through empowerment stimulated or tapped their internal strengths. Wai explained, "Somehow, I felt empowered in that session. It was maybe exciting, maybe stimulating, sometimes overwhelming. A good sign because I got some-thing out of it, something to think about or feel, then that's something I consider successful." Mai Li described her experience as follows: "She helped me gain deep respect, the way she talked to me."

Sharing and Bonding   For Wai and Mai Li, sharing and bonding with their counselors evoked feelings of respect, inspiration, and safety. Wai's experience of having a Hispanic counselor who incorporated traditional (culture-specific) ways into his approach in counseling was reassuring for him. He explained, "Some of those things he said inspired me and made me more aware and respectful of diver-sity." Mai Li expressed a similar sentiment: "If I have a good rapport, I feel safe. She could hold the things I shared with her with respect and tenderness. I could see the care, her love."

Essential Qualities   For both Asian participants, experience was most impor-tant. Wai said, "I think well educated, experienced, yeah. If the credentials are the same, experience is most important. However, if that experience makes that person more stubborn, then I would stay away." In agreement, Mai Li's comments were as follows: "I respected her very highly because of the experience that she has had. I don't care too much for young people, honestly."

In Summary

Credibility for the Asian participants was experienced as empowerment by the quality of the therapeutic relationship, that is, clients feeling safe, validated, and hopeful; the counselor bonding with the client through collaboration; mutual respect; the counselor's self-disclosure; and the counselor possessing the essential qualities of skill and competence. From their perspectives as clients, credibility was empowering clients by getting them involved, having them take responsibility for their own therapy, and teaching them using their inner resources; sharing and bonding resulting from a strong rapport, mutual respect, and feeling safe and inspired; and the most essential quality to these two counselor-clients, experience.

CULTURE

Cultural Knowledge

Sue, Arredondo, and McDavis's (1992) call to the counseling profession expanded the concept of multicultural-counseling competencies by including the counselor's understanding of the worldview of the culturally different client. According to Sodowsky and Johnson (1994), "Worldview is related to the person's individual perceptions and to social, moral, religious, educational, economic, or political inputs shared with other members of one's reference group such as one's cultural group, racial/ethnic group, family, state, or country" (p. 59).

From a humanistic perspective (being open, respectful, and collaborative), the Asian participants envisioned cultural knowledge as powerful when it originated from the client.

Wai commented, "Learn as much as you can about their culture. Don't impose that knowledge on them, like, don't just use them or categorize them. Increase the sensitivity and understanding."

Mai Li noted,

> Collaborative, a very inquisitive stance. I get a great curiosity about that person. That person sees herself as a person who can instruct me, and that changes the dynamics quite interestingly. And it happens in [a] therapy room where the cultural differences of the counselor become an asset.

Dialoguing   To the Asian clients, dialoguing involves patience for the language-different client to translate to his or her own language and back again to English, time to develop trust, and a feeling of sheer vulnerability.

Wai shared,

> I struggled to pick out the right words in English; I want to be very accurate. If you were of a different culture, I would explain more, and I can process more stuff. If that person can be patient, I will be OK. Listen more, don't assume.

Mai Li shared, "Holy ground comes to me. It's like a stranger walks in, and just because you are a counselor and you have professionalism behind you and training and so on, they are coming to bare their soul before you."

Culture-Centered Networks and Interventions   The Asian participants see a grassroots, immersion-in-the-culture approach as much more effective for involving the people from their countries and ethnic backgrounds in counseling. Hickson and Mokhobo (1992) have suggested introducing indigenous helpers into existing therapeutic interventions and a model of cooperation and collaboration, where the counselor and the indigenous healer refer clients to each other when appropriate, as options for integrating indigenous models of helping and traditional counseling and therapy.

Wai said,

> Tailor-make something like parental educational stuff; more people will come. Or a social activity, a party, picnic, an activity to celebrate the Chinese festivals, the Chinese New Year. If more indirect, they'll come. Say counseling, they won't do it, or a room with just you and I—no way.

Mai Li stated,

> Family therapy, I can see that as working very well because you don't just deal with the individual client, you can all dive in. Get the elder person to be the one, court him to give the answer. He becomes the facilitator. Support him and his authority. Don't work against that authority.

HOMEGROWN REPRESENTATION

Speaking about their homelands of Malaysia and Hong Kong, the Asians see the greatest threat to their people in counseling as a shortage of bona fide, qualified counselors. Mai Li said, "[There are] church pastors if they are Christians. There's hardly any counselors in town." In concurrence, Wai said,

> In this country [the United States], minority counselors are hard to get here. Clients may have a better chance to see minority counselors in big cities versus secluded, rural areas. We don't have recognized counselors in our country [China]; we have social workers and psychologists; there's even a shortage of them.

IN SUMMARY

In the category of culture, cultural knowledge emerged as important. In addition to the openness, respect, and collaboration necessary to gather knowledge of the client's culture, the Asian participants saw dialoguing with the client as building trust, creating a safe environment, and allowing the time and safe space for clients who had a different native language to make the needed affective and cognitive translations.

Counseling is not a part of Asian culture; therefore, counselors can create ways that are compatible with the culture to encourage Asian clients to use counseling services. Some of the suggestions the Asian participants made are congruent with Zhang's (1994) experience and value system as a Chinese person. Zhang, a People's Republic of China school counselor, came to the United States to learn American counseling theories, skills, and techniques. During his eighth week of attendance, he saw what he called a theme of "individualism" permeating American counseling. He concluded that unless American counseling theories and skills were altered, they would be inappropriate for modern-day China.

Last, in their Asian (birth) countries, the Asian participants felt that the biggest need was for increased numbers, meaning that there simply are not enough trained, professional counselors.

5

The Hispanic/Latino Client's Story

*T*his chapter provides an overview of the research on Hispanic/Latino clients' experiences in mental health. Next there is a discussion of the Hispanic/Latino study participants' experiences as they relate to the chapter theme. Using the Hispanic/Latino participants' experiences as a center, the chapter also highlights the intragroup differences existing among Hispanics/Latinos and provides discussion of counseling relationships that Latinos deemed successful and unsuccessful from the personal and professional experiences of the Hispanic/Latinos participants and bias, culture, and credibility factors addressed in Chapters 1 and 2 directly related to Hispanic/Latinos. The chapter concludes with implications and recommendations for counseling and psychotherapy with Latinos.

THE HISPANIC CLIENT'S EXPERIENCE

Well, I was very fortunate because of where I was, working in San Diego in Southern California. So, just the sheer numbers, the exposure. I worked in a clinic in an agency that was part of a health center that was just on the other side of the border. And every person in that agency was bicultural or bilingual, except for their director. They were all Spanish, they were all bilingual in Spanish and English. And they were from all different, mostly from [Mexico], but they were people from different Latin American countries. At one point, we had an African American counselor. We also had someone who was Filipino. The Filipino was a psychologist and more in an administrative position. The only group that was not represented was Native Americans. But the dominant representation was Hispanic. The clients were about the same.

—Angelica

Hispanics Changing the Face of America

Living in California, I had a lot of friends and I work with a lot of people who are Mexican American. And I was different, really, from [them], even though I was Hispanic and spoke Spanish, very different from my own orientation and native culture. And I have friends, good friends, and my very best friend is Mexican American. I feel a real close tie, I'd say it's almost like my second, sort of adopted culture. I feel comfortable with that culture, very comfortable. That may be the reason I made so many friends that are Mexican Americans and from the Mexican background. I like their foods and like a lot of things about Mexico. I am interested in their history and their art, and things like that. In addition, I had a lot of exposure to people from the Middle East because of my first years in college in Miami. In that area, there are a lot of people from Iran.

I have friends in Japan that I feel very close to, and I also feel very comfortable in that culture. I enjoyed it very much. I have a lot of things that are Japanese in my home. I also adopted some of their culture. Since I lived in Japan, I never wear shoes in my home again. Always keep the shoes outside; never bring shoes in the house. Just one of the things that I adopted, that's become a part of my family. Eating their foods. I love things I learn from that culture. And values, when we are eating.

—Angelica

As mentioned in Chapter 4, Southern delegates were opposed to the passing of the Immigration and Naturalization Act of 1965 that lifted restrictions regarding the number of immigrants from non-European developing nations (mostly countries within Africa and Asia), fearing that it would (a) flood U.S. cities with immigrants, (b) take American workers' jobs, and (c) change (i.e., upset) the ethnic makeup of the United States. The irony of it all is that the loss of American jobs is due largely to outsourcing by major companies, rather than jobs being taken over by immigrant populations. And the anticipated drastic change of the U.S. ethnic landscape was not the direct result of influx of people from the developing countries of Africa and Asia, but rather is a flood of people from Latin American and Spanish-speaking countries (the majority of whom come from Mexico, our neighboring country). In fact, according to U.S. Census figures (U.S. Census Bureau, 2008a), Hispanics have experienced the largest growth of any racial or ethnic group in the 21st century. This means that it is Latinos, not the anticipated Asians or Africans, who are changing the face of the United States.

The 2000 U.S. Census counted 35.2 million Hispanics, who accounted for 12.5% of the total population. This group had experienced a 61% increase since 1990, when the Hispanic population stood at 21.9 million. Approximately 35.3 million people now self-identify as Hispanic Americans. By 2050, the number is expected to increase to 97 million—nearly one-fourth of the U.S. population. Mexican Americans are the largest group, comprising almost two-thirds of Hispanic Americans, with the remainder being of Puerto Rican, Cuban, South American, Central American, Dominican, and Spanish origin. They are largely found in the southwestern states of California, Texas, Arizona, Colorado, and New Mexico (U.S. Census Bureau, 2008a).

Hispanics tend not to identify themselves as a racial group (even though the U.S. Census has identified five racial categories) or a single ethnic group, but as a cultural group with enormous diversity. Though research indicates a shared cultural identity (mostly Spanish speaking and Roman Catholic) for Hispanics and Latinos, there is no one shared identity but, rather, a self-identification that makes lumping them into one category impossible. This is problematic mainly because they self-identify from a variety of nationalities (e.g., Mexicans, Puerto Ricans, Cubans, and Dominicans), countries from South America (e.g., Argentina, Bolivia, Brazil, Chile, Colombia, and Ecuador) and Central America (Belize, Costa Rica, El Salvador, Guatemala, Honduras, Nicaragua, and Panama), and traditional racial groups (White, Black, American Indian, and Latino). In fact, Black people in

Central and South American countries have begun to refer to themselves as *Afro-Latinos*, *African Latinos*, *Afro-Hispanics*, or simply terms related to their country of origin such as *Afro-Cuban* and *Afro-Brazilian*.

In other words, indigenous cultures (e.g., Aztec, Maya, Inca, and Arawak) and African culture, as opposed to just Spanish culture, have largely contributed to the development of the Latino identity. To some groups, the African ancestry is more powerful than the contribution of their Hispanic identities.

Their skin color, like that of African Americans and American Indians, reflects a rainbow of human skin colors from ivory white to ebony black, from vanilla with almost no melanin pigment to the darkest ebony hue—or, in other words, from almost black to nearly colorless. In short, Hispanics have a common heritage, values, rituals, and traditions, but there is no such thing as a homogeneous Hispanic group.

The Hispanic Experience in America

Let me just begin with telling you how I see things. First of all, I see myself as a lucky person. For one thing, America is a great country. There are a lot of opportunities, although we encounter obstacles, we encounter things that tend to want to hold us back. I still believe that it is a great country, and I still think there are opportunities in this country. And when I look at that from a global perspective, I see we are more fortunate as Americans than people in other countries, even Mexico or Canada and some of the bigger countries like Great Britain. I still think that we are a lot better off than most other people in the world. So, I see it from that perspective.

—Alexias

Latinos have a complex lineage and thus a complex history that date back centuries. Hispanics/Latinos have resided in parts of North America for centuries. In fact, their American citizenry predates European American dominance. Not only did California, Texas, and New Mexico belong to Spain and then later to Mexico, but also Hispanics were residents in those states when the United States' original colonies were the property of Great Britain. In addition, Spanish settlers founded some current U.S. cities (e.g., Albuquerque, Santa Fe, Pensacola, and St. Augustine) before the 13 colonies were founded.

Nevertheless, as a group, both males (e.g., Vasco de Balboa, César Chávez, Horacio Rivero, Pedro Almodóvar, and Rubén Darío) and females (e.g., Dolores Huerta, Linda Chávez, Helen Ochoa, Joan Baez, and Dora Hernandez) have made important contributions to the United States and to their own people. Yet, too often, their accomplishments are not noticed or recognized. Their contributions have spanned the fields of literature, fashion, science, medicine, business, education, politics, the arts, and mental health, and have played major roles in the construction of this country. Inherently, Hispanics are an integral part of the fabric of the United States that began with the European exploration of this country and continued through its ascent to world power status.

Further, Hispanics/Latinos have also fought bravely and served proudly in the U.S. armed forces, aiding the United States in its fight for independence, for example in the Revolutionary War and the War of 1812. In fact, significant numbers of

Hispanics served during World War II; in the Korean, Vietnam, and Persian Gulf Wars; and in every other major war, and they have remained loyal in spite of the discrimination and abuse of their ethnic group.

HISPANIC OR LATINO?

If I was in a group of Hispanics, I would say I am Uruguayan.

—Angelica

I am speaking on my behalf and my own perspectives and my own views of the Mexican American culture. So I am not trying to generalize that all Mexican Americans or Hispanics think and see things the way I do. I am just speaking for myself.

—Alexias

As previously mentioned, to marginalized groups, the affiliation names given to their groups touch on identity and cultural affirmation; thus, it is important for them to be able to self-identify. As American Indians and African Americans feel about U.S. Census labels, many Hispanic/Latinos feel that the label *Hispanic* is government imposed.

Recent polls taken indicate that the term *Hispanic* is the most popular and preferred by the young generation and those who are native born. Still others prefer the name *Hispanic* because they want to remember and honor their Spanish heritage, and other Hispanics want to honor simply being a U.S. American.

Conversely, those who self-refer by the term *Latino* believe that those who prefer using the word *Hispanic* are ignorant that the latter is derived from imperialist Spain—the country that dominated and led the conquest, massacre, and colonialism of many Latin American countries—as its name for the cultural diaspora it created. Typical aspects of Spanish colonialism include racial and cultural inequality between the Spanish and the Latin American people, political and legal domination by the Spanish, and exploitation of Latin Americans. Also, there are those who simply object because the word *Hispanic* (which means of Spanish origin and Spanish speaking) was created and developed in the 1980s to create a U.S. Census category.

To some Hispanics and Latinos, the term *Latino* underscores ties with Latin America rather than Spain. The word *Latino* also traces its roots back to ancient Rome (Latin is the language from which Spanish and Portuguese developed) and is more inclusive, encompassing Latin American countries such as Cuba, Puerto Rico, the Dominican Republic, Mexico, and others that do not speak Spanish such as Brazil. Many *Hispanics* are referring to themselves as *Latinos* because they wish to honor their current culture and the culture of the indigenous people who lived here prior to the Europeans rather than imperialistic Spanish origins from centuries ago.

As a result of the difference in preferences among Hispanics/Latinos and to simply be inclusive for all the reasons stated above, in this chapter the terms *Hispanic* and *Latino* will be used interchangeably.

A MENTAL HEALTH PROFILE OF HISPANICS

When I came to counseling, I felt that the therapist was in a power position and that I came to him with this problem, and he was going to help me find a solution. He was in power, and he had more power over me. Race may have played a role. When I was growing up, my grandfather told me that the White man was right, and the White man had the power because they are the ones who paid us and put food on the table. So maybe, that's why, subconsciously or not quite in a conscious way, maybe, I chose a White man. Maybe I thought he knew more and could help me deal with this problem because he was White.

—Alexias

I had changed physicians, and I went back to my previous physician to explain and let him know why I was making the change. It was nothing against the physician. Before I could say anything, he assumed it was because the second person, the other person I chose, spoke Spanish and he didn't. And that was not the reason at all, and I was a little bothered by that.

The assumption was that I would be more comfortable with someone who spoke Spanish, and that was not the case all. And it was an assumption he made based on my being Hispanic. It was based on a stereotype. It was an erroneous assumption. Actually, he was Hispanic, too, but he didn't speak the language. Actually both physicians were Hispanics, but one speaks the language, and the other one doesn't. In counseling, there may have been a few times when the counselor had been trying to understand or to determine something based on what they knew about Hispanic cultures.

—Angelica

The environmental stressors and historical and sociocultural factors surrounding Hispanics' economic and education status suggest that, as a group, Hispanics are in great need of mental health services. Couple this with the large number of Hispanics who are U.S. immigrants, and it is not a surprise that Hispanics are experiencing multiple stressors associated with past and present discrimination on top of having to adapt to a new culture. To start, their educational status parallels their work status, both of which parallel their immigration conditions. For example, Cuban immigrants have the highest percentage of formal education, are the most financially affluent, and have the most professional and skilled jobs. Their profile, however, is in stark contrast to that of Mexican American, Puerto Rican, and Central American immigrants, most of whom came to the United States as unskilled workers.

Latinos have high poverty rates: 14% for Cuban Americans, 27% for Mexican Americans, and 31% for Puerto Ricans, respectively, compared to a poverty rate of 13.5% for all Americans (U.S. Census Bureau, 2000a). However, as a group, 36% of Hispanics compared to 9% of non-Hispanics don't have a high school diploma. The low educational status of Hispanic youth places them in low-skill, and thus low-paying, jobs.

In addition, those stressors associated with acculturation lead to increased risk for mental health problems. For example, Latinos, specifically Latino youth, have high rates of substance abuse, more anxiety-related and delinquency-type problem behaviors, suicide ideation, and depression, which often are unreported, undetected, and inadequately treated compared with other ethnic and racial groups.

Although a large number of Hispanics are depressed, the depression seems to be related to physical health. To further compound Hispanics' mental health status, of all racial and ethnic groups in the United States, Hispanic Americans are the least likely to have public or private health insurance. Their rate of uninsurance, at 37%, is twice that for Whites and more than twice the national rate of 16%. In addition, Hispanic Americans, both adults and children, are less likely than Whites to receive needed mental health care, and of those who seek out care, they are more likely to go to primary care doctors than to mental health providers.

Overall, compared to the national average, Hispanics have less formal education. According to the *Surgeon General's Report* (U.S. Department of Health and Human Services, 2001), nearly half of Hispanics (56%) over 25 years old have a high school diploma, and only about one-tenth have a college degree. However, academic attainment varies significantly among Hispanic subgroups. For example, 70% of Cubans, 64% of Puerto Ricans, and 50% of Mexican Americans 25 years old have graduated from high school.

Last, Hispanics are caught in the system and are thus disproportionately represented in high-need populations such as inmates, Vietnam War veterans, refugees, and individuals with drug and alcohol addictions.

In terms of language, 43% of Hispanic adults have poor English language proficiency. In 1990, 40% either did not speak English at all or did not speak it well. As a result, due to language barriers, Spanish-speaking clients have difficulty with accessing mental health and health services in such matters as scheduling medical appointments, understanding instructions, and taking their medicine. In the mental health profession, there are only 29 Hispanic mental health professionals for every 100,000 Hispanics in the United States compared to 173 Caucasian providers per 100,000 people.

Regardless of the source, Hispanics face disparities in the recognition, diagnosis, and treatment of mental illnesses, specifically clinical depression. Ironically, however, adult Mexican immigrants have lower rates of mental disorders than U.S.-born Mexicans. Thus, for long-lasting mental healing, Hispanics as a group, like African Americans, need a mechanism by which they can process the negative effects of historical abuses (e.g., colonialism, racism, oppression, and immigration) on their mental health. A type of group healing is a necessary precursor to the individual issues that Hispanic clients present with in counseling.

COUNSELING HISPANICS

The number one rule, more specific to my culture (Uruguayan) than other Hispanic cultures, is that you don't talk to anybody; basically, you keep things to yourself. The second one is that you don't go outside. You talk to someone in your family or a very close friend. Someone who is seen as a part of the family. When you say family, it could be someone you are very close to. You know. It could be an uncle, a second cousin. It could be a great-great-aunt. You know. And then, the next thing is acceptable.

You see, I grew up with people who are not that religious. I didn't grow up with talking to the priest kind of thing. But I, I guess, I have seen it more in people, my friends that come from Mexico who would think of it. Those who haven't managed their problems, they would think of talking to a priest before talking to a counselor. Maybe talk to a physician for another one. Especially, because, physicians in our countries, in Latin American countries, are much more familiar, more family oriented. They take their time. The physicians are contemporary support systems, as far as my generation.

—Angelica

One factor that might have prevented me from going would be if I had gone to my parents first, or if I gone to someone in my Mexican American culture and shared that problem with them. They might have talked me out of it, out of coming to counseling, by explaining, "This is how you deal with it, and this is what you have to do." I think that it would have been a cost and some money that would have prevented me from going.

—Alexias

Like the other groups of color, Latinos tend to shun counseling, drop out, or have unsuccessfully counseling relationships largely due to cultural differences. Hispanics, like Asians, are family oriented. Therefore, it is important to know that the *familial* is central in traditional Hispanic culture; it is both a social process and a cultural practice. For example, in the collective experience of immigrants, specifically those experiencing difficult social conditions of relocating to a different culture, adherence to family ties becomes a resiliency factor in their survival and adjustment.

Given the historically oppressive experiences that Hispanics have suffered, it should not be a surprise that Hispanics are presenting with mental health issues. Consequently, Torres-Rivera, Phan, Garrett, and D'Andrea (2005) have argued that a more revolutionary, radical worldview is needed to augment therapy with Hispanic clients. As a result of historical colonialism and oppression, it is not surprising that they propose using a social justice, political, and revolutionary counseling approach, one that incorporates the ideologies of Paulo Freire, Ernesto "Che" Guevara, and Don Pedro Albizú Campos, when working with Hispanic clients.

Second, counselors working with this group desperately need tools such as counseling techniques and strategies that address the cycle of intergenerational abuse resulting from immigration as well as historical oppressions. With the realization of a need for a more radical counseling approach, one with systemic changes and that reconnects Hispanics to their cultural resilience, Hispanic clients may report more successful counseling outcomes and experiences.

Thus, from cultural and systemic lenses, the social justice, revolutionary, political approach of Torres-Rivera et al. (2005) appears to an appropriate worldview tradition for viewing Latino cultures and this Hispanic/Latino case study.

CASE 3: THE HISPANIC/LATINO STORY: ALEXIAS AND ANGELICA

Well, beginning with my marriage, multicultural marriage definitely, it's not just a matter of accepting even his culture, but also making it a part of mine. In a way, being adopted by that culture. I learned to enjoy Indian food. I like to go to Indian restaurants when one is available. So, appreciating that. That's my main exposure because that's my family.

—Angelica

Angelica

Angelica is a 38-year-old married family therapist. She has earned a bachelor of arts (BA) degree in international psychology and a master of education (MEd) degree in counseling, and is currently pursuing a PhD in counselor education.

She is a licensed marriage, family, and child counselor and a licensed professional counselor (LPC). Her specialty area is marriage and family. She has memberships in the American Counseling Association (ACA), American Association for Marriage and Family Therapy (AAMFT), Association for Multicultural Counseling and Development (AMCD), International Association for Marriage and Family Counseling (IAMFC), Arkansas Counseling Association (ArCA), and Arkansas Association for Marriage and Family Therapy (ArAMFT).

Acculturation   Angelica identifies her race as White and her ethnicity as Hispanic and Latin or South American, but in a group of Hispanics, she classifies herself as Uruguayan. Although Angelica realizes that her strongest identity is with the Hispanics, she considers herself bicultural. "I am probably going to be feeling most at home with the Hispanic friends, people who have a Hispanic background who have some level of acculturation, bicultural, and have been here a few years." When I asked her to explain what *bicultural* meant to her, she said,

> Regardless of even their racial identity, they may be Asian American, they may be Hispanic American, but it's more of where they are at in terms of not being one culture or the other exclusively, but really being bicultural. Having really integrated two cultures in sort of a unique group.

Racial Identity   Angelica self-administered both the White Racial Identity Attitude Scale (WRIAS) and the People of Color Racial Identity Attitude Scale (POCRIAS) and obtained the highest score in the final stages of both instruments, scoring 47 out of 50 on the internalization stage of the POCRIAS and 39 out of 50 on the autonomy stage of the WRIAS.

Multiple Perspectives   Angelica's whole being lit up when she began to talk about how cultural diversity and her adopting various aspects of many cultures have bought so much richness to her life. Her personal and professional multicultural exposure spans from various ethnic and racial groups residing both in the United States and in the international community. To illustrate the degree of her cultural diversity, she gives several examples of the depth of diversity in her life. To begin with, she has a multicultural family: Her husband is from India, and they not only have a child from that union but also adopted their daughter from Colombia. Angelica has a best friend and countless other friends who are Mexican American.

In addition to her exposure to various ethnic groups here in the United States, she lived in Japan for 2 years and in Colombia for several years, has traveled widely, and had lots of contact with Middle Easterners, Indians, and others from South American countries. Traces of these cultures are visible in her everyday life, from the decorations adorning her home; to the manifestation of cultural values; to the diversity of religious, cultural, and national celebrations; to her enjoyment of foods and artworks from many cultures. For example, she talks about the steps she took to adopt her husband's culture:

> It's important to make that a part of our household, in terms of values, religion, foods, and decorations for the house. I mean everything, art. He's Parsi; it's

more associated to Indian culture, East Indian. He's Zoroastrian, his religion is. My children are being raised in that religion. For me, it was important to learn to cook Indian food.

Discussing her views on human diversity, she replied,

In general, it's more of a Western view. I have come to more of a relativistic, integrated kind of way of looking at things because of my being bicultural, being in different places, and my own growth as a person. Being in counseling, seeing myself as a helper, as a healer, as being people oriented, has had a major influence. Being more interested in relationships and being relationship oriented.

Later in the interview, she continued her reflection on human diversity with these remarks: "So, I see myself as a richer person because of it. So, to me it's part of reality or also a plus. It's enriching. It's what life is about."

Angelica's document described the racial and ethnic breakdown of her clients by percentage as follows: 5% Asian (mostly Filipino), 40% Anglo and Caucasian, and 55% Hispanic (mostly Mexican American). Angelica, when asked to rate herself in the area of multicultural and cross-counseling skills, when thinking of her future growth and development, found it very difficult and complex to commit to a definitive number. She replied,

In terms of knowledge and awareness, I would say maybe, hmm. I don't know. Maybe, let's say right now, an 8. Let's say now an 8, but it's probably not really an 8 because—but let's say an 8. Because years from now, if I continue. Because I see it as a process, and if I continue becoming more aware and gaining knowledge, I am going to go back and say, "That wasn't really an 8, Angelica. Now, it is an 8; that was a 6." Because there's no end to it, really. Skills, I'll say a 5. The skills, I would need, I would want more skills, in terms of how to adapt to different cultures, meaning how to adapt and what to adapt, what to take, what to bring. And that's, let's say a 3.

Alexias

Alexias chose to use his middle name as his pen name. He is a 48-year-old, third-generation Mexican American with very strong ties to his community. He is currently employed as a counseling psychologist in a large research university setting. He is an LPC in Texas and has teacher and bilingual education certifications. He described his specialty area as Spanish. He holds professional memberships in the Texas Psychological Association (TPA), the American Psychological Association (APA), and the local psychological association.

When asked to describe the affiliations that link him to the Mexican American group, he replied,

We spoke Spanish. Spanish was my primary language. I still speak it, and I understand it. I understand the culture, the holidays, the birthdays. I am active in the Mexican American community. I am active in the church. The church that I go to is predominantly Hispanic, Mexican American. I am a member of a couple of the organizations in the community, and I get involved in the community. I have community people, because of my position here at the university, who send me letters about issues that are happening. They want me to know what's happening, and they also want my opinions about what's happening and my representation in certain things.

Later in the interview, Alexias continued with other examples that bond him to his Hispanic and Mexican American culture:

Expressing feelings, as well as processing thoughts, I am much more comfortable with Spanish. I was diagnosed with some dyslexia and some dysgraphia. Dyslexia is that I miss words when I read them, the words. Dysgraphia is the thought processing. But it seems like in Spanish, it seems to me like I don't have that kind of problem because Spanish is my primary language, the one I learned to speak first.

Like Wai and Joshua, he is better able to process things in his own language: "When I read words in Spanish and process things in Spanish, it seems to make more sense and is clearer to me than when I tried to do it in English."

Acculturation   Alexias identified his ethnicity as Mexican because, as he said, "My grandmother was of Mexican descent. I'm of Mexican descent."

Racial Identity   Alexias self-administered POCRIAS and obtained a high score in stage 5, the internalization stage.

Multiple Perspectives   Alexias grew up in a neighborhood that was predominantly African American and Hispanic with maybe one or two Anglo families living there. He remembers the Anglo family as having a small store, and having children with whom the Hispanic and African American children didn't play and whom they rarely saw. Rather, it was the African American and Mexican American children who played together and ate together. His exposure to Whites began in the northern states. The Whites in the North, according to him, "seemed more respectful of us and treated us in a more fair sense." While in Germany, the German people were very nice and didn't seem to show any discrimination or prejudice. In addition, he had been in contact with American Indians, whose culture reminded him of his own culture and with whom he felt accepted and very comfortable. He shared meals with Taiwanese Chinese residents and African students from an apartment complex he managed.

Alexias's document delineating the racial and ethnic breakdown of his clients by percentage was as follows: 8% African American, 60% Anglo and Caucasian, 30% Hispanic (mostly Mexican American), and 2% other.

HISPANIC/LATINO CLIENTS: EMERGENT THEMES

Biases

Gender   The Hispanic participants, as clients, were drawn to counselors of the same gender. For Angelica and Alexias, having a counselor who shared their gender was a more powerful multicultural consideration in selecting a counselor than either race or ethnicity. Gender and gender biases in the Hispanic/Latino community are more fully covered in Chapter 7.

Socioeconomics   The Hispanic participants viewed the socioeconomic bias as three tiered: (a) being unaffordable, (b) being fundamentally for people of upper and middle (mostly White) socioeconomic status (SES), and (c) uniquely problematic for acculturated clients.

Alexias commented,

> If it would cost money, that would have prevented me from going. I wanted to be a part of the American pie; I also inherited the problems that went along with that kind of job. For a lack of better words, a White man's problem that I had to deal with, so I had to go to a White therapist to help me deal with it instead of someone in my culture who didn't understand.

Angelica commented, "Counseling is really a middle-class, at least upper-class phenomenon. It works mostly for people who have resources and are educated, also for people who don't have resources when you are able to reach those people."

Ethnic, Racial, and Cultural   Due to their race or ethnicity, the Hispanic participants felt that their education, skill, experience, and position as counselors have been challenged. In order to retain minorities in counseling, we have to address those biases.

Angelica commented,

> Until we come to a realization that those biases are in there, we will continue to lose minority clients. I wonder if some people, potential clients, doubted my expertise or position because I was different, have a different accent. Relating to some Asian groups for me has been very difficult.

Alexias commented,

> I have had some experiences where they didn't feel comfortable because I was Hispanic. White students questioned my education, my training—whether I was licensed or experienced. Minority students accept me as a counselor, as a therapist, whether they have been Black, Hispanic, and Asian.

In Summary

Hispanic participants' gender bias navigated toward same-gender counselors. Both Angelica and Alexias felt that counselors of the same gender could understand their gender struggles better than a person of the opposite gender. In terms of socioeconomic bias, counseling, according to Angelica, is an upper- and middle-class phenomenon and unaffordable for the lower socioeconomic class. It has a double-edged sword, meaning that it tends to be unaffordable and unappealing to less acculturated, more traditional Hispanics, yet those who embrace it find themselves trying to cope with the problems that accompany being socialized into the middle class as well as those lingering from their cultural backgrounds.

CREDIBILITY

Counselor's Perspective

Empowerment   These Hispanic participants, in the counselor role, felt very strongly that *empowerment* connoted helping clients ascertain their own inner spirituality or strengths.

Angelica commented,

> People pretty much come with some resources, and some direction, self-direction. They may be requesting specific directions. The purpose is to help, to help the person find that direction and goals. Oftentimes people just lack information.

Alexias commented, "Counseling is to have an understanding of what the clients' problems or their concerns are, and then help them understand and learn how to deal with it and to take care of themselves from hereafter."

Bonding With the Client   To Angelica, bonding with the client was a combination of relationship building and timing. She said,

> Timing is the key. Counselor's ability to stay with you, to understand exactly, to grasp the issue, make the right interpretation, ask the right questions. You trust her to keep your confidence with your life. It's that human aspect and the expertise.

Alexias, on the other hand, viewed it as a mishmash of relationship building and his personal attributes. He said, "I am an idealistic person who wants to help others and understand things better. I've had Asian students, Hispanic students, and Arabic students come to see me."

Essential Qualities   As counselors, these Hispanic participants interpret *essential qualities* differently. For Angelica, what seems important is a combination of the counselor's skill and experience and the client's readiness. Angelica stated, "It's the skill level of the counselor and the client's readiness to be there. How experienced this person is and how good they are. It's more in terms of experience, life experience." Alexias, in contrast, focused more on the counselor's understanding and sensitivity to cultural differences. He stated, "A sensitive counselor, an understanding counselor. Sensitive to cultural difference, the issues, the problems at hand, the presenting problems. I'm always trying to know, learn, and experience more."

Client's Perspective

Empowerment   As a client, Angelica's perceptions of empowerment are similar to her perceptions as a counselor of the bonding and sharing. That is, to her, it is a combination of the client's readiness and the counselor's timing and skill.

Angelica commented, "My own level of readiness, whether it was distress at the time or confusion. And the counselor's ability to stay with me, take me to the next level. Challenging me and sort of providing the right amount of challenge."

Alexias saw this empowerment as one that fosters internal action: "The way he put that empowered me to go back and use the power that I should have had or been thinking of having to do that."

Sharing and Bonding   Once again, for Angelica, bonding involves timing. However, in this instance, she explained it as not only the rapport-building skills of the therapist but also, simultaneously, her degree of readiness skills as the client. She said, "It's a combination of where I am, where I was at the time. And then, it's sort of a right match with where I am at the time, which you are as a person."

For Alexias, the therapist's sharing was the catalyst that helped him develop trust. He explained,

> I feel the therapist by nodding, by sharing and saying yes, and giving me positive feedback, positive reinforcement, I think that's what developed my trust in him so that I could open up and talk to him and feel comfortable.

Essential Qualities   For Angelica and Alexias, as clients, having an older counselor was essential or preferable. Angelica said, "I respect the person who is older, older than me. Personal and professional experience." Similarly, Alexias discovered that his successful counseling experience was with an older therapist, and the unsuccessful group-counseling experience was with a younger, inexperienced therapist.

> He was an older therapist; he seemed very perceptive and very sensitive. He was pacing himself to me. The group and the therapist, now that I think about it, weren't as experienced as I thought or she needed to be.

In Summary

For these Hispanic participants in the counselor's role, credibility was achieved through empowering clients to tap their inner spirituality; bonding with the client through relationship building, personal attributes, and counselor's timing; and the essential qualities of skill, experience, awareness of a client's readiness, and understanding and sensitivity to clients' cultural differences. From the client's perspective, these Hispanic participants achieved credibility through empowerment that results from the synchronism of a client's level of readiness, the counselor's awareness and ability to take advantage of it, and the empowerment that fosters internal action. Credibility was also achieved through sharing and bonding that involved the client's degree of readiness and the therapist's rapport-building skills, as mechanisms to develop trust. Last, credibility is seen in their preference for an older, seasoned therapist who had developed cultural sensitivity.

CULTURE

Cultural Knowledge

For the Hispanic participants, it was important to acknowledge the clients' cultural differences and understand the cultural perspective and how cultural differences might be misinterpreted in counseling encounters, but not without understanding the importance of allowing for the client's unique, individual perspective.

Angelica commented, "Realize that this person may have a totally different worldview. Acknowledge that difference; put yourself in a posture of "I need to learn from you." Be open, flexible, consider culture as a determinant, integrate the uniqueness of the individual."

Alexias commented,

> Traditional psychotherapy says that if the client does not maintain direct eye contact, then he is resisting. In the Hispanic culture, if we maintain eye contact with you, we are challenging your authority, [showing] disrespect. Understanding that culture difference, whatever little might be there [is important].

Dialoguing

I'm curious, I guess; I'm curious. And I like to understand people.

—Angelica

For the Hispanic/Latino participants, dialoguing is a combination of curiosity about the clients' cultural stories and a genuine effort to understand. Angelica illustrated, "I like to understand people, behavior, or why things happen. Counseling is an ideal place to do that. You have an excuse to sit down and ask and understand why something happened." Alexias, as a counselor, illustrated,

> The language was simple. They didn't say things that were beyond my understanding. I've had students that are Asian, Hispanic, Arabic; I've tried to make them feel comfortable and be honest with them. When they tell me something I don't understand, I say, "I'm sorry, I don't understand."

Alexias, as a client, illustrated,

> They were understanding and sensitive to my issues and my cultural differences. Them telling me that it wasn't a Hispanic problem, but it was a problem that as a Hispanic I was dealing with. He made comments like "Is this the way you grew up? Do you want it to be that way? How is it that you want it to be?" It was a validation of my feelings and experiences.

Culture-Centered Networks and Interventions   For counseling to reach the traditional and low-SES clients, the Hispanic/Latino participants believed that more outreach to natural networks such as the extended family, community, and clergy was necessary. Alexias's thoughts were as follows:

> Get more involved in terms of visiting the community, talking to the people in the community, trying to understand them, reading research about them. If there were problems, you went home to Mom and Dad to talk about it. If they couldn't help, you went to Grandma, an uncle, or an aunt.

Angelica's thoughts were as follows:

> Work on it by being less traditional in your counseling practice, and more inviting. Inviting people to come over and going to visit their homes. Visit the priest, or whoever the healer may be in the community. It takes effort and going beyond what your training taught you.

HOMEGROWN REPRESENTATION

In addition to bringing more minorities or multicultural groups into the counseling field, the Hispanic participants felt there was a need for more bilingual or multilingual counseling professionals. Angelica commented,

> Bring more people who are Native Americans, African Americans to the field, other perspectives. People who speak a second language. I know people who can afford to go to counseling, who want to go, but want a Spanish-speaking person. If there isn't one, then they don't go.

Alexias commented,

> Hire more minorities. At the time I was going to counseling, there weren't any minorities. I would have preferred a minority counselor, probably a Hispanic counselor, and a Mexican American counselor, someone who would understand the background and how we grew up.

CONCLUSION

A large amount of research on the effect of cultural orientation on the counseling process among Hispanics has focused on the correlation between college students and variables such as preference for an ethnically or racially similar counselor, expectations from counseling, and preferred counseling orientation. Arbona, Flores, and Novy's (1995) study suggested that ethnic identity may be a salient issue for Mexican American students regardless of their level of acculturation.

For the Hispanic/Latino participants in this study, it was important to understand not only the client's worldview but also acculturation patterns, and sense of ethnic and racial identity. This knowledge may help counselors guard against misinterpretation of communication due to cultural differences. Also, they felt that efforts made to connect with clients' social and natural support systems and to recruit more people of color in the counseling profession would, in fact, result in better services to clients of color.

6

The Native American Client's Story

One of the things I would look at on any scale like that—I still feel that even at that, American Indians look at themselves differently than any other race in America because we are of this country.

—Woodro

STORIES OF PROUD PEOPLE

We all have those kinds of things. I see others, Indian people whom I am more knowledgeable about. I accept them first as Indians and then within their various tribes.

—Woodro

A Sovereign Nation

I preferred American Indian. At one time, people were saying Native American in reaction to American Indian. All of these years we've been known as American Indian. The census, I think, is one of the reasons why a lot of people reacted, because during the census, when they first used Native American, a lot of people signed Native American because they were born here, and they are American regardless. You know, the way I look at it, it is American Indian.

—Woodro

*N*ative Americans are unique among the groups of people of color not only because they are members of federally recognized *sovereign* nations that exist within a nation but also, mostly, because they are the natives of North America. Due to the impact of historical factors on the experiences on American Indians and Alaskan Natives—specifically, the systematic, genocidal attempts to destroy their people and ways of life—any discussion of them, as with African Americans, must occur within a context of history and demographics, and an examination of contemporary American Indian culture.

The complexity of identity for Native Americans today is difficult to understand. This complexity is even more pronounced in multitribal urban areas and further complicated by changes in U.S. Census data procedures, specifically the Census Bureau's change in enumeration procedures from ascription to self-identification.

This switch to self-identification, on the one hand, led to a reclaiming of ethnic identity and major growth in the American Indian population. On the other hand, it also led to ethnic switching (changing one's racial identification), ethnic fraud, and internal suspicion among Indians.

Even so, there are multiple terms for Native Americans (Natives, Native Americans, American Indians, Indian, Amerindian, First Indian, Original Indian, First Nations, and Native American Indians). The terms *American Indian*, *Hawaiian*, and *Alaskan Native* (the latter term refers to Indians, Eskimos, and Aleuts) mean those who trace their heritage to any of the original peoples of North and South America and who maintain tribal affiliation or community attachment. In essence, these were self-sufficient and self-governing peoples who thrived in the Americas before Western Europeans arrived in the Americas and Russians arrived in Alaska.

The legal definition of *Native Americans*, according to the U.S. Bureau of Indian Affairs (1988), is a person who is an enrolled or registered member of a tribal nation or whose blood is one fourth or more genealogically American Indian ancestry. Congress defines *Native Hawaiian* as "[a]ny individual who is a descendant of the aboriginal people who, prior to 1778, occupied and exercised sovereignty in the area that now constitutes the State of Hawaii" (Native Hawaiian Government Act, 2009).

It should be noted that the American Indian nations do not use this definition to define *Indian* or determine who their people are. Hawaiian tribes (who identify themselves as *Kanaka Maoli*) are seeking federal recognition through enactment of the Native Hawaiian Government Reorganization Act (NHGRA) of 2007. This bill, commonly known as the Akaka Bill for its main sponsor, Senator Daniel Akaka of Hawaii, is currently before the U.S. Congress awaiting a hearing of the full senate. The bill is expected to schedule a vote and pass in 2010.

A Demographic Profile

In terms of demographics, there are approximately 4.1 million Native Americans and Alaska Natives, and they account for less than 1.5% of the U.S. population according to the 2000 census (U.S. Census Bureau, 2001a). Of these combined populations of Alaska and American Natives, about 4% are Alaska Natives (Population Reference Bureau, 1999). There are 517 federally recognized native entities (196 in Alaska and 316 in the continental states; as mentioned in this chapter, Hawaiian tribes are awaiting federal recognition), 304 federal reservations (53% of all Native American people live on reservations), 365 state-recognized tribes, more than 50 tribes without any official recognition, and more than 250 different spoken languages.

American Indian beliefs are deeply rooted in their culture and history. They believe everything is sacred from the tallest mountain to the smallest insect. They believe that they are a part of everything and everything is a part of them; therefore, they honor the creator, Mother Earth, and every living thing. Yet, American Indian history is characterized by military genocide, ethic demoralization, forced immigration and displacement, and present-day contemporary societal issues such as drug and alcohol abuse, poverty, and major health issues. Thus, viewing American Indian history from different time periods is a tool to understand their specific cultural experiences, worldviews, characteristics, traditions, and customs.

THE NATIVE INDIAN EXPERIENCE

The Social and Political History of Native People

Exploring Native peoples' social and political history and their relationship to the U.S government, though briefly, provides a better understanding of the diversity of American Indian tribal cultures and ultimately a better understanding of contemporary American Indian life. This means that an investigation of American Indian history is a necessary catalyst to identify the sociocultural, psychosocial, economic, political, racial, and mental health barriers that characterized their history.

Backpedaling in time is a necessary step in order to understand the historical elements that have led to Hawaiian Native, Alaska Native, and American Indian clients' mistrust of mental health services as well as mental health practitioners. This means that in order to fully embrace the mental health of Native Americans, mental health clinicians need to become familiar with the events that transpired during the major time periods of American Indian history beginning with the era before Christopher Columbus, the era between Columbus's arrival but prior to the Civil War, and from the Civil War to the declaration of the state of sovereignty of Native tribes. For the Native Hawaiians, they lost their sovereignty in 1898, when Queen Lili'uokalani was overthrown with the annexation (colonization) of Hawaii.

THE AMERICAN INDIAN GENOCIDE

Corresponding to these major historical epochs, scholars (Garrett, 1995; Heinrich, Corbin, & Thomas, 1999; Senier, 2003) have identified five key stages in American Indian history. The time span covering the first two, beginning in the 1400s after the arrival of Christopher Columbus up until the 1920s, comprised a lengthy period of genocide. It has been called the *American Indian Holocaust*, the *500-Year War*, and the *world's longest holocaust* (in the history of modern humankind; Legters, 1988). The stages are (a) the removal stage (1600s to 1840s), the reservation period (1860 to 1920s), (c) the reorganization period (1930s to 1950s), (d) the termination period (1950s to 1960s), and (e) the self-determination period (1975 to the present). The stages can be a framework for understanding the emergence of mental health problems surfacing in the American Indian nations and their response or lack of response to mental health services as a result of these adverse and horrific historical experiences of being in the United States.

However, it is important to bear in mind that the Indian nations' battle with the early Europeans began before the 17th century and prior to the removal stage, not as brute force but, rather, their exposure to infectious diseases such as smallpox and syphilis, which nearly wiped out (estimates up to 75–90%) the American Indian population. The American Indians' immune systems simply could not protect them against exposure to the deadly diseases they contracted from the early Europeans, including those that did not usually kill Europeans such as measles, chicken pox, and rubella.

Removal

The first stage, the removal stage, occurred between the 17th and mid-19th centuries. It was characterized by sometimes voluntary (but more often involuntary) Indian migration and the forceful removal of American Indians from their land—with and without policies and with and without treaties. It was during this period that the saying "A good Indian is a dead Indian" was coined; and a U.S. government policy was created not just to relocate but also to isolate and ostracize American Indian tribes living east of the Mississippi River, forcing them to relocate to those lands west of the river. Further, in 1823, the U.S. Supreme Court ruled that Indians could occupy lands within the United States but could not hold title to those lands.

Also, during this era, the United States negotiated nine treaties that literally stripped the Southern tribes of their Eastern lands in exchange for less desirable lands in the West. It should be noted that though there were some conflicts, the Indian nations attempted nonviolent negotiation tactics with the United States, including adopting a posture of coexistence; assimilating to and adopting European ways, including Western education and agriculture; and owning Black slaves to work those farms.

This virtually untold and unwritten historical chapter of American Indian history as slaveholders really muddies the water for framing a discussion on the history of African Americans and Native Americans as well as the ally–rival, slave–slaveholder historical relationship between Native Americans and African Americans. Though the implications are critical for understanding the experiences of these two groups of color with mental health and the training of mental health clinicians, it is certainly beyond the realm of this book.

Reservation

The reservation period was the second stage. It was set apart by the Dawes Allotment Act of 1887, following the allotment of granted reservation land to individual tribesmen during this period. It was characterized by the sentiment of "Kill the Indian, but save the person" similar to the Christian belief of "Hate the sin, but love the sinner." In 1887, after the bloodiest Indian wars ended, the U.S. government shifted strategies from the removal and relocation of Indians and made a concerted effort to civilize them through granting them citizenship, a formal education, and an allotment of land.

Congress passed the Dawes Allotment Act, which allotted portions of reservation land to tribal members via each family. It stipulated that the Bureau of Indian Affairs would hold the deeds to the land for 25 years before the Native Americans could get title. The government then sold the leftover reservation land at bargain prices. In essence, this legislation, which intended to integrate American Indians into the rest of U.S. society, like earlier governmental initiatives became one more method of swindling Indians out of their lands (Horsman, 1999). In addition to losing surplus tribal lands, many Natives lost their allotted lands as well, and had little left for survival. By the early 1900s, the population of American Indians was less than 5% of the estimated original population at first European contact (Thornton, 1987).

As an aside, Indian life on the reservations, for the reservations' 150-year history, for the most part has been pitiful, shameful, and a sham. From the beginning of the reservation era to the present, reservation boundaries were violated and encroached on with governmental interference or restrictions. The Indian people lived in impoverished conditions. In other words, the Indians were given the poorest quality land, expected to live in the poorest conditions, and stripped of their natural resources; their traditions and cultures were attacked; and they were left without much means for rebuilding any effective economy. In the meantime, the government turned a profit off the land while the inhabitants got poorer. All of this has resulted in more economic and social ills for American Indians, especially on the reservations.

Reorganization

The third stage is called the *reorganization period*, which occurred between the 1930s and 1950s. As a result of passing the Indian Reorganization Act of 1934, the government returned certain lands to Indian tribes. This act was put in place as a sort of early stimulus plan to aid in the reformation (specifically, the development) of Indian lands, people, and resources. It was to create credit, vocational, educational, and business systems, and organizations for the welfare for American Indians and Alaskan Natives. It was a measure to create and strengthen the economic foundation of Indian reservations, and simultaneously decrease federal governmental control of the Indian nations and increase their self-governance.

Termination

Fourth, the termination period was filled with governmental relocation programs aimed at ending the Indian Nations' reliance on the federal government and ultimately integrating the Indian people. Indians called it being *hoodwinked*. Instead of independence, they received interference and exploitation; instead of treaties, they received mistreatment; and instead of increased independence, there was increased poverty. There is also no denying that Native Americans and Alaskan Natives have not fared well with mental health services. In fact, like other groups of color, they have been violated and exploited by the mental health systems. Thus, mental health professionals are obligated to protect the human rights and to take necessary precautions not to violate the human rights of indigenous people in counseling situations.

Self-Determination

Last, the self-determination period began in 1973 and continues today. It is described as increased tribal sovereignty following a period of American Indian activism, and it picks up where the Indian Reorganization Act of 1934 failed.

Indian attempts to achieve sovereignty today have come with economic hardship similar to that of developing nations. American Indians living on reservations have the highest unemployment rate in the nation combined with the lowest life expectancy rate, except for pueblos and reservations that have oil wells or casinos.

Forward pedal to 2008, and find that tribal governments are desperate for change and, as a result, push for greater self-determination to deal with their peoples' problems. In this effort, they reach out to the government for aid, and the U.S. government's response has been that self-determination is a central component of sovereignty. In essence, reservations are sovereign entities and as such are responsible for their own affairs without interference. In short, there will be no help.

Keep in mind that this follows closely on the heels of centuries of interference, promises and broken promises, relocations and re-relocations, lies and more lies, military genocide, ethic demoralization, and forced immigration and displacement. There have been multiple roadblocks, both historical and contemporary, that have prevented Indian independence and sovereignty.

After the U.S. government systematically stripped Indians of their autonomy, it now has the gall and audacity to say, "You are on your own." This sounds awfully similar to African American stories, such as those of the Reconstruction period for former slaves. A recent example is contemporary welfare reform (which disproportionately affected those of color)—that is to say, the unsuccessful welfare reform (welfare-to-work or back-to-work) initiative aimed at eliminating poverty and ending poor people's dependence on federal and state governments—in which welfare made people dependent and then was snatched away.

In addition to extreme poverty, Indian nations are wrestling with social ills such as alcohol and drug abuse, juvenile delinquency, suicide, lack of medical care, lack of quality educational facilities, and high incidence of crime. This means that it is imperative that clinicians working with Native American populations understand that their problems reach far beyond psychopathology alone.

Mental health professionals are bound by fundamental ethical principles, especially *nonmaleficence* and *beneficence.* In the mental health field, the principle of *nonmaleficence* originated from the Hippocratic oath and stands for *do no harm* to our clients, whereas the principle of beneficence stands for the proposition to do good for our clients. Therefore, it is mental health clinicians' responsibility to first acknowledge Native American clients' autonomy in a system that has historically unfairly victimized them, and protect the self-determination of our Native Indian clients in counseling.

A MENTAL HEALTH PROFILE OF NATIVE AMERICANS

I'm becoming very proud of who I am and what I have done and who I was. And having that experience and knowing I am a stronger person for it. I have to go back to the Vietnam War, because to me that was the most negative experience, but it was also the most positive. Being in the military, being in the Marines, at that time. Coming home to a nation that didn't appreciate it. And, but, to look around and hav[e] Indians who did. And they regarded us as veterans, regardless of what the rest of the nation felt.

—Woodro

The historical and sociocultural factors that American Indians have endured over the last 500 years, including the seizing of Indian land, the elimination of Indian people, and the separation of Indian children from their parents, certainly have led to major distrust of White people and governmental services, including mental health. As previously mentioned, the five key stages in American Indian history from the arrival of the first Europeans to the self-determination stage were characterized by violence, exploitation, and cultural rape of Native people. This 500-Year War has culminated in a loss of lives, culture, and dignity, and in widespread and extreme poverty for the Indian people. This economic hardship and the environmental stressors associated with the American Indian Holocaust have, in turn, led to poor physical and mental health for American Indians. Economic hardship is even more pronounced on Indian reservations.

In additional to the American Indian Holocaust, American Indian service in American wars, such as the Vietnam War, also increased their risk of having mental health disorders such as suicide (and suicide ideation), clinical depression, post-traumatic stress disorder (PTSD), and drug and alcohol addiction. Overall, major and large-scale studies of mental illness among American Indians are lacking. In fact, there are few, if any, empirically grounded rigorous studies that can inform clinical mental health personnel for Alaskan Natives, Hawaiian Natives, American Indians, or other indigenous people.

COUNSELING NATIVE AMERICANS

Some of the things that Indian people have provided me have been a unique experience with other tribes. In that sense, participating in true cultural ways that are distinctly different from anything in America [and] have been here for thousands of years.

—Woodro

It is unpardonable that there is so little empirical research on American Indians and Alaskan Natives; specifically, large-scale studies are fewest for them in comparison with the other major groups of color. Nevertheless, extant research has found that American Indian people, specifically elderly and adolescent American Indians, have significantly higher rates of mental health issues such as the prevalence of depression and alcohol and substance abuse, respectively (Berkman et al., 1986; Curyto et al., 1998; Kramer, 1991; Chapleski et al., 1997; Manso, 1992). As with the other groups of color, Indians are overrepresented in high-need populations.

Similar to Hispanics and Asians, emotional distress in American Indians is also largely displayed and manifested physically, resulting in physical illnesses (Ackerson et al., 1990; Manson et al., 1990; Somervell et al., 1993). What's more, they are, as Woodro stated in the opening quote, "[d]istinctly different from anything in America"; there are culturally specific mental illnesses exhibited by American Indians and ones that cannot yet be diagnosed (Manson et al., 1985).

Access and Affordability of Mental Health Care

We need more empirical research by minority counselors and scholars with an agenda, with their specific minority, focused on their specific minority. We need Native Americans doing research on Native Americans.

—Lioma

Notwithstanding the underutilization of as well as the lack of data on American Indians' use of mental health services, affordability and access to mental health care are difficulties. Access to mental health services is limited primarily due to lack of money, no insurance, not living on reservations where there are mental health and health care clinics, and not enough Native American mental health practitioners. In terms of language, similar to Hispanics and Asians, a large number of American Indians and Alaska Natives need English translators. Also, like the other language minority groups, culturally there are often not words in their language that correspond to mental illness, making access to and utilization of mental health services problematic.

Next, according to U.S. Census Bureau (2008) statistics, at the turn of the 21st century, American Indians and Alaska Natives twice as often lived in poverty and were twice as likely to be unemployed or underemployed compared to European Americans. Further, only a small percentage (20%) have access to medical care on reservations (via clinics); in total, one half (50%) have employer-provided insurance, 25% have Medicaid, and one fourth (25%) have no health insurance. The last factor affecting the access and availability of mental health services for American Indians, especially those with major mental health diagnoses, is the infinitesimal number of American Indian and Alaska Native psychiatrists in the United States (only 29) and the small number of other mental health professionals available.

Nevertheless, mental health is one area in which Native American groups have taken the lead and clearly demonstrated *self-determination* for their people. Although a large number of Native American people are in dire need of mental health, Native Americans are exercising self-sufficiency and reaching out for healing within their own communities. As a proud and resilient people, they are rising up, regaining control of their lives and the welfare of their people, and slowly rebuilding the mental health of their own communities.

CASE 4: THE AMERICAN INDIAN STORY: LIOMA AND WOODRO

There are people differences because you can have four Cherokees in the same room, and they won't believe the same thing. So, it is more traditions passed down by the families and things. You have that in other cultures too. There is a dichotomy; there are similarities and there are differences.

There is the tendency for the dominant group to focus more on the similarities and not the differences, and things get kind of fuzzy. And you can't look at the differences unless you are a part of the group.

—Woodro

Woodro

During the middle of the interview, Woodro looked up at me with a gleam in his eye and a hint of a grin on his mouth and said, "Sometimes it works to my advantage to let people think I am an old, backwoods Indian. Some people," he continued, "believe that folks who speak like me, with a rural, northeastern Oklahoma, kind of Ozark-Southern accent, are ignorant." With a wide grin, he admitted, "I use that to my advantage a lot of times."

Woodro is 50 years old and refers to himself as an American Indian. He is a former high school English teacher. He earned a bachelor of arts (BA) degree in English and a master of science (MS) in education, and is currently pursuing a doctorate of education (EdD) in counselor education. He considers his specialty areas Indian studies and education.

Acculturation   From early on, Woodro said, he was raised in a very traditional Cherokee family. Woodro's pen name is actually that of his grandfather, who died when he was 4. According to Woodro, speaking about his grandfather, "He was one of those full-blooded Cherokees who didn't look Cherokee, but spoke the language and lived the lifestyle." His grandmother, who also spoke Cherokee, looked Cherokee and was Cherokee. His mom also was Cherokee, but his stepfather was Navajo.

When asked about affiliations and ties that bind him to the Cherokee Nation, he replied simply, "Birthright." He explained that it was "the way I was raised. The community I was raised in. My grandfather, my grandmother, my mother as being Cherokees. Contemporary, same thing, our history, our language, our traditions."

Speaking about how language has influenced him or bonded him to the Indian community, he stated, "I speak the language very little. I will be, quote, a novice. I would speak the same language in Cherokee that a baby understands." He sensed that for people who speak Cherokee fluently, it's a way of thinking, and therefore they speak and understand things completely differently: from a Cherokee perspective rather than from an English-language perspective.

Multiple Perspectives   Woodro believed that there are very distinct differences and much diversity among his people. In fact, it is those differences, rather than similarities, that determine the degree and quality of their interactions with each other; they accept each other by tribe. Woodro stated,

> With American Indian people, the first thing they will do maybe is become familiar with each other. Even the way they approach each other is different. A lot of times, we will come up and shake each other's hands and introduce ourselves and do it in a professional manner. And then, you sit back and you kick back and you talk about your tribe and you understand each other from that perspective.

Discussing further his exposure to people who are culturally different, Woodro said,

In growing up, in my earlier years, I was under the impression that the world was round, that everyone was Cherokee. Then, I became aware, when I got a little older, that it wasn't that way. Then, going into public high school in Tahlequah, it was different. And after that, after graduation and a semester here at Northeastern, I joined the Marine Corps and was exposed to much diversity. I mean, you had Asians, you had Blacks, and you had people from rural areas. You had them from all states. You had Marines from inner-city ghettos, Marines who were street smart. You had people who were just rural, and to a degree, you had people who were very naïve to very sophisticated. And then going from stateside to Okinawa to Vietnam and from Hong Kong and places like that, where you are exposed to world cultures, and you get a better idea of what true diversity was about.

Woodro's document depicting the racial and ethnic breakdown of his clients by percentage indicated the following: 90% American Indian (no tribal breakdown available), 5% African American, and 5% Anglo or Caucasian.

Racial Identity   Woodro self-administered the People of Color Racial Identity Attitude Scale (POCRIAS) and obtained a high score in stage 5, the internalization stage.

On a scale from 1 to 10, in the area of multicultural or cross-cultural counseling, he gave himself "maybe a 10, maybe even more."

Lioma

My diary entry regarding an interview with Lioma reads,

July 15, 1997 I simply could not shake Lioma's words, "I feel safer in the Indian world than I do outside of it," from my mind. She said, "You know, I could have left my purse, I could have left stuff on a blanket at an Indian gathering, and nobody would bother it, unless it was a tourist that came up. I felt safe; it is an understanding that we have, you know. I've never heard of Native American youth stealing from other Native Americans." And then she added as an example, "In the library the other day, I mean I've really got really cautious on campus holding stuff. But one of the guys in the classroom was Mississippi Choctaw, and he was sitting next to me in the library. And I said, 'Hey, I'm going to go down here.' And he said, 'Yeah, I'll watch it.'" As she described the trust and bond that she enjoyed in the Indian world, I had a sense of envy, maybe reminiscence, when that sense of trust and affinity was also found in the African American community. But now instead, there is a fear, a loss of a feeling of safety that once came from simply being in the company of my own people.

Today, I can only think what a wonderful gift and legacy Lioma has.

Lioma is a 38-year-old married American Indian, who refers to herself and her race as Native American and her ethnicity and culture as Cherokee. Unlike Woodro, Lioma is not visibly Cherokee, but grew up pretty much having been told from early childhood that she was Cherokee. Her father is non-Indian, and her mother's appearance, like hers, is not visibly Indian. She described her mother as half-blood Cherokee and Swiss. Like Woodro's, her pen name is that of a grandparent.

Lioma earned a BA in education and a master of arts (MA) degree in guidance and counseling, and is currently pursuing a PhD in counselor education. She is a licensed professional counselor (LPC) in both Missouri and Arkansas, and declares her specialty area as school counseling. She is a certified school psychological examiner and a national certified counselor (NCC), and she procured certifications in elementary education (K–8), secondary education (K–12), and guidance and counseling (K–12). She holds professional memberships in the American Counseling Association (ACA), Association for Specialists in Group Work (ASGW), American School Counselors Association (ASCA), National Career Development Association (NCDA), Association for Multicultural Counseling and Development (AMCD), Association for Counselor Education and Supervision (ACES), American Counseling Association of Missouri (ACAM), Arkansas Counseling Association (ArCA), and Association of American Indian and Alaskan Native Professors (AAIANP).

Lioma, like Woodro, speaks and understands a few words in Cherokee, but she does not speak the language. She grew up in a rural area and, also like Woodro, recognizes that there can be certain advantages to resorting to rural colloquialisms or clichés. Lioma explained,

> I guess I've used colloquialisms specific to growing up in a rural area. You know, like I'd say, "Everybody had their own row to hoe," and people would look at me and say, "What do you mean?" When I was a school counselor in a sawmill and timber industry area, they didn't have row crops. They didn't have any idea of knowing some of the things I said coming from an agricultural, farming area. I try to watch that, but there are some differences that show up.

Acculturation   I asked Lioma why she referred to herself as Cherokee, and she responded, "The reason is that basically, when I think of my people, that's what I think of. It's stronger than just identifying on paper. I'm very active with my people."

In distinguishing *band* from *tribe*, Lioma explained,

> Band is the geographic group, and it is usually smaller than a tribe. Traditionally, it has been like 7,500 people. Bands today maybe have up to 500, maybe 600 people. Historically, they lived in the same geographic area. For example, there's a White River Band that is predominantly in Southwest Missouri, Northeast Oklahoma, Northwest Arkansas, and Southeast Kansas.

When asked to discuss what affiliation and ties she had to the Cherokee Indians, she talked about her ancestry being Cherokee and gave a short synopsis of her band's history:

> The Cherokees Band, some of them left the Trail of Tears. Some of them were here before the Trail of Tears, members of the old settlers. So, it is a descendent group, our ancestry. Our tie is a familiar tie to a specific geographic area and the bloodline.

Lioma said that she is currently using her Indian name, and aside from commitments to saving the Cherokee language and learning to speak it when the opportunity arises, she described her more current ties to the Cherokee Nation as

I'm very much active in the political structure of my Cherokee people. I participate in purification types of ceremonies, traditional dances, I wear traditional regalia. Well, I wear a Cherokee tear dress when I dance which is reminiscent of the Trail of Tears and the suffering people had. Most of my people were over in this area, Western Cherokee. So that's more reminiscent. I have drumming tapes and things that I listen to. Sometimes, when I'm writing a paper or something, I'll put it on. I enjoy that. I keep ceremonial stuff around the house. One of the big things is to use tobacco for special blessings or stuff. It's called doctoring tobacco. And I have some of that that I may use for certain things. There's an interesting corn soup, eating corn. The traditional three sisters: the corn, beans, and squash. We eat a lot of stuff, tend to fry things. It's hard to separate from Southern cooking. But, one thing that I do and have done for years, that people find strange, and I didn't know any difference, is wild green onions. In the spring, I'll pick wild green onions and scramble with eggs. And you have a meal called wild green onion supper. That's very traditional. I grew up with that.

Multiple Perspectives   Lioma is married to a Jewish American, and like Angelica, she has an interdenominational, intercultural, and interracial marriage. Her husband has been adopted by the Cherokee tribe. She defined her ethnicity and cultural referent group as Cherokee; more specifically, she is a member and a group leader of an active Cherokee band. Lioma's exposure, like Mai Li's, began early in life.

My dad is German from what I can tell. But, he won't talk about anything. I got that from my grandmother when she was alive. I don't know anything about his dad's family. I suspect that there is some African American blood, and they don't want to own up to that because of the plantation era. My mother is Cherokee from both sides. My grandfather and my grandmother were both pretty much strong Indians. Except my grandfather became a Baptist minister. And at that time, preaching meant that you gave up being Indian and became White. He was more acculturated than my grandmother. His parents were Cherokee and Choctaw.

Lioma's cultural upbringing discouraged rating oneself in a competitive, bragging way. She cited several incidents where she felt uncomfortable, even anxious, over being forced to rate herself. She shared,

I do remember twice in my life in education programs (master's and doctoral programs) feeling an intense anxiety in class. The first time was in a reading diagnostic course that I had to have. We had to do a self-evaluation. And just that fear coming up and anxiety of "I can't do this. I can't rate myself high." I don't remember what my rating was, but it had to be lower than what the professor expected. Because the professor kept me after class and said, "Lioma, you cannot rate yourself this way" [i.e., too low]. I remember. I had a double whammy. I felt this fear and anxiety of self-evaluations, and then I had the fear or the impact of this professor keeping me after class.
    Then the other time was in a doctoral program on the first day of class, and I was told, the class was told, … that we would be competing against each

other for points. Again, this anxiety came up because I didn't want to compete with people in the class. I was thinking that "I am going to have to drop this class." That was the point in my life where I was going to say, "I am not doing this. This is against what I believe." And it's really uncomfortable.

Because of her apparent discomfort with this kind of question, I acknowledged her reluctance and uneasiness with this kind of activity and gave her the option of not responding. When I asked Lioma to rate herself in the area of multicultural and cross-cultural counseling, Lioma gave herself an eight in these areas. She replied, "I think that it would be different with different groups."

Racial Identity   Lioma self-administered the POCRIAS and scored in the internalization stage. Lioma's document demarcated the racial and ethnic breakdown of her clients by percentage as follows: 10% American Indians (primarily Cherokee and other tribal groups, such as, Chippewa, Seneca, Miami, and Ottawa), 5% African American, and 85% Anglo or Caucasian.

AMERICAN INDIAN CLIENTS: EMERGENT THEMES

Biases

Gender   Both Woodro and Lioma felt that females were respected and even cherished in the Indian Nations more than in U.S. mainstream society. The phenomenon of gender bias with American Indians is explored in more detail in Chapter 8.

Socioeconomics   Socioeconomics, as related to clients who cannot afford to pay, according to the American Indian participants, is addressed through American Indian social service programs. Lioma said, "Counseling will be sought if it is something that is paid for by some service project, meaning it was free." But personally, she said, "The family group stuff was covered by insurance for the most part. In the couples counseling, it was unfair that I had to pay $22 and he had to pay $10."
Woodro stated,

> Usually, American Indians are at the lower extreme of the economic ladder. Therefore, paying for counseling would be prohibitive and the lack of finances would be a factor. Therefore, agency counselors are likely to be providing services to low-income American Indians.

Ethnic, Racial, and Cultural   As American Indians, both Lioma and Woodro have experienced bias as a result of their race, ethnicity, and culture.
Lioma commented,

> Anglos make statements like "Why don't they just leave the reservation?" "Why are the Indians taking welfare?" or "Do we all wear feathers at home?" It is a greater comfort level if it's an African American client with me being Native American, than a White client, if they know that.

Woodro commented,

> The first thing they notice is skin color. And that denotes a certain way of looking at people, and brings forth certain stereotypes about people. I have certain attitudes and stereotypes about them. In counseling, you have to eliminate those kinds of things.

In Summary

Bias, in the subcategory of gender, was an antithesis of that in American culture, in that the female point of view is not only respected but also actively sought after by American Indian men, unlike the case with White men. For clients who are of low socioeconomic status, counseling services are provided through American Indian bureaus.

Historically, American Indians have been exposed to racism and discrimination in this country. Textbooks, films, research literature, and the media have perpetuated stereotypical and negative images of American Indians as savages, murderers, alcoholics, and so on. Their history and culture have been immensely misrepresented and misunderstood. Nevertheless, as American Indians, these participants have managed to move beyond the inquisitions and biases that occur when people assume or realize that they are American Indians. The findings of this study demonstrate some of the ways they remain mentally healthy and at the same time work at eliminating biased attitudes and behaviors in counseling settings.

CREDIBILITY

Counselor's Perspective

Empowerment   For both American Indian participants, as counselors, *empowerment* meant using counseling as a medium for helping clients discover their inner resources and answers for themselves. Lioma commented, "Empower the client to be able to cope and to make decisions about their own lives and to be satisfied and feel comfortable about and with those decisions."

Woodro commented, "Clients want to know more about themselves, find a resolution, be empowered. They are looking for answers, and ultimately all the answers are within them. They need the counseling to bring it forth and validate it."

Bonding With the Client   Bonding with the clients, for American Indian participants, involved client-centered conditions such as openness, acceptance, immediacy, and rapport building. Lioma articulated that it is "an opportunity to gain a sense of security, safety, and trust. Openness and a willingness to build rapport, helping clients come up with their own strategies and coping skills."

Woodro asserted, "You can't fool a client. It is that acceptance, immediacy, connectedness to the counselor, trust. If you don't feel that, you can always say, "It's a piss-poor experience; I don't want to do it again."

Essential Qualities   Essential qualities ranged from Woodro's self-responsibility philosophy to Lioma's humanistic approach. Lioma stated, "Empathic, warm, genuine, respectful. Being nonjudgmental, yet willing to confront incongruencies," whereas Woodro said, "I see people as being responsible for themselves."

Client's Perspective

Empowerment   For Lioma, simply being understood was empowering when she was a client, whereas for Woodro, it was being able to resolve his own problems. Woodro stated very definitely, "I can resolve my problems myself, the difference between a healthy way and an unhealthy way of being." Lioma, in describing a successful counseling encounter, said,

> He blatantly said, "Tell her she's going to hell if she leaves me." And they said, "No, if she believes that, she already knows that, and there's no need for us to say anything." They understood. One of the few times in my life that I had felt that empowered.

Sharing and Bonding   As clients, feeling connected and understood were key ingredients in the bonding and sharing that occurred in their successful counseling encounters or entrance into counseling. Lioma said simply, "I sensed from them that they understood." However, for Woodro, it was that connection to others who had undergone what he had. He stated,

> I feel one thing that really helped me to get through the crisis in my life that went on for several years as a veteran was the need to connect with other veterans. Dealing with connectedness with other veterans enticed me into the situation.

Essential Qualities   Both Lioma and Woodro, as clients, have discovered that high skill level and a nondirective approach are essential qualities for an effective therapeutic encounter. For Lioma, it was success in a more conventional counseling encounter; however, for Woodro, the counselor was a traditional healer.

Lioma commented, "The skill level was pretty high with the couples counseling. But, it was a more nondirective Rogerian type of thing."

Woodro commented,

> He would show up, sit down, and say, "Hey Chief. What's going on?" And we would talk and talk, and then he would go. Days later, I would think something he said was pretty profound. I didn't think he knew what he was talking about at the time.

In Summary

For the American Indian participants, credibility through empowerment, bonding and sharing, and essential qualities was achieved through Rogerian techniques such as the encouragement of clients' inner resources, self-responsibility, and client-centered conditions (authenticity, empathy, acceptance, honesty, and therapeutic rapport), As clients, the participants felt more connected and understood by those counselors who exhibited high skill levels and a nondirective approach.

CULTURAL KNOWLEDGE

A critical component is to acknowledge cultural differences and assess whether you as a practitioner feel comfortable discussing cultural, ethnic, or racial issues. Any counselors of color involved in a cross-cultural counseling relationship who lack cultural knowledge run the same risks of therapeutic ineffectiveness and propensities toward overpathologizing as do White counselors (Rollock, Westman, & Johnson, 1992). This frustration felt by Lioma as a client in multiple-family counseling, as she tried to explain what the concept *bloodline* meant to her, is an example of therapeutic ineffectiveness. Lioma commented, "They didn't understand the concept of bloodline. I was trying to explain. I remember at one point I said, 'You don't understand.'" In another statement, Lioma warned, "Whatever meaning the client assigns to a situation is the truth. Seeing it from that particular perspective of not being part of the dominant culture, that is difficult."

Woodro summarized the importance of culture knowledge with the following statements:

> Looking from more than a broad, general sense of Black, Asian, American Indian or White. Every individual has different characteristics, attitudes, ways of being. Look at the client as an individual who has a racial, ethnic background. To our people, being alien and differences are seen as good.

Dialoguing

The American Indian participants felt that, verbally, there was more silence or less talk with American Indians because of a need to be prudent when speaking for fear of being misunderstood. To them, American Indian communication reflects a high-context, less verbal culture with more of a focus on listening.

Lioma explained,

> I thought very carefully about what I was going to say and how it was going to be interpreted. Even though it wasn't a different language, it was like processing it as you would get [it] out, thinking about it and being very cautious. When I'm with Native Americans, there's talk and chatter going on, but it's not the same. A lot of high-context, nonverbal things.

Woodro explained,

> With American Indians, there's a degree of silence; it's being careful in wanting to choose the right words. It makes a White person very nervous. You choose carefully what you do say; you don't want to be misunderstood. "Don't worry about it; all you have to do is listen to the drums." I never understood what they meant until that day, then, hearing the drum and what they had to say.

Culture-Centered Networks and Interventions

The American Indian participants advocated a more experiential approach, which includes an immersion in the culture of the client and an awareness of the indigenous support systems in that client's culture. This need for nontraditional, culture-specific counseling endeavors with the American Indian population is well documented in the literature.

Lioma shared,

> Getting out in the field, going to the reservations, Indian activities. Get a better understanding of modern-day Native Americans. Going to urban areas, the Hispanic communities, the Italian communities, actually doing some work. An awareness that the support systems are out there.

Woodro shared,

> More experiential activity. Understanding that for the Navajo, for healing purposes, the sand paintings that they do are a part of the treatment. Sweat lodges, there is a lot of symbolism associated with it. We need to look at those differences as strengths also.

Herring (1996) cautioned non–Native Americans to be very sensitive to and careful with the use of indigenous healing techniques, using them only under the supervision of a Native healer.

HOMEGROWN REPRESENTATION

Homegrown representation for American Indians was a need for specific groups to conduct research on their own ethnic groups and to hire more people of color. Lioma advocated for more inside perspective, that is, people of color conducting research on their own ethnic groups. She believed, "If you get a Native American author, that would at least get you a little closer." Woodro noted, in terms of a diverse faculty in academe, universities' tendency to opt for White women to satisfy the diversity piece. He commented, "I've seen White women become a minority in regard to the legal definition. And a lot of times, what I would see are White women become hired before a minority man."

IN SUMMARY

Balance and cycle–circle were reoccurring themes in the interviews with the American Indian participants. Balance, according to Garrett and Myers (1996), is a desired state wherein one is in harmony with the universe. Disharmony is a result of being out of balance, when we lose sight of our place in the universe. Further, American Indians' circles of life surround us, are within us, and consist of the many relationships of our existence.

In describing her worldview, Lioma said, "It is all in a cycle, and you can't say that one thing is higher than another thing because it is all together and the best thing to do is be balanced and have it all." In describing how natural support systems can be integrated into counseling, once again, the theme of balance appeared. Lioma replied, "The support systems would be used first, and it would be when there is a sense of disharmony and imbalance or anxiety that's created that [people would] need assistance from someplace else."

Similarly, with Woodro, the themes of balance and circle–cycle reoccur throughout the interview. For example, balance was found in over 10 statements or phrases he made during the Standard Open-Ended Interview Guide (SOIG) interview, such as the following: "I like to think I'm a fairly balanced person," "That there is a relationship that is balanced," "Balance that the person has to attain," and "There is a particular way of looking at how people stay in balance."

For the Native American participants, this complex category of culture means doing some background work, such as counselors immersing themselves in the culture, familiarizing themselves with cultural nuances and traditional techniques, and grasping the role of silence or little verbal communication in the Cherokee Nation in an effort to better understand a Native American client in counseling situations. They felt it was important to hire racial and ethnic minority faculty with a specific research, teaching, and service agenda for their specific racial group.

There have been a few researchers who hold a similar view that there is a need for and an advantage to having members of a particular racial or ethnic group conduct research on their own group (Mio & Iwamasa, 1993; Parham, 1993). Both Native American participants advocated not for *only* but for *more* researchers of color doing research on their own group. They believed that differences can be better understood from members within that racial or ethnic group. In other words, people who are of a specific group, though they see themselves as connected, naturally recognize their intragroup differences.

7

Gender
Gunpowder and Lead

The women of this world—as the women of Texas, and women of the United States of America—must exercise a leadership quality, a dedication, a concern, and a commitment which is not going to be shattered by inanities and ignorance and idiots. … We only want, we only ask, that when we stand up and talk about one nation under God, liberty, justice for everybody, we only want to be able to look at the flag, put our right hand over our hearts, repeat those words, and know that they are true.

—Barbara Jordan (Blue & Naden, 1992)

GENDER ISSUES

I have had mentoring experiences. Ironically, they have all been with African American males. I have yet to have a female African American mentor in the program, but I do have an African American female mentor who kind of guides me along throughout the program, as far as things I should keep in mind; that's why she has been there. She is not a professor; she's an administrator, but she does have a PhD in counseling.

—Shawn

This chapter provides an overview of the literature on the experiences of groups of color in mental health based on gender with a subsequent discussion of the experiences of male and female participants of color (in each ethnic and racial group). Using the participants' experiences as a focal point, it will compare and contrast male and female participants' responses to the factor of *gender bias* addressed in Chapters 3 through 6, highlighting the similarities and the gender differences existing within the African Americans', Asians', Hispanics and Latinos', and Native Americans' experiences with mental health services. The chapter will conclude with multiethnic, multiracial, feminist, and gender implications and recommendations for counseling and psychotherapy with people of color.

Although gender and sex can be seen as overlapping and fluid categories with multiple meanings, *gender* in this chapter is used to refer primarily to the social experiences and expectations associated with being female or male. *Sex* refers to the biological and physiological features that characterize and define men and women. *Gender bias* is a construct that frequently occurs in this literature. *Bias* is defined as a partiality or prejudice. The term *gender bias* is applied to beliefs, attitudes, or views that involve stereotypes or preconceived ideas about the roles, abilities, and characteristics of women and men. Gender bias often is modified by and intersects with biases related to race, class, culture, religion, age, ability, and sexual orientation.

Gender and People of Color

If I am a Black feminist, serious in undertaking self-love, it seems to me that I should gain and gain and gain in strength so that I may without fear be able and willing to love and respect, for example, women who are not feminists, not professionals, not as old or as young as I am, women who have neither job nor income, women who are not Black. And it seems to me that the strength that should come from Black feminism means that I can, without fear, love and respect all men who are willing to love and respect me.

—Jacqueline Jackson (1981)

Gender as previously defined is a socially constructed byproduct of our social experiences and expectations. As such, all humans are situated in a historical as well as cultural process. That is to say, for people of color, gender plays out differently than it does with Whites or European Americans, and differently among each ethnic and racial group. For example, *gender* for American males and females of color—including those in the lesbian, gay, bisexual, transgender, transsexual, queer, questioning, intersex, and allied (LGBTQIA) community—as with European American males and females, is grounded in multiple complexities interwoven in to class, geography, ethnicity, and other cultural variables. This means that gender, for people of color, is a derivative of each person's separate ethnic group's historical and contemporary experiences of being marginalized in the United States. Consequently, gender is complex and fluid.

For females of color, gender exists with multiple complexities; their class, race, ethnicity, and gender statuses create unique combinations, rather than separate statuses that have simply been added together. Unfortunately, it is within these aggregates, the private spaces, that African American women are most wounded, hurt, and demoralized (hooks, 1989). Similarly to females of color, Brooks and Good (2001) put emphasis on the fluidity and complexity of gender identity for men of color and the importance of mental health professionals treating gender for men of color as a unique culture, one that makes them particularly susceptible to gender role identity conflict and distress.

Among African Americans, Hispanic/Latino Americans, Asian Americans, and Native Americans, their racial and ethnic identity, traditional gender roles, and gender identity often clash with those of mainstream Americans. This clash of cultures for men and women of color creates gender conflict and psychological distress, and it adversely affects their help-seeking behavior. Thus, an important first step is to place this discussion of gender and gender roles within a cultural framework that addresses the cultural conflicts existing between groups of color and mainstream society, and also within a global context that addresses the clashes between American Western culture and the countries of origin for some people of color. This broadens our understanding of the complexities of gender roles in communities of color.

Next, gender and mental health among groups of color require mental health professionals to recognize the economical, social, and psychological effects that historical assaults, genocide, and intentional efforts to dismantle and depower families of color have had on the social construction of gender and gender roles, specifically femininity and masculinity, for men and women of color. This means that any understanding of gender for men and women of color is predicated on an understanding of the complexity of their multiple identities as a result of their collective and unique identity, ethnic history, and culture.

There is the full range of gender roles beyond those of males and females that exist in groups of color and among all cultures. Although this chapter does not directly address nontraditional gender roles and LGBTQIA gender identity and gender roles for people of color, it does, however, recognize them as another dimension for gender identity in communities of color that has major implications for gender and counseling. Thus, acknowledging the existence of nontraditional gender roles, nontraditional sexual identity and orientation, and multiple genders in counseling people of color is another critical component in understanding gender roles for groups of color. Not to do so is hypocritical as well as naïve, and would leave this chapter on gender unproductive, full of loopholes, and a bit dangerous.

VIOLENCE AGAINST WOMEN

Many years ago when I was a student in San Diego, I was driving down the freeway with a friend when we encountered a Black woman wandering along the shoulder. Her story was extremely disturbing. Despite her uncontrollable weeping, we were able to surmise that she had been raped and dumped along the side of the road. After a while, she was able to wave down a police car, thinking that they would help her. However, when the White policeman picked her up, he did not comfort her, but rather seized upon the opportunity to rape her once more.

—Angela Davis (2000)

While running through the park at 6:30 a.m., I was listening to and enjoying the lyrics of Miranda Lambert's song "Gunpowder and Lead":

He slap my face and he shook me like a rag doll
Don't that sound like a real man
I'm going to show him what a little girl's made of
gunpowder and lead.

As I listened, I saw the connection to the song and the vulnerability and plight of so many women all over the world. After the song ended, it occurred to me that the song title would also be a most befitting title for this chapter on gender.

Befitting not because of the violence, but because it sheds light on spousal abuse. In other words, it has become an anthem for women who have been abused.

Violence Against Women of Color

[Feminism] asks that women be free to define themselves, instead of having their identity defined for them, time and time again, by their culture and by their men.

—Faludi (1991)

Any conversation on gender issues for women of color must include a dialogue on the darker side of traditional gender roles: violence against women, specifically domestic and sexual violence. This includes American women of color with national ties to other countries. Globally, in addition to domestic and sexually violent behavior against women, every day unthinkable and hideous violent offenses such as the human trafficking of women (e.g., in Saudi Arabia, Mexico, and Thailand), genital mutilation (e.g., in Kenya and Eastern African countries), sex work (in all countries), the prostitution of female children (e.g., in Thailand, Mexico, and Brazil), and the burning of wives (e.g., in Pakistan and India) are committed against women. It behooves us as U.S. women to remember that as a nation, "Only one generation separates us from that era of silence" on violence against women, in particular domestic and sexual violence (Davis, 2000).

As illustrated in Angela Davis's (2000) opening quote for this section, for women of color, gender is often an inseparable phenomenon from violence of all types. As a result, violence is exacerbated and elevated. For instance, women of color and marginalized women (e.g., poor women, women with disabilities, elderly women, lesbians, and those in custodial care) are frequently the most vulnerable to all forms of sexual assault, violence, and abuse of power (Field & Caetano, 2003; Hindin & Adair, 2002; Jasinski & Dietz, 2004). The abuse occurs in multiple arenas such as inside families, societies, countries, prisons, and the medical, educational, and mental health sectors. By and large, women of color face the greatest obstacles in obtaining protection, needed services, and prosecution.

Time and again, women of color are portrayed as sexual objects, erotic, promiscuous, and/or animalistic, and thus as sexually available and unworthy of protection. As a result of such stereotyping, women of color are victimized not only in American society, within their families, and within their ethnic and racial groups but also by the criminal justice system that is in place to protect them. For example, courts have taken sexual assault, marital rape, date rape, and domestic violence less seriously when the victims are Black, Asian, Hispanic, or American Indian (Cattaneo & Goodman, 2005).

MEN OF COLOR AND MASCULINITY

It is a peculiar sensation, this double-consciousness, this sense of always looking at one's self through the eyes of others. ... One ever feels his two ness,—an American, a Negro; two souls, two thoughts, two unreconciled strivings.

—Dubois (1903/1996)

Gender is fluid because it takes on different contexts in American society as opposed to within specific ethnic cultures. In fact, the traditional gender role identity, specifically masculinity, for White men in mainstream society often remains out of reach for men of color. For example, the institution of slavery castrated the African man's masculinity. Being a slave with no say-so over either himself or his family took away his ability to provide for and protect his wife, children, or even himself and fulfill the traditional American male gender role of provider and protector of his wife and children.

For African American, Hispanic, Asian, and American Indian men, their traditional gender roles were reconfigured in the slavery, refugee, immigration, and forced migration experiences—legal and illegal (e.g., the immigration experience of Hispanic Americans, the forced relocation experience of American Indians, and the forced immigration or slavery experience of African Americans). Some Hispanics did not come over the border, rather the border came over them. This means that there were Hispanics who resided in the United States (New Mexico, Arizona, Texas, and California) when these territories belonged to Mexico.

In other words, for men of color, the overarching question becomes how being a male, given their experience in a dominating oppressive system, has been influential in their constructions of masculinity and their maleness (Alford, 2003; Heppner & Heppner, 2008). Racism, in particular for African American men, has had dire psychological consequences for their masculine identity. This means that their gender, like their racial identity as men of color, also has been pushed to the margins and created internal conflict for men of color who are unable to meet the traditional standard of White masculinity.

Certain cultures are thought to adhere more strictly to traditional male gender roles than others. To understand male gender for men of color, gender must be viewed within the context of the ethnic, racial, and cultural differences existing between White men and men of color, both heterosexual and gay. For example, African American men frequently express conflict about their gender role expectations—trapped between the unattainable role of society's definition of masculinity and the culturally specific expectations of the African American community.

From the violence perspective, although research shows that violence crosses multiple boundaries including age, ethnicity and race, socioeconomics, religion, geography, and sexuality, men of color have certainly been perpetrators of violence against women in both the United States and countries abroad (Campbell, 2004; Chen & White, 2004; Field & Caetano, 2003). The sexual assault and violence mentioned in the "Violence Against Women " section of this chapter are primarily attacks on women by men. In other words, as people of color, these men of color have two adversarial, oppositional identities. On the one sleeve, they wear a racial and ethnic identity grounded in oppression, and on the other sleeve, they wear a gender identity grounded in privilege and domination.

Nonetheless, many of the recent publications regarding counseling and psychotherapy with men and women from a gender perspective (e.g., Brooks & Good, 2001; Pollack & Levant, 1998) stress the importance of understanding how a client's ethnic and cultural background influences his or her experiences with socialized masculine and feminine gender roles. However, despite this emphasis, the empirical literature still tends to overlook people of color.

GENDER STORIES FOR MEN AND WOMEN OF COLOR

First, the counselors of color expressed a personal bias in terms of having a preference for the gender of the counselor. In all but one of the cases, the female participants indicated a preference for a female counselor. The male participants also indicated a gender preference, but not as specifically as the female participants. The Asian and the Hispanic males indicated that they felt less threatened by a male counselor, and the American Indian and African American male, though not excluding male counselors, felt that a female counselor was preferred.

The African American and American Indian males actively sought the feminine perspective. For them, the female viewpoint was needed and respected. Woodro, the American Indian participant, explained, "I always feel I need to connect with a female and get that perspective. I noticed that a lot of Native American men, that they do have a female mentor." Similarly, Joshua, the African American participant, said, "If I need input into sensitivity, I get the female figure. And if it is a male issue, I talk to a female again, and if I really want a male's opinion, I get a male."

This difference may be due to emic cultural differences, with Hispanic and Asian men coming from patriarchal societies whereas American Indian and African American men come from more matrifocal communities. Thus, it would seem likely that the latter two cultural groups might seek a female counselor. If the gender of the counselor is going to play a major role in the success of counseling experiences for clients of color, then perhaps we should be asking clients of color for their preference in terms of the gender of the counselor during the initial intake interview.

All of the participants except Wai, the Asian male, indicated that the feminine perspective was very important in their lives and their preference for a counselor. Wai felt intimidated by females and therefore sought a male counselor. Similarly, Mai Li, the Asian female, felt intimidated with the thought of having a counselor of the opposite gender. Because of the sexual attraction she thought to be naturally present in male–female dyads and the power image associated with the European American male, she was very uncomfortable with a White male counselor. For the American Indian participants, the female matrifocality was an understood and taken-for-granted phenomenon.

I found that some of the counselors, as clients, felt that having a same-gender counselor in some cases was better because of the similar gender journeys; therefore, there was a natural understanding and sensitivity that did not require a lot of explanation. For example, Angelica said, "There are things another woman would know instantly. You don't have to explain." And Alexias explained, "We were both males, and he understood me, and I understood him."

GENDER AND AFRICAN AMERICAN CLIENTS

Even in the doctoral program, let's put this on camera. When I first applied to the doctoral program, I was applying to the counseling psychology program. They had never had a Black male in this program. Never. My

GRE [Graduate Record Examination] scores were great. Everything from the educational point of view was great. I had a good chance of getting into the program. And I sat through the interview, and I thought I did great in the interview and everything. And I came back; I was turned down.

The feedback, the official feedback that I got back from this program was that I was too aggressive and overbearing. And it disturbed me so that I went to all my instructors and asked them had I been aggressive and overbearing in their classrooms, and they said, "No, we found you to be a bright, young intelligent man, and we enjoyed your feedback." Finally, one of my instructors, one of my mentors, told me, "I am just going to be honest with you. You are Black, you are a man, and you are not the smallest guy in the world. You are automatically perceived as being aggressive." And so, from that, all of this has been a great big cultural shock.

—Joshua

African American Females

In my family development class this semester, we discussed issues on race. Some people had very different perceptions of how Memphis is on the issue. Some thought it was a great place to live and that there were no racial problems. The minority groups [African American and Asian American] seemed to think citizens of Memphis have a lot of work to do. The professor made the comment that when he sees people, he does not see "color." While his intentions are well taken, that would be an insult to me. Being African American or Black is so much a part of me, just as much as being a female—so how can one not see my paper-bag-brown color?

Racism, prejudice, sexism, and discrimination will always be present as long as the Earth is here. People are real good about doing workshops and presentations on these topics. It seems as though people want to talk all of the time, but I'm interested in the actions after the talk is over. Talk is cheap; show me.

—Shawn

On the one hand, the African American woman is in a fight for civil liberties for her and her gender counterparts. On the other hand, as a Black person, she has had to fight not only for liberation but also for freedom (from bondage, lynching, the selling of her children, physical and sexual abuse, and modern-day welfare reform) for herself, her race, her man, her children, and her family (both male and female). Thus, due to their historical and current realities relating to gender and race, for African American women, feminism cannot be their central focus. Rather, they must integrate race, class, color, and gender in a collective liberation struggle with Black men for race empowerment and with White women and other women of color for gender empowerment. To further add to the African American woman's stress, trauma, and depression, there are many venues (e.g., film, books, and literature) that continue stereotyping and portraying her as the superwoman and/or as the hypersexed, nonvirtuous, or matriarchal woman.

There are several factors affecting African American women's use of counseling services, mostly relating to trust, self-esteem, feeling powerless, and lacking power stemming from the historical mistreatment of Black people and women. In addition, many African American women simply cannot afford counseling, whereas others enter counseling only because they are forced to go as a result of being trapped in a system such as the penal system, child protective services, drug rehabilitation, or welfare.

Despite such need for effective mental health services for African Americans, there is a dearth of research appearing in the literature devoted to the perceptions and use of counseling services by African American women, notwithstanding a need to identify effective counseling that is culture and gender appropriate. The good news is that in recent years, more scholars have focused specifically on the mental health of African American women (Brown, Abe-Kim, & Barrio, 2003; Brown & Gary, 1985).

African American Males

Well, I remember having a family therapy course, where we were sharing information and I was as usual— Black men in graduate school are few and far in between, and you have more Black women. But I remember, we were in this session one day, and I got to sharing some information that happened to me as a counselor. And we were just sharing experiences. I happened to say that "two young ladies came into the place where I worked at the time." And when I said, "Two young ladies," I was really attacked by the instructor at that time and the other classmates. And I couldn't understand why. And they informed me that I was being sexist, as well as being a chauvinist, by using the term lady.

And I informed them that from my ethnic background, from my perceptions, a lady is one of the highest terms you can attribute to a woman. They then informed me or enlightened me that lady comes from the White male Southern mentality and is viewed as being a derogatory term for a woman. And that the term now, which was the term then, was to simply refer to a female as a woman. And I kindly informed them that I once referred to my mother as a woman and almost got knocked over the head. So, I didn't consider that a good experience.

—Joshua

The social construction of African American manhood in mainstream American culture is rooted in images of *Black men as beasts* (Gould, 1981; Hoch, 1979; Turner, 1977), *Black men's rage* (Grier & Cobbs, 1968), and *Black males as an endangered species* (Parham & McDavis, 1983). These images result in part from (a) White slave owners describing Africans as physically aggressive, sexually uncontrolled, and in need of the Whites' control and protection, thereby providing the rationalization for their enslavement; (b) African American men's responses to frustration and anger over the denial of their manhood, identity, and personhood; and (c) the growing concern over the survival of African American men as a result of the massive social ills (e.g., drugs, violence, and gangs) plaguing African American communities. These images of African American males are illustrated in the following two incidents shared by Joshua in the "African American Clients' Gender Stories" section.

In summary, African American men's (like African American women's) environment often includes poverty, the criminal justice system, unemployment, inequitable educational opportunities, and negative media images. The African American man's masculinity is trapped between living up to the ideal White masculinity and an oppositional one that has been socially constructed and culturally defined by the African American culture. Regardless, his male gender identity— which has become synonymous with his masculinity—has been and continues to be unpredictable. That contrasts with the case for White men, whose masculinity is culturally validated and affirmed; the African American man's masculinity has to be earned and proved on a day-to-day basis.

It is important for counselors to be aware of their own biases and stereotypes based on negative portrayals of African American women, for example as *baby mamas* (with *baby mama dramas*) and *welfare queens*, or African American men as *deadbeat dads*, absent from families and remiss as providers. Most importantly, counseling should not be part of and privy to either the further masculinization of Black women or the castration and demasculinization of Black men.

Rather, counselors must source their techniques and strategies from the indigenous traditions and strengths of the African American community that liberate rather than victimize. From a gender perspective, a Black feminist consciousness or liberation counseling model would enable both African American men and women to become more aware of the social problems that are stifling the Black race. In particular, the African American man must tap that Black feminist consciousness—the way his African American mama raised him to treat a lady. His consciousness must be raised so that he realizes that sexism, violence, and woman abuse are critically dysfunctional to his liberation as an African American man (Marbley, 2005).

African American Clients' Gender Stories

First, Joshua shared two incidents that highlighted his experiences as an African American man: The first, discussed by him in Chapter 3, was a memory of a painful and unpleasant childhood scene in 1970 that happened during a high school field trip, where White people emptied a swimming pool when he stuck his big toe in. The second, discussed by him in this chapter, involved a university denying him admission solely on an image of him being too aggressive and overbearing. Hunter and Davis's (1992) findings suggest that because of the interlocking dynamics of race, culture, and class, African American manhood has been stereotypically, narrowly, and wrongly defined.

With both Joshua and Shawn, having a female figure to confer with was very important in their selection and seeking of guidance or counseling. They both felt that having a female perspective offered something of value and comfort to their well-being. For Joshua it was balance and sensitivity, and for Shawn it was comfort and safety.

In fact, much of the earlier research (Lerner, 1972) that suggested that African Americans are more apt to discuss their personal issues with females than with males still rings true today. Chatters, Taylor, and Neighbors (1989) summarized the following demographic factors in their article on helper networks among African Americans:

> Overall, respondents were more likely to discuss their problems with women than with men. Respondents consulted mothers at a higher rate than fathers, sisters more than brothers, daughters more than sons, and other female friends more than male friends. Women also had larger helper networks than men. (p. 674)

Another study, of African American adolescents (Coates, 1987), showed that gender differences also exist in the selection and utilization of social support systems. Coates found gender differences in the structure and support characteristics of African American adolescent social networks. Some of the differences she found were that males and females differ in the numbers of females and of males they identify as network members, in their estimates of the number of people they know and in frequency of contact.

Shawn commented in her interview,

> I don't know if I would've felt comfortable, necessarily, with a male, regardless of his race. I felt that I was opening up myself to be vulnerable. For me and my comfort level, women were preferable. It just so happens that I was asked if I preferred a male or female, and I said female.

GENDER IN THE ASIAN COMMUNITIES

My bigger problem is having a Caucasian male therapist because it's always a sense of a dominant White middle class and superiority.... Back home, it's always in the news; it's always superiority with men. Emotionally, it's still a thing I have to work past. It's always a sense of dominant White middle class. I am a woman minority. It's my own issue.

—Mai Li

Gender issues in mental health in the Asian community, like the other experiences of women and men, must be approached with an appreciation and respect for the larger social, political, and historical contexts in which they live. This means that the cultural predictors of gender issues may vary from those of other ethnic groups and between Asian males and females (Chen & White, 2004; Tsai, Ying, & Lee, 2001). Sexism, accompanied by violence against women, is the most insidious and historically pervasive type of *ism* and discrimination of all. Globally, gender roles and gender role stereotypes, specifically, are achieved and maintained by cultural beliefs and norms based on the devaluation of women both within dominant cultures and, to a smaller degree, within each ethnic community.

Thus, gender-related issues associated with gender roles, gender stereotypes, and gender differences are culturally defined, culturally specific, and acted on within the person's cultural context. Asian men and women gender identities and images, like those of other groups of color, have been stereotyped negatively and portrayed pathologically, and simply neglected and overlooked in multiple venues such as the media, textbooks, pop culture, scholarship, and the field of mental health.

For example, in Asian communities, sometimes it is the patriarchal social and cultural structures that reinforce those gender roles and gender identities that become the instigators of domestic violence and gender inequities in Asian communities, specifically those cultural beliefs about how women behave and how they should behave.

It is critical for mental health professionals to know and respect the Asian cultures and the different customs and religions that exist among the many co-cultures. Also, mental health professionals should be aware of the damaging effects of immigration on Asian refugees (e.g., Vietnamese and Cambodians) and the particular needs of Asian American veterans such as Native Hawaiians and Japanese. For example, both may suffer from posttraumatic stress disorder (PTSD) emanating from the experience of being in a war or war zone, and having experiences such as torture, death and near-death experiences, and marginalization. This can be further aggravated, in the case of Southeast Asian refugees, by the trauma associated with fleeing their home countries and the immigration experience of coming to the United States.

Asian Females

In the beginning, it was all right. It was an Asian American who provided therapy for me. In the beginning, it seemed all right; she was taping. In the fifth session, I got really mad with her because I had been telling her about issues in my family and so on. She had been respectful up to then. In the fifth session, she made some very nasty remarks about my father, and so I became very defensive of my father. So, I was defensive in the session and she was like, nonapologetic, you know.

—Mai Li

Tremendous diversity exists within the Asian community with respect to mental health–seeking behavior and knowledge, socioeconomic status, educational level, cultural traditions, and specific mental health care needs and issues.   This means that Asian women face specific factors such as cultural barriers, physical differences, and sexual and racial biases that may influence their mental health, mental health care, help-seeking behaviors, and access to and ability to pay for mental health care.

Asian women, in contrast to White women but similar to the other groups of women of color, tend to have fewer social, legal, and financial resources available to them. Thus, their mental health issues are often domestic and sexual (violence, family, and/or marriage related), acculturation related (adjusting to the U.S. culture), and socioeconomic (housing and employment) in nature. This is especially true of immigrant women and those from less wealthy and developing nations. For Asian American women, the rate of serious psychological distress increases with lower levels of income, as it does in most other groups of color. As a result of these stressors, a lot of concern has been expressed about the prevalence of mental health issues among, and barriers to and accessibility of mental health services for, Asian women.

For example, although violence is pervasive for all women, compared to other women of color, violence against Asian women is the least reported. Many Asian women remain silent not only because of fear of reporting and a lack of resources, but also because of cultural shyness and reserve, lack of self-confidence, fear of family disgrace and shame, and cultural beliefs that they deserve the abuse. They are often murdered by their husbands and partners after a secret lifetime of physical, mental, and emotional abuse, or they commit suicide to escape the abuse.

Apart from the usual stressors related to being women of color (racism, sexism, classism, and violence), East Asian, South Asian, and Arab women have to deal with stressors relating to their physical images, attire, and religion (specifically Muslim women). For example, media portrayals and the mail ordering of East Asian women (Glodava & Onizuka, 1994; Hodgin, 1991; Narayan, 1995) play roles in perpetuating violence against Asian women. Therefore, extra care to create a power-free, empowering counseling environment that is culturally sensitive, and strategies that integrate their ethnic and gender identities, is paramount when working with Asian women from oppressive environments.

Asian Males

> I would also like to see people taking care of each other and themselves psychologically, emotionally, and at the same time taking care of their physical health, especially in my country. Chinese pay lots of money just to take care of their mental health and pay herb doctors. There are so many men who spend lots of money just to get tablets or on some of the Chinese herbs they have to boil every day to drink. In the Chinese tradition, we eat the saliva of sparrows and spend a lot of money to buy the saliva of sparrows. They don't trust the counselor because they don't really trust themselves. That's sad. They trust the herbs, and they trust the psychics.
>
> —Wai

Traditional Asian men, as a group, like most men all over the world, tend to embrace traditional male gender roles that reflect their culture and an affirmation of masculine identity associated with such traits as dominance, success, and self-reliance. That is, in relation to male gender roles, men from Asian cultures, by and large, share several cultural values related to their masculinity such as responsibility for and to family, male as authority, and not expressing emotions.

As a caution, do not confuse affirmation of Asian cultural identity with affirmation of a sexist male-dominant system, especially traditional patriarchal gender roles. In other words, it is important that mental health clinicians do not legitimize power and power domination by perpetuating the notions of male domination and gender hegemony in the name of Asian culture.

Nonetheless, mental health research on Asian male gender roles is clearly missing from empirical research. The extant research shows that there are differences for Asian Americans on the basis of gender. For example, although Asian American men (and women) are more likely to help themselves, seek help from family and friends, or use avoidant coping strategies, Liang, Alvarez, Juan, and Liang (2007) found that Asian men who experience racism-related stress were more likely than Asian women to seek support to cope. Another study (Hall, Teten, DeGarmo, Sue, & Stephens, 2005) found that loss of face was a protective factor against sexual aggression in Asian American men. Although some Asian groups (e.g., Japanese and Chinese) have utilized counseling services to a degree, all in all, Asians, especially Asian men, are less likely to use mental health services.

The Asian Clients' Gender Stories

> If 10 is positive, I would rate myself very high in the sense of respecting. I hold a viewpoint like this: I am not asking for men to do one thing and women do the same—like lifting weights or cooking up meals—you know what I mean? I don't see doing exactly the same as total equality. But the chance for us each to have equal chance—even though I am aware that some of us, we weren't born equal.
>
> If someone is born in a very poor family, actually that underprivileged person, no matter how hard he may try, he may never compete good enough with maybe a very good background person. People I don't think that that is something that can be equal because there is no way that we can really work on it, but I would think

that as long as the person would like to try, and no matter if it is a man or woman or anything, I would really say, "Go for it." I would really shoot for that. In that perception, I would rate myself at an 8 or even a 9.

—Wai

Gender bias for the Asians showed a number of overtones. On the other hand, Wai had no gender preference, but Mai Li felt strongly about having a female counselor. Wai had an experience with a female counselor and felt very intimidated. Wai reported,

> I don't have a gender preference; the counselor would have to be empathic, genuine, person centered. With the female counselor I had in Hong Kong, I felt a little intimidated by her; she had a confrontational, interpretive style. The important thing is that the counselor has experience.

Mai Li wanted to avoid the possibility of sexual innuendoes with a male counselor and was very intimidated by the thought of having a Caucasian male therapist. Mai Li reported,

> I think I would feel better with a female. A female could understand me more. With a male, it could be sexual attractions. Naturally, in my horizon, I don't want to deal with that. I would feel better with an older female.

Cooke and Kipnis (1986) found that female therapists used significantly fewer influence attempts and interrupted their clients significantly less often than male therapists. Some attempts have been made to look at power differences as they relate to gender in counseling relationships, but the majority of studies (Bem, 1974; Fong & Borders, 1985; Heilbrun, 1986) have examined the relationship of gender role orientation to behavior. Those findings are inconclusive regarding gender role orientation and gender and counseling effectiveness.

GENDER IN THE HISPANIC COMMUNITY

Different experiences, legal standing, English language proficiency, health insurance status, length of residence in the United States, gender roles, familial and community traditions and customs, and knowledge and beliefs in regard to the U.S. mental health care system are all factors that affect the Hispanic community's help-seeking behavior, ability to access needed mental health care, and success with counseling services. Therefore, it is important to begin any discussion of gender and Hispanics from the historical perspective and treatment of males and females in contemporary Hispanic cultures and current issues affecting their status (e.g., legal or illegal immigration) in the United States, as well as the cultural variations among individual families, different countries of origin, and clients' degree of acculturation.

The gender discussion should be from the perspective of the traditional hierarchal gender roles existing within the Hispanic community. For example, research shows that Hispanic women, specifically first-generation immigrant women, are more likely to hold traditional gender roles than White women and women of color.

A significant concern for Hispanic immigrants and those in traditional marital roles and family structures may be centered on efforts to maintain their traditional functions such as socializing children, including teaching them values and morals, and providing family members with nurturance, affiliation, care, and economic and financial support in a culturally different society. In fact, as mentioned in Chapter 5, historically the United States has made deliberate attempts to dismantle and disempower Hispanic families by, for example, limiting the male's ability to fulfill his responsibility to support and provide for his family by his relative displacement in the new global economy and relegation to a low social status.

This means that Hispanic cultural values in relationship to gender differences sometimes clash with those of other Latin cultures and often clash with mainstream American culture, making counseling, in particular couples and marriage counseling with traditional Hispanic cultures, challenging at best. Likewise, a discussion of Hispanic men's and women's construction of gender in their community must be scaffolded from a perspective of a cultural group with massive diversity, that is, acknowledging that Hispanic men and women are of many different shades of color, self-identify from many different countries, and are from many traditional ethnic groups with different cultures and traditions.

In contrast to other traditional groups of color, in most Latin and Hispanic countries, the culture is more associated with clearly defined hierarchal gender roles and gender role expectations for men (*machismo*) and women (*marianisma*) that are closely associated with the sustainability of the family and the traditions in the culture. In fact, along with gender roles and general role expectations, Hispanics' gender identities are shaped by strong ties to family and community (*familismo*), and reinforced by the strong value placed in the Hispanic female's role of childbearing within the family structure, all of which play a significant part in counseling Hispanics.

Even in modern times, Hispanic cultures are marked by strong gender chains of command and gender role divisions, which serve to reinforce images of submissive women and dominant men. Traditional feminine gender roles involve being obedient, chaste, and reliant on men. In contrast, the masculine gender roles involve being authoritarian, manly and virile, and autonomous. It should be noted that the function and meaning behind gender role expectations vary among Latin countries and have shifted over time, becoming for males more dominating and sexist and for females more passive and submissive. This shift results perhaps from Hispanics' acculturation and migration to the United States, specifically shifts in the meanings of the words *machismo* and *marianismo*.

For example, *machismo* (although it originated from the meaning of the Spanish word *macho*, meaning masculine), the belief that males are superior over females, in traditional Latin countries and Spanish cultures referred to the male role as one of provider and protector of his family. It now has been confused and interpreted as referring to the Hispanic male as the domineering, abusive partner. Similarly, *marianisma*, the Hispanic female gender role, traditionally was not viewed by Hispanic males as being inferior; rather, the female's role was respected and revered as that of caretaker for the children and keeper of the home and family.

Latino Females

> My closest relationship to people from Uruguay will be my parents because they haven't acculturated to the same degree, obviously, that I have. There are many things that are cultural. Sometimes it is hard to tell what is personal or my uniqueness. The same with the culture. There are some things that are distasteful; they do not go with you, who you are now. A lot of the people from Uruguay—I mean, these are generalizations—they are very proud and arrogant. Very much identified with European. Very European in ancestry, you know, people from Spain, people from Italy.
>
> —Angelica

Hispanic women have, like Hispanic men, made outstanding achievements and contributions to our nation in every arena—a lot of which, like those of all women, have gone unnoticed and unrecognized. Yet Latina, like White women and other women of color, are yet to achieve equity. Regardless of the shift in role expectations within the Hispanic community, Hispanic women are the recipients of historically oppressive, abusive, and violent systems, and are often victims within their own homes and families. Hispanic women emigrate from patriarchal countries that have systematically launched, and continue even today to tolerate, abuse against women.

Latino Males

> In the Hispanic culture, men don't cry, but I remember crying in the counseling session. Crying because my feelings were hurt, crying because of frustration. And yet, the therapist, I felt, was sensitive enough to encourage me and tell me it was OK and men could cry too and we are human beings. So that process was kind of a good thing for me. It made me feel that if I go to counseling, I could talk to people, and don't have to feel macho, I don't feel I have to solve it my own self or pretend that nothing's wrong, you know, things like that.
>
> —Alexias

Granted, gender role beliefs, particularly notions of gender role differences, similar to those of Asian men, are strong among Latino men (especially those with traditional and cultural ties to the Latino culture). Latinos are, nonetheless, a heterogeneous group with multiple complexities and views that may play out differently among male and female GLBTQIA individuals. For example, their masculinity (masculine gender role) is a direct product of their cultural heritage, with the older Latino men being more traditional in contrast to the younger Latino men being more acculturated (Lazur & Majors, 1995; Ramirez, 1993), which may be different with people from South American countries rather than from Mexico or Puerto Rico.

As previously mentioned, Hispanic men, as a group, are expected to be tough, dominant, and in control and to avoid such characteristics associated with femininity such as emotionality, vulnerability (e.g., weakness and helplessness), and intimacy (above all, showing affection to other males). Yet traditional masculine gender roles for Hispanic men clash with the dominant culture's masculine ideology, creating gender role conflict for traditional Hispanic men that in turn leads to psychological distress and symptoms, especially for Hispanic male immigrants.

It is important for mental health professionals to be aware that although men in traditional Hispanic cultures are often viewed as cold, domineering, aggressive, providers and protectors of the family, and able to control their emotions, it does not mean that Hispanic men are not also sensitive, nurturing, loving, supportive, and the caretaker of the children, especially for those men who embraced the positive side of *machismo*. Nonetheless, in the Hispanic community as well as in Latin countries, dominance, aggression, and control, the more dangerous facets of conservative male gender roles, can be oppressive and lead to violence, in particular domestic violence against women.

Gender and Hispanic/Latino Clients

In terms of the gender preference, at one time I did prefer a male therapist before my own training as a therapist. Now, I have no preference. However, in some situations it would depend on the circumstance as to whom I would prefer.

—Alexias

As a counselor, being a woman has helped me definitely. In general, my experience tends to seek a female. Males, in general, tend to seek a female in my experience. As a client, it is hard to tell because I haven't had a positive experience with a male. If he was Hispanic, it would be worst [laughs]. If I had to go to a male counselor, I would go to an Anglo [laughs].

—Angelica

For Hispanic men and women, their gender affects most aspects of life, including those factors that influence their mental health, such as help-seeking behaviors, access to mental health resources, methods of coping with conflict and stress, interactions with others, self-evaluations, and spirituality. Understanding gender role expectations, stress, and strain in the Hispanic community from a gender perspective may be critical to counseling outcomes and Hispanic clients' success in mental health. For that reason, it is important that mental health professionals examine traditional gender roles and family systems in Hispanic populations in order to understand their impact on mental health counseling with Hispanics.

On the surface, gender roles within Hispanic families may vary from being ultratraditional to being acculturated to the majority culture with little trace of traditional Hispanic behavior. For example, Hispanic immigrants may willingly (or out of necessity) acculturate more toward mainstream culture. Yet it is important to recognize that these cultural gender role expectations can still hold with acculturated families, and the shift away from traditional gender roles may stress and strain the partnership and the family, and drastically affect their mental health and counseling outcomes. It may also impact their choice of and comfort level with male or female counselors.

Therefore, mental health practitioners need to be armed with knowledge and have an awareness of traditional gender roles within mainstream society. Keep in mind that these roles and expectations play a significant part in the ways that Hispanics seek, react to, and continue with counseling, and even how a therapist might define a successful counseling outcome.

The Hispanic/Latino Clients' Gender Stories

The Hispanic and Latino participants, as clients, experienced an innate and powerful connection that sort of naturally occurred with same-gender counselors regardless of race or ethnicity.

Angelica commented,

> My experience has been to seek a female. As a client, the experience I had with a male wasn't very good. If a male can really understand, from his male perspective, my worldview, the trials I go through because I'm a woman.

Alexias commented, "He was White, and I was Hispanic, with different cultural backgrounds; we were both males, and he understood me and I understood him."

For Alexias, as a Hispanic, he felt White females, as members of an oppressed group, could understand his experience as a member of another oppressed group. He explained, "The group leader was female, and I felt comfortable. She understood prejudice and discrimination; she was a White female in a male kind of profession."

GENDER IN THE NATIVE AMERICAN NATIONS

I was raised to believe, being from a matriarchal society, that the women initially bond with the child, and that bothered me after a while. In my own experience, in my own family, my wife stayed home with the children until both of them were at the age when they could go to a private, at that time, Montessori school.

—Woodro (from critique)

Historically, traditional gender roles in the Native American nations have varied greatly from sovereign nation to sovereign nation, from region to region, from tribe to tribe, and in some cases even from band to band within a particular tribal nation. Although there are some similarities in gender roles among all ethnic groups, in comparison to the other groups of color, gender identity is more fluid and more polarized.

For example, though not covered in detail in this book, in North American Indian cultures, there were and continue to be multiple sexualities and gender tribal categories, more recently referred to as *two-headed spirits* (Pilling, 1997). In other words, people with multiple or uncommon gender identities were integrated into the tribal nations. That is to say, in traditional American Indian cultures, gender variation and gender flexibility in men and women were not only accepted but also welcomed, honored, believed to be of a higher order, and held sacred, and these individuals were seen as having spiritual gifts (Underhill, 1939).

In almost stark contrast to Hispanics' well-defined hierarchal gender roles, Native Americans' gender roles are ill-defined and unspecific. For Native Americans, gender roles (cultural rules and expected behavior) were based more on the survival of the tribal nations and less on sex roles (biology and genetics). In other words, for both males and females, gender role expectations are firmly rooted in the protection and survival of their nation—that is, until the 19th century, when American Indians were forced to adopt and incorporate Anglo traditions and gender roles.

American Indian Females

We survive war and conquest; we survive colonization, acculturations, assimilation; we survive beating, rape, starvation, mutilation, sterilization, abandonment, neglect, death of our children, of our loved ones, destruction of our land, our homes, our past, and our future. We survive, and we do more than just survive. We bond, we care, we fight, we teach, we nurse, we bear, we feed, we earn, we laugh, we love, we hang in there, no matter what.

—Allen (1986, p. 190)

Since the beginning of time, women in the world have shared a similar traditional gender role and occupied lower status, yet overall the experiences of American Indian women have been quite different from those of White and European American women, immigrant Asian women, migrant Hispanic women, enslaved Black women, and colonial women. To start, women have always maintained very active roles in the American Indian tribal nations and often have been placed in a higher status than women in other cultures.

In the past, American Indian gender roles have been strongly matrifocal and matrilineal as opposed to matriarchal (although the terms are sometimes used interchangeably). A *matrifocal* community is one in which the women manage domestic relationships, not in authoritative dominance over others, but in a more mutual, shared-governance manner consistent with traditional female gender roles. In other words, Native American women were the fulcrum or center of their families and their tribal nations. By contrast, matrilineal societies are ones in which lineage, ancestry, or descent and family property are passed down through the wife's family. Thus, American Indian women own and inherit family property.

Further, when the survival of American Indian people was threatened or in danger, American Indian women rolled up their sleeves and hunted for food, made weapons and tools, and fought in battle alongside the American Indian men to defend their families and their native soil. Because of the roles that American Indians have undertaken, it is not surprising that American Indians, in contrast to other ethnic groups including Whites and European Americans, have adopted a more collaborative, egalitarian relationship between the genders. As an example, women and men often shared equally in social, economic, and ritual roles.

Last, as members of a matrifocal society, Native American women were seen as being caring and nurturing, fostering and valuing cooperation, and valuing interdependence, quite the opposite of a matriarchal society of women dominating. Instead, Native American women fulfilled traditional female gender roles in the family, when necessary took on traditional male gender roles, and still respected men and valued women. In essence, their identity was grounded in their family, their people, and their spirituality.

Ironically, however, American Indian women experience the highest rates of sexual and domestic violence (due in part to living on reservations with their sometimes severe poverty) compared to women from the other ethnic and racial groups (Bhungalia, 2001). Although more data need to be gathered on violence against Native American women, according to the U.S. Department of Justice (Bureau of

Justice Statistics, 2003), 70% or more of violence experienced by Native American women is committed by persons not of the same race.

Similar to other women of color, they are not only victimized at home but also revictimized by the police and the criminal justice system. That is, police fail to come when they call, courts ignore them, and U.S. attorneys do not prosecute the crimes against them fairly; their excuse for doing nothing about the abuse of women is supposedly confusion between federal and tribal authority.

American Indian Males

I came back from Vietnam with a lot of issues that a lot of veterans had: guilt, survival guilt, anger, rage. The gambit: alcohol, substance abusing. And then I was asked to become part of the kind of things with other veterans who were involved in traditional dance things—a warrior society.

—Woodro

In some ways, with only the broadest characteristics in common, there were similar traditional gender roles of provider and protector for Native American males, in that they learned to hunt food, and men and older boys learned to be warriors in some nations. In other nations such as the Navajo, the Hopi, the Zuni, and many Pueblo, Indian males learned to be not only warriors but also healers and spiritual leaders. They were also taught how to be generous, wise, strong, and brave. American Indian male gender roles, as with those of Native American women, have historically been focused on the importance of the survival of their people sustaining their cultural traditions and practices, and regenerating their culture.

Due to historical abuse and current discrimination, poverty, and social ills in the Native American community, both masculine and feminine roles have been muted, resulting in major social, mental, and physical ills. Therefore, healing in American Indian men is paramount as there is a need to reestablish a sense of connection to their cultural roots and traditions in order to fulfill their functions as providers and protectors of their people. As a result, mental health professionals should made use of indigenous and culturally sensitive mental health modalities that maintain Native American values and restore their cultural traditions.

Gender and American Indian Clients

And part of it with me is that I consider myself as walking in two worlds.

—Lioma

Of all the ethnic groups, the mental health and health issues of Native Americans (and, perhaps, the most severe) are more closely tied to the effects of their forced relocations and genocide experiences in the United States. As a result, mental health healing is needed to deal with the emotional trauma of Native people caused by the denigration of their customs, beliefs, and traditions, and the historical saga of their lands. This is especially true of Native American women. It is precisely that resiliency and strength to survive that should be the bases of counseling for both women and men.

Also, because of both current and historical conditions of American Indians resulting from continuous exposure to abuse, what is needed (as proposed by Sue, Ivey, & Pedersen, 1996, in multicultural counseling and therapy [MCT] theory) are traditional healings, strategies, and treatment plans that are firmly grounded in the helping traditions that are indigenous to American Indian people. Perhaps a vastly different, radical worldview is needed to make therapy more effective for Native American clients, as with the one proposed by Torres-Rivera, Wilbur, Phan, Maddux, and Roberts-Wilbur (2004) for Hispanic clients. Last, but equally important, is mental health professional involvement in social justice and advocacy efforts to stop the violence against Native American women and all women.

Native American Clients' Gender Stories

Perhaps the gender differences of the Native American participants' experiences of gender bias may be the result of the matrifocality prevalent in the Cherokee Nation. Accordingly, it is significant that Lioma is a female in a culture in which being female is cherished; therefore, the gender bias experienced by females in the United States and other male-dominated cultures is simply not a part of her experience. As opposed to Lioma, Woodro, as a male in a female-centered culture, is more aware of the female perspective.

Lioma commented, "Each of the times I went, there was male and female counselors, so I really don't think gender was an influence. Female perspectives are on equal footing with male perspectives in my culture; I seek both." Woodro commented, "A lot of times, American Indian men want a female perspective. That isn't valued in other cultures."

Again, for American Indians, *bias*, in the subcategory of gender, appears to be a direct opposite of the gender bias of White American culture, given that American Indian men, unlike White men in the majority culture, not only seek after the female viewpoint but also highly value and treasure it.

In summary, traditional Native American gender roles have been very different from those of the traditional mainstream culture, in that the female perspective was well respected and actively sought out by American Indian men, unlike White men in the majority culture. However, historically, as a result of American Indians' acculturation and adopting and exposure to racism, sexism, and mainstream culture in the United States, their gender roles have become more aligned with those of the mainstream culture. This is especially true in how Native American women are respected and treated.

CONCLUSION

For men and women of color, their multiple identities, groups' historical experiences, traditions, and culture all impact their gender role identities. This collision of cultures with mainstream cultures can create gender conflict and psychological distress for both males and females, and has major implications for counseling people of color. This may mean that understanding the mental health of groups of color necessitates mental health professionals to be sensitive to the economical, social, and psychological historical assaults on families of color. It also requires sensitivity to the assault of those factors on gender and gender roles in terms of the manifestation of femininity and masculinity for men and women of color juxtaposed against those of White men and women.

Last, it requires awareness, knowledge, and skill sets to work on gender issues specific to males and females of color, mainly a multicultural approach grounded in a gender perspective. This means that effective gender counseling with men and women of color is contingent on mental health professionals having an understanding of the complexity and uniqueness of their multiple experiences as a result of their communal and cultural identities, experiences, and histories as well as individual experiences, and the skills and training to work effectively with these issues. This means that acquiring skills and training with gender issues is incumbent on mental health professionals to understand the complexity and uniqueness of the gender identities of men and women of color.

Section III

The Art of Forgiveness

8

The Follow-Up Interviews
12 Years Later

LOVED FEELING

I want to work on helping them to love and accept themselves as what they are. To love is important; I want to love by showing acceptance and empathy to these people who feel that they are just not adequate. I want them feel that they are being loved. Feeling being loved by others is important in each and everyone's developmental process. Children, yes, they need to have that being loved feeling when they are very young, and this is significant to their healthy development as a person.

—Wai

During 2008, I completed follow-up interviews with seven of the eight individuals in this book. I had not had contact with some of them since the initial study. Others I had developed and maintained a professional relationship with during the last 12 years.

Despite numerous efforts to contact Mai Li, she did not respond to any of my efforts. Thus, I gathered current data on Mai Li from her public records and interviewed Yuchen as an added Asian female voice. To create the follow-up instrument, I used information from the original Standard Open-Ended Interview Guide (SOIG) to construct the follow-up questionnaire. Using the original questions as a template, participants were asked to reflect back on the last 10 years when answering the questions. Following is an update and a comparison of the demographic data compiled on these counselors.

At the time of the follow-up, more than 12 years later, the females ranged in age from 38 to 54 with a mean age of 48.5, and the men ranged in age from 52 to 67 with a mean age of 57. All remained married to the same individuals; Shawn, who had been engaged during the initial study, married her fiancé during the time between the initial and follow-up studies.

In an attempt to acknowledge the various cultural and ethnic differences exist-ing within each case study and any changes in their perceptions of their cultural identities, participants were asked to again identify their ethnic group and racial group separately. Surprisingly, there were some changes. Lioma, who identified her ethnic identity as Indian/Native American 12 years ago, now identifies as American Indian. Also, Joshua, who earlier identified his ethnicity as African American, now identifies ethnically as African.

Other demographic data gathered again were types of degrees, specialty areas, licensures, certifications, marital status, employment status, professional member-ships, and the modalities of counseling services they have used as clients and as service providers. In terms of professional organizations, four (Angelica, Hispanic female; Wai, Asian male; Woodro, American Indian male; and Joshua, African American male) of them have discontinued their memberships in professional men-tal health associations, and five (Lioma, American Indian female; Shawn, African American female; Yuchen and Mai Li, Asian females; and Alexias, Hispanic male) continue to be affiliated with professional mental health associations such as the American Counseling Association (ACA) and American Association of Marriage and Family Therapy. Although there has been shifting around for Alexias, Woodro, Joshua, and Angelica within the same employment place, only Woodro and Angelica have kept the same jobs they had 12 years earlier. Shawn, Joshua, Woodro, and Wai have dropped their professional mental health licenses. Wai is not licensed because he returned to China, and counselors are not licensed in China.

Of the original participants, all but Alexias completed their doctoral degrees, with Shawn being the last to complete (she attained her PhD in 2007). Lioma, Mai Li, and Angelica are in the professoriate: Angelica is an adjunct professor and Lioma is an associate professor, both in counselor education, and Mai Li is an assistant professor in marriage and family therapy programs, all of them in state universities. Half of the original participants (Alexias, Angelica, Woodro, and Joshua) remained in the South-Central United States; in fact, they did not move at all. Wai returned to China, Mai Li moved to the West Coast, and Lioma and Shawn moved to the Midwest.

Woodro (American Indian male) and Shawn are no longer in the counseling field, and Lioma does very little outside her role as a counselor educator. Wai, Woodro, Shawn, Alexias, and Joshua are administrators. Shawn returned to the public schools; Joshua transitioned from working for other mental health agencies and now owns his own agency. Woodro continued in his same position with added responsibilities, and Alexias and Wai are in college student counseling programs. Wai, Mai Li, Alexias, Angelica, and Joshua are in private practice, and Joshua now does only pastoral, clergy-based counseling. Mai Li and Angelica, who are licensed professional coun-selors (LPCs), are also licensed marriage and family therapists (LMFTs).

YUCHEN

When I asked Yuchen why she chose her pseudonym, she said that it was because Chen is her mother's last name and she liked it and Yu is her father's middle name (it means *jade*) and she liked it too. Yuchen is a 35-year-old Chinese American female (a naturalized citizen). She is married and currently working as a mental health clinician. She is an LPC with a master of education (MEd) degree in counselor education. She was pursuing a PhD in educational psychology and changed to a PhD in counselor education and supervision.

CASE 1: THE AFRICAN AMERICAN STORY: JOSHUA AND SHAWN

Joshua

Over the past years, Joshua has worked for a mental health agency and a nonprofit agency, and established a church-based agency. In terms of worldview, philosophy, and theoretical framework for counseling diverse clients, over the prior 10 years, Joshua developed a more biblical worldview and approach to counseling philosophy and modalities. For example, he uses Gestalt from a scripture-based paradigm. He felt that *counseling* in his culture had changed over the previous 10 years. He noted, "A lot of counseling (services, care, and clinical work) has become more culturally aware."

Joshua felt that the role of education in counseling remained very important. He continued his diversity training in the area of racial recognition groups. However, he felt that human diversity in counseling had not changed much over the decade, even in the training and preparing of counselors to work in a multicultural setting. Thus, he described his experiences as a counselor in the last 10 years as "illuminating."

In his counseling, he discovered that differences in speech styles and recognition of words, terms, and phrases (especially the cultural lingo) can become communication barriers that hinder the development of trust between culturally diverse clients and counselors. In contrast, he felt that simply "listening" would facilitate the development of trust and that it is the most effective tool for counselors working with African American clients.

Over the past 10 years, he has enjoyed many successful counseling encounters and a few unsuccessful ones. Therefore, at this juncture in his life, he felt that only time and availability could prevent him from participating in counseling.

Shawn

The youngest in the group is now approaching 40. She, like Joshua, is very involved in her church, and her church keeps her connected to and grounded in the African American community. She, like Woodro, is no longer in the counseling field. She took an educational assistant position in the public schools in the Midwest.

In the past, she was a behaviorist and totally against using prescription medication. As a behavioral counselor, tools were needed to modify behavior without the use of medication. In her current job, she is a part of a culture that supports the use of medication. She has witnessed firsthand the positive effects of medication for some children, who, without their medication, would be out of control and unable to participate in classroom activities, gym, music, or meals during the school day. She now appreciates the benefits of prescription medication in conjunction with behavior modification techniques.

She felt that diversity counseling is still difficult. In her experience, many people of color know what counseling is and that it can be beneficial, but taking that initial step is sometimes scary. She is not yet convinced that African American people understand what counseling is and the work that is necessary on their part as clients.

Nevertheless, as a mental health professional of color, she has found it difficult to advocate multicultural ideas. To her, it seems that "the world as a whole wants to lump everyone together" (and not see racial or cultural differences).

As a client, she has not participated in counseling since she had a few sessions as a student more than 12 years ago. If she needs counseling, affordability would be a concern, along with child care, the office hours of the counselor, and the sex of the counselor (with a preference for one of the same sex). She would need to make sure that her health insurance would cover the costs.

As a mental health professional working with culturally diverse clients, Shawn felt that the cultural background of the client and the counselor must be considered. She explained,

> Some terms may not be understood, the rate of speech, the expectations, and how the initial session is focused. There are different experiences with each client and counselor, so it's important to listen to the other person and feel comfortable asking questions when they arise. I still think some adult clients believe, "If a person doesn't look like me, how can they understand where I'm coming from?"

For clients of color, she felt listening was essential. Along with listening, mental health clinicians must be willingness to be open and nonjudgmental, and allow time. She believed that time facilitates the development of trust. For mental health professionals working with African Americans, she suggested that the client be viewed as an individual with a culture and experiences that make him or her truly unique.

Recommendations

Shawn and Joshua provided the following recommendations for working with African American and Black clients.

Shawn recommends the following:

1. View the client as an individual with a unique culture and experiences.
2. Do not make assumptions if there is something the counselor has not been told by the client or family member.

Joshua recommends, "Listen."

CASE 2: HEARTS WITH LOVE AND CARE:
THE ASIAN STORY: MAI LI, YUCHEN, AND WAI

I'd select a counselor who has a heart with love and care.

—Wai

Mai Li

Mai Li did not complete the follow-up interview. From her public profile, she is currently an assistant professor at a state university on the West Coast. In addition to her responsibilities as an academician, she is involved in numerous projects relating to the Asian population, including a palliative care community partnership program for terminally ill Asian patients with cancer. The program's main goal is to minimize barriers for and provide culturally and ethnically grounded palliative care to this Asian population. She also works with Asian immigrants, women, and families.

Twelve years earlier, her work was more diverse and encompassed a broader range of clients. Her clinical work was primarily in a university campus–based clinic that was housed within the marriage and family therapy program. Her clientele ranged from families and individuals to college students and adults, children, and adolescents from the surrounding communities and smaller towns.

Yuchen

After graduating with her master's degree from a program in counselor education, Yuchen worked for a state youth commission as an associate psychologist and later at a state prison, where she is currently employed and does individual and group counseling, mental health evaluation, testing, and crisis management. When asked about her philosophy of counseling for the past 10 years, she said,

> I have been exploring my philosophy of counseling. At the very beginning, I don't think I had a philosophy, though I claimed to be an existentialist. But in counseling sessions I just put together different techniques to get things going. Now, I espouse the humanistic-existential philosophy.

Looking through her worldview at her work with clients over the last 10 years, she moved from being what she described as *color blind* to realizing that she needed to do much more than read a diversity textbook. She started examining how each major counseling theory may or may not help diverse clients, looking at the world through the feminist theorists' eyes, and examining how her attitudes and prejudices may intentionally or unintentionally harm culturally diverse clients.

Over the past 10 years, she had witnessed a major shift from counseling being stigmatized in Chinese culture to Chinese people being more open-minded now. Further, she said that 10 years ago, there were very few counselors in China, and people knew very little about what it was. Now people are beginning to realize its importance, especially after the earthquake in Sichuan, when many counselors and psychologists helped to counsel the survivors.

To the question of the role of education in counseling, she felt that clients needed to be educated about some basic facts of counseling, human behaviors, symptoms of specific disorders, and treatment options so that they can have a better understanding of their problems and have a better sense of control. She also stressed that in the last few years, she developed a better understanding of the oppression and discrimination that people who are marginalized endure. She was more sensitive to diversity issues and has more compassion toward diverse clients.

When asked how the decision process to participate in counseling changed over the last 10 years, she responded,

> When I was a graduate student, there were many resources where I could get counseling for free. My decision process was based on (a) was I in a lot of pain? If yes, I would call and make an appointment. (b) Did the counselor understand me? Did he or she like me? If yes, I would continue. If not, I would try to switch to somebody else.
>
> Now I need to pay for counseling. My decision process is simpler: (1) Am I in a lot of pain? (2) Can I afford counseling? (3) Is the counselor a good match for me?

Yuchen discussed her experiences as a client over the last 10 years as at first seeking counseling in order to get adjusted to American culture and deal with her anxiety: She stated,

> I saw my first counselor for only one session. To me, she was a typical American woman, very assertive and outspoken. She was almost intimidating. Plus, I felt it was a big stigma to seek counseling. So I didn't come back. I worked very well with my second counselor. His personality was closer to mine. I made a lot of progress working with my anxiety. More recently, I saw a counselor for marital problems. She mainly does reality therapy. She was good at conceptualizing problems and disentangling thoughts. When I tried to explore my feelings and gain more insight, she did not seem to be interested. So I stopped seeing her.

In terms of her counseling experiences in the last 10 years, she said, "At first, I was very insecure and often felt lost during counseling sessions. Now I am more confident and know more about what I am doing." The discrimination that she experienced as a client related to her religion. She stated,

> My second counselor assumed I was a Buddhist, although I indicated in the intake form that I was a Christian. He asked me how my life was influenced by Buddhism, and I told him not that much. I told him I was a Christian. He was embarrassed and apologized. He was a very genuine and caring person. That incident didn't affect our relationship. It just made me realize the stereotype people hold toward Asian clients. The same thing happened with my site supervisor.

The discrimination, racism, and prejudice she experienced in her professional roles were due to her nationality. She stated,

> When I was doing internship at the Student Counseling Center at Tech, most students did not want to be assigned to work with me. They said they didn't feel connected to me. The internship coordinator did a couple of role plays with me and told me I had good skills.

When asked about unsuccessful counseling outcomes as a client, she said,

> I terminated counseling sessions prematurely several times because I didn't feel comfortable with the counselors. The main reasons were they tried to give me advice, they appeared too animated during the session (I am a very quiet person), they didn't feel comfortable with the topic I brought up (e.g., I talked about a friend who is homosexual and the counselor appeared embarrassed), they didn't take me seriously (I wanted to talk about my anger problem, but the counselor didn't think I had an anger problem), etc.

Thus, when asked what counselor characteristics (similar or dissimilar) she considered when selecting a counselor, such as race, ethnicity, culture, and socioeconomic status (SES), she responded, "I would like to have a counselor who is as similar to me as possible in terms of race, ethnicity, culture, SES, and personality. I haven't found one like that."

Wai

> In the counseling process, I encourage clients to trust in their inner self and learn to help and take good care of themselves. I like to see that more people are able to self-help and provide peer counseling to others. I respect each unique individual and support his or her way of living.
>
> —Wai

Twelve years later, Wai lives in China and works with Chinese clients in Hong Kong. Two years earlier, he started doing training and therapy in Canton, the southern part of mainland China. He has become more phenomenological, and empathy has become more important in his counseling process. That is, he allows respect, love, and acceptance of his clients for who they are and where they come from to guide his practice. He stated, "In their difficulty and hardship, I was there by them and traveled with them side by side to the point that they can be independent and happier."

He also felt that his evolving philosophy of counseling informs his clinical work. He explained,

> In the beginning, I worked more from the remedial and problem-solving perspective. Recently, I'd like to do more educational, developmental, and preventive work. I prefer more and more to work with parents to raise healthy children. I'd like to have more parents as my working partners and to help and train them to be positive parents to bring in a healthy second generation.

As a result of this shifting he made over the last 10 years, Wai now works with different people, most of whom are grassroots—poor people, mostly children and their parents. He truly has worked the gambit of including gamblers and their families and clients with emotional or depressive problems. He also trains teachers, counselors, volunteers, parents, social workers, and church workers in how to be what he describes as "helpful counselors and loving parents."

According to Wai, over the last 10 years in China and the Chinese culture, Chinese people appear to have accepted counseling more. However, there are still some stigmas. *Therapy* per se carries a stronger pathological connotation as opposed to *counseling*. The words *training* and *coaching* are less stigmatized and more educational. The terms *helping*, especially *peer helping*, are more acceptable to the public in general. Chinese people are also more ready to seek counseling when it is more affordable.

Since leaving the United States and returning to China, Wai learned to acknowledge and appreciate the individuality of humanity and the massive differences that exist within, for example, the Chinese community in China. He noted,

> I have worked with Chinese people in a very Chinese community. However, there have been differences among Chinese. Chinese in Hong Kong are different from Chinese in Canton. The more I understand their specialness, the better I can relate with them and work with them. Motivated by enjoying working with different people, I have been quite prepared to work with people coming from different areas in mainland China.

Unfortunately, Wai discovered that this growth and change in China, specifically the focus on material things, have not been without cost. According to him, "Sometimes, or most of the time, I feel lonely and like I'm fighting the battle all by myself." He said that he tries very hard not to discriminate, but he felt that he had made some mistakes in that area.

> I think misunderstanding. We see people and understand them with my learning and experiences. Those would affect me. Sometimes I'll see people positively with my learning and experiences, but sometimes I'll see them not as positively because I can't cut off my history and background when relating to and perceiving others.

To facilitate the development of trust, Wai believes that it is important to love, appreciate others, and humble ourselves. Risk taking is also important, as is willingness to admit that you are wrong. His trust is not based on others' trustworthiness, but rather he trusts because trusting is one of his virtues.

He stated that counseling is only a process and a tool. Thus, as a tool himself, he sees himself as an inspirer and motivator for people to grow and change to become better and to mature. He believes that happiness is important and that we need to love each other and treat each other equally and fairly for people to become happier and full of energy. Last, he firmly believes that self-trusting is an important factor to all of us in our personal development.

In his role as counselor, Wai has experienced unsuccessful results with clients as well as multiple successes with his clients. For example, he has worked with clients who don't agree with his convictions about counseling or life, those unwilling to do internal exploration and open themselves up, and those who found it hard to experience their emotions. There were also those who weren't willing to invest the necessary time and effort needed and wanted a quick fix, and those who merely wanted advice.

As a result of his personal growth and his successful and unsuccessful experiences with clients, he now knows that successful outcomes with clients are achievable, real, and sustainable. He affirmed,

> I've helped children who've experienced intents of killing themselves to regain the living motivation because they experienced more love and care from their parents. I've help depressed clients who felt listened to and understood. They expressed that they don't have to *be* somebody to feel loved and cared.
>
> I've helped gamblers who've become effective peer counselors helping other problem gamblers and their families. I've helped people to regain the ability to self-love and self-appreciate. I've helped parents who felt and experienced themselves more energy and ability to love and accept their children as *who* and *what* they are instead of continuing putting too much pressure onto their children. I've helped people resolve their childhood and developing trauma. I've helped people reconcile with their own self and become free and happy again.

In closing, he said that he felt that it was important for counselors to be open and be ready to receive whatever may come up. To be humble and ready to learn are virtues that each clinician should have.

Recommendations

Yuchen offered the following recommendations for working with Asian clients:

1. Don't assume we are all Buddhists. Don't assume we like advice. Silence is a way to show respect.
2. More community outreach and more in-home counseling are needed.

Wai suggested the following recommendations for working with Asian clients:

1. Be open, and be prepared to be flexible.
2. Be humble.
3. Be ready to learn (that is a virtue each counselor should have).
4. Counselor and client must work together to help the client in need.

CASE 3: THE LATINO STORY: ALEXIAS AND ANGELICA

Alexias

Every individual has some diversity in themselves that it would be unfair to try and define a specific orientation for one group or the other.

—Alexias

Professionally, Alexias has gone from being a clinician to an administrator and back to a clinician. The change has been from working directly with people to administering and managing people back to working with people again. This change is also reflected in his professional affiliations, which changed from national to more local, regional, and state-level associations of the ACA and American Psychological Association (APA). It is also evident in his greater focus on his successes as a counselor rather than as a client; in contrast, I noticed that 12 years earlier, he focused more on his positive and negative experiences in counseling as a client rather than as a counselor. He acknowledged,

> I tried administration for a short period in my life, six years, but I realized that the deeper I got into administration the further it took me away from working with people directly in therapy. Therefore, I came back to counseling.

Philosophically, Alexias switched from a cognitive-restructuring philosophy centered on irrational beliefs from early childhood experiences that he believed impacted on his clients' adult lives and the lives of other people in their personal lives and social associations to a more eclectic approach in counseling diverse clients. Alexias stated, "In my years of practice I have learned that you listen to the individual closely as to what their concern may be, and then determine what counseling orientation is more appropriate for that issue." He further stated,

> Counseling has changed tremendously in my culture in the last 10 years. It has gone from using traditional values and norms that were practiced in the Hispanic culture to incorporating some of the dominant culture's values and norms. This is part of the new generation's acculturation into the dominant culture at large. There are more interracial marriages today than when I was growing up. The more we get educated as a culture, the more accepting we become of counseling.

In terms of prejudice, racism, bias, and discrimination, Alexias has adapted a sort of quiet resignation and acceptance of biases as a part of life. He says that in some form or another, biases, prejudice, and discrimination have been a part of his life.

As a result of these negative experiences, Alexias said that one of the most detrimental communication barriers is not to listen to the client of color without prejudices or assumptions. Examples include having a counselor treat him or talk to him without respect and in a condescending manner, and assuming that what he had to say was not important or significant. He felt that prejudicial behavior from the counselor most definitely will hinder the trust between a client of color and a culturally diverse counselor. In contrast, he felt that empathy and genuine openness show that you care, and the desire to want to help will facilitate trust. He later shared concrete examples of his experiences with prejudice:

> I remember very clearly some clients telling me when I worked for the counseling center, after doing an intake interview, that they wanted to be seen by a White therapist. Others wanted to know how much experience I had in counseling and if I had a college degree. I had one person confront me and ask me how much experience I had counseling White people. In my position as an

administrator, my immediate supervisor was always questioning my decision making. This person was more than likely a micromanager, but in my perspective, this person did not think I could make wise decisions because I was Hispanic. I could sense in the nonverbal behavior the prejudice.

Although Alexias did not elaborate, this time around gender took a backseat to race and ethnicity in terms of counselor and client characteristics, similar or dissimilar, that he considers when selecting a counselor. Years earlier, he felt strongly that having a male therapist was important. He now explained, "I considered race, ethnicity, and culture in selecting my counselor."

All in all, Alexias thought that counseling does work for people of color. As a therapist, according to him, counselors have to identify the best way to approach that particular person of color. He added that in his work with people of color, he realized there is still much more research that needs to be done on counseling them.

Angelica

As I have grown, and hopefully matured both personally and professionally, I have become more patient, flexible, and accepting as a person and as a therapist. I have also developed spiritually, which is reflected in my view of human beings and the purpose of my work. My philosophy of counseling has turned more practical and spiritual.

I do not classify myself as a "Christian" counselor, nor do I impose my own views or beliefs. However, I am either more open or willing to recognize the mystical nature or divine force that permeates and transforms my work. Ten years later, I can say with certainty that my effectiveness as a therapist is intrinsically connected to something greater than myself. I find that I am less effective, and even cynical, the moment I lose touch with this spiritual dimension.

—Angelica

Angelica's work setting remains mostly clinical, but has expanded to include teaching and consultation opportunities. She describes her clinical practice as community oriented, with a primary focus on serving a people-of-color population in need of bilingual and bicultural services. The nature of her work tends to be more missionary than profit oriented.

Angelica felt that the past decade had not adequately prepared her for working in a multicultural setting but, rather, has given her opportunities to observe, corroborate, reinforce, amplify, question, and apply previously learned knowledge. She thought that a combination of personality traits (e.g., openness and curiosity), personal background, and exposure to a wide variety of cultures, formal training, and clinical experience is what led to the formation of the necessary knowledge and skills to work effectively with diverse populations.

Because of the limited psychiatric support in her region, she developed a closer relationship with physicians, especially family practice providers. This development, which reflects a widespread trend, has forced her to become more knowledgeable regarding medical terms and conditions, as well as to stay up-to-date on psychotropic therapy.

She found it ironic (and empowering) when a medical doctor would ask her, a nonmedical doctor, for suggestions regarding the type or choice of psychotropic medication. This was a situation that would have been extremely rare a couple of decades ago, "Not to mention an eyebrow raiser in the academic setting!"

Similar to Alexias, and her responses in the interview she did 12 years ago, Angelica, looking back on the impact of cultural differences, has become even more appreciative of our common humanness and uniqueness as individuals. Her interactions with hundreds of clients have shown her that, sometimes, an existential or analytical orientation may be the most appropriate approach to use with a client of color. She has also become more willing to consider, and even support, nontraditional approaches, as long as they seem to work for a particular individual. This means that her ethics have become more personal and less dogmatic. In her own words,

> I cannot speak for the members of my culture, but I can share my observations and experiences. In general, I have seen greater acceptance of counseling as a means to healing or self-improvement—sometimes even among those with no formal education or material resources. I have also observed greater acceptance and utilization of counseling by males, even those from traditional backgrounds.
>
> For me, it has been satisfying and a bit surprising to see that differences in the degree of acceptance or utilization of counseling do not seem to be associated with acculturation. In other words, I have not found predictable differences between the new immigrant or less acculturated minority clients and the more acculturated ones.

Regarding views or expectations of counseling itself among the Hispanic/Latino population, Angelica observed that expectations tend to be more realistic than traditionally (or stereotypically) expected from a non-Anglo population. In general, she felt that the average person does not seem to expect counseling to be a practical, direct, short-term, or easy problem-solving mechanism. In her opinion, the concept of counseling or psychotherapy among Hispanics and Latinos is more diverse and sophisticated than typically described among scholars. And this observation still applies, even among new immigrants with little formal education and limited exposure to American institutions.

Experiences as a Client   Angelica continues to participate in counseling as a client at different times in her life. The only change she saw in the decision process was that her reason to seek counseling, with time, depended less on a personal sense of crisis and more on a pressing need for self-examination, personal growth, or change. She felt that she had also become more careful and particular about whom she chose as a counselor.

Experiences as a Counselor   Her experiences as a counselor have been varied and, for the most part, positive. However, she felt that none of the counselors who she worked with directly addressed relevant issues of diversity (except for gender—mostly brought up by female therapists). In all cases, she felt that her knowledge and experience in the areas of diversity and counseling were superior to those of her peer counselors.

Last, there is still a lack of counselors of color. According to Angelica, "I have not yet had the opportunity to have a provider who is also a member of a minority group. I suspect (and hope) that my experience would be different."

Discrimination   For Angelica, discrimination—gender and religious differences in particular—are still alive and kicking. She shared the following example:

> I've been mostly aware of gender discrimination, particularly regarding compensation, in all professional roles—especially administration. The most overt experience of prejudice and discrimination I had occurred in a private (religious) academic setting. I had been invited (and encouraged) to apply by the program head, who I had known previously in various professional roles. I was the best qualified candidate for the position. Yet my application to teach a course in multicultural counseling was turned down because of my religious views or/and affiliation. Although I did not take it personally (actually, I was glad I had this experience before joining the organization), I was appalled—to say the least.
>
> What was most disturbing to me was that an institution of "higher" learning was narrowing and shaping the education its students would receive. I felt sad and concerned for the students (and future professionals), who were, in my opinion, not getting the training necessary to be in the real (diverse) world. To me, the irony of the situation is still mind-boggling. How can anyone justify such a contradiction: Offer to teach a course on "diversity" but exclude qualified candidates because of their diverse background?

Recommendations

Alexias and Angelica provided the following recommendations for working with Hispanic clients.

Alexias recommends the following:

1. Have a strong cultural awareness of the Latino/Hispanic culture.
2. In regard to counseling styles, use a psychoeducational approach.
3. Integrate group counseling, family systems, and cognitive restructuring in counseling work with Hispanic/Latino clients.

Angelica recommends the following:

1. Check your biases.
2. Question all stereotypes.
3. Begin from a person-centered orientation.

CASE 4: THE AMERICAN INDIAN STORY: LIOMA AND WOODRO

Lioma

Lioma is tied to the American Indian culture personally and professionally. She has a tribal membership, and she is involved in several professional American

Indian organizations such as the Indian Professors Group, American Educational Research Association (AERA) Indigenous Peoples Special Interest Group (SIG), and Association for Multicultural Counseling and Development (AMCD) Native American Concerns group.

Her philosophy of counseling remains very existential but with what she describes as more pragmatic approaches and techniques. Her philosophy of life and theoretical framework have also remained fairly consistent, though she felt that she was better at articulating them now.

Her worldview, in contrast, has altered slightly. She explained, "I have mellowed as I've aged; I'm not as quick to judge or search for underlying meaning when working with diverse clients. I just accept what they bring to me."

She believes that counseling is dependent to some degree upon educating individuals to transfer self-awareness and self-determination into their lives. She posed the question "How can counseling be effective if clients are not taught to transfer learning into new situations in the future?" Thus, her concept of counseling within American Indian cultures has broadened from thinking that counseling is primarily about substance abuse issues to a healthier view of counseling being for helping individuals who need to work on daily functioning issues.

Her views on human diversity are more integrative at this point in her life. She put it in plain words: "I see more inclusive diversity, such as individuals possessing multiple identities instead of just one identity being important."

Lioma has not been a client in the past 10 years. She felt that there was just a subtle change process that occurred in her when she considered going to counseling. She didn't believe that it was any conscious decision to change her participation in counseling; rather, it just seemed to happen.

Similarly, her counseling experiences have been limited to educating others to be counselors. She has, however, been in counseling-related situations as a court appointed special advocate (CASA) and as a foster parent. She also continues her training with continuing education credits and attending professional conferences and workshops, and she enjoys these experiences.

In her opinion, the barriers to effective communication that negatively impact trust between the client of color and a culturally diverse counselor are socially constructed prejudice and oppression. On the contrary, in order to facilitate the development of trust, each individual needs to reflect and uncover his or her socially constructed views of diverse cultures. This reflection allows openness to diverse cultures when people are exposed to the *other*.

Woodro

Woodro describes himself as an American Indian who is an enrolled member of the Cherokee Tribe, has been reared in a tribal nation, and works for a tribe. He has been employed by the same employer for more than 12 years.

Although he is no longer working in the counseling field, he often employs the skills gained in interpersonal relationships not to counsel, but to better understand fellow employees and friends. This is extremely helpful for those experiencing difficulties that may require counseling because with his counseling expertise, he can encourage them to seek counseling. In essence, the skills he acquired often influence his professional and personal interactions.

Woodro was adamant that his worldview will never change. As an American Indian, he interacts in the Indian environment. His Indian culture also informs his professional demeanor in interactions with many non-Indians. He accepts people unconditionally for who they are: "One might call it Rogerian," he said, "but this is the way I was reared in my own community."

He believes that counseling and education work hand in hand. One must, at times, provide the client an education regarding his or her own lack of knowledge or awareness.

In terms of his evolving views on human diversity, through life experiences, he has always viewed the human environment as diverse beyond culture and color. Working in an Indian nation, he has not experienced any of the discrimination, racism, or prejudice that some may have perceived or experienced in their professional roles.

Woodro felt that there is a need to develop trust between clients of color and a culturally diverse counselor. Most importantly, trust is a two-way street. To facilitate the development of trust, he believes that the mental health professional and the client must be willing to get to know one another from a community perspective—the life experiences that influence and impact them.

Recommendations

Woodro and Lioma offered the following recommendations for working with American Indian clients.

Woodro recommends the following:

1. Build trust by not coming on too strong.
2. Get to know the client.

Lioma recommends the following:

Genuineness and openness to learning from your client

TRANSFORMING THE COUNSELING PROFESSION TO MEET THE NEEDS OF PEOPLE OF COLOR

These counselors in their roles as both counselors and clients offer the following suggestions on what is needed to change the counseling profession to tackle the needs of people of color. Lioma did not believe that counseling needed transforming. According to Joshua, two simple things are needed to transform the counseling profession in order to meet the needs of people of color, namely, "sensitivity and research."

Woodro noted, "It is my opinion that the counseling profession is more aware of culture, color, and diversity, but would benefit from working within an environment that one might call out of the comfort zone—more diverse, in other words."

Wai stated, "If there are more people of color who come out to do counseling, to educate people on counseling, to help, to write, to share, and to publish, the counseling profession can meet the needs of people of color."

Shawn felt the counseling profession has been and is being transformed to meet these needs.

> At times, a client might be fortunate to have a diverse staff from which to choose from, which is a step in the right direction. Continuous education on the part of the counselor is necessary as well as a willingness from the counselor to work with people of color without being judgmental.

MULTI-LIFE-FUNCTIONING CHANGE

Last, each of them was asked to use a word or phrase that captures counseling. Following are their responses:

Alexias: "I feel strongly about counseling."
Wai: "A way of relating with myself and others."
Joshua: "Essential."
Angelica: "Inspiring."
Lioma: "Multi-life-functioning change."
Woodro: "Empowering."
Shawn: "Hopeful."
Yuchen: "Fascinating."

DOES COUNSELING WORK FOR PEOPLE OF COLOR?

Last, to the question "Does counseling work for people of color?" Joshua's answer was a reverberating "Absolutely!" Shawn said, "It works if the client has the *right* counselor and if the client is willing to do the necessary work to make counseling successful." Lioma believes that counseling works as a catalyst for change in all people regardless of color.

Wai sees counseling as a better way of relating. He shared,

> Counseling has helped me to be more sensitive and have more understanding of myself. I believe I can use it to work with different people and with counseling knowledge and skills; I can be more sensitive and understand people of color more.

Alexias thought that if the counseling profession sits back and applies the old psychotherapeutic approach that if people need help they should look for it, this is "wrong. In order to serve people of color, the counseling profession needs to go out and collaborate with the public schools, community centers, nursing homes, and take counseling to the people." Last, but not least, Woodro summed it up with a resounding "Of course it works; nothing to discuss."

9

Drum Majors for Justice
Social Justice Efforts for Women and People of Color

ARETHA FAYE MARBLEY, RACHELLE BERG,
GREG JOHNSTON, SHARHONDA CRYSTAL
KNOTT DAWSON, and JULIE MERRIMAN

Nothing Short of a Radical Revolution

Yes, if you want to say that I was a drum major, say that I was a drum major for justice.

—Martin Luther King Jr. (1968)

THE ENTRANCE OF SOCIAL JUSTICE

*M*ulticulturalism has been seen as the *fourth force* in counseling. This revolutionary force was seen in 1991, when Pedersen edited a special issue on multiculturalism in the *Journal of Counseling and Development*. Multiculturalism in counseling has flourished over the past 30 years. Many strides have been made to appreciate the diversity of issues facing counselors when viewing clients through a multicultural lens. The American Counseling Association's Code of Ethics (2005) requires that counselors become more aware of the diverse needs of the client, regardless of culture, ethnicity, gender, sexual identity, or religious affiliation. Empirical evidence has provided momentum that continues to support the need for cultural and ethnic sensitivity in mental health professionals.

Yet the maltreatment of groups of color remains buried deep in society and in the consciousness of the mental health field. Multiculturalism has certainly been a

137

powerful force in eradicating some of the damage done to people who are culturally different. To a large degree, multiculturalism shies away from issues of social
justice resulting from the history and politics of race, ethnicity, and gender and the
interlocking of those statuses with socioeconomics.

Indeed, multiculturalism has been a powerful and transformative movement,
but not as revolutionary and radical as others such as the civil rights, feminist, and
American Indian movements—at least, not enough to constitute a revolution. In
essence, multiculturalism, though necessary, is not enough. Rather, an advocacy of
a social justice perspective picks up where the diversity conversation ends.

In an evaluation of the multicultural counseling movement, D'Andrea and
Heckman (2008) provided five main themes that have come forward from the
almost 2 decades of publications. They are (a) sensitivity to the significant ways
that cultural factors affect human development, (b) awareness of the competencies
needed to effectively promote the healthy development of persons from diverse
cultural groups and backgrounds, (c) thinking about types of professional training
strategies that help foster the development of culturally competent counseling professionals, (d) knowledge of a broad range of research findings relevant to multicultural counseling, and (e) understanding of the present and future challenges that
the counseling profession faces within the context of a society that is undergoing a
rapid transformation in its racial and cultural demographics.

Social justice is called for when a population group is systematically discriminated against, and counseling alone cannot meet the needs of the client. Equity
implies fairness. All populations strive to be treated with equity in all areas of society. These areas may include political, economic, or religious networks. When one
or more aspects of our social network break down, advocacy is needed. A counselor
must be aware of systematic discrimination within population groups, and work to
change those social structures. This is our challenge as counseling professionals.

Therefore, there is a need to reach beyond the tenets of multiculturalism and
even the dialogue about our differences in order to change the delivery of mental
health services to people of color. Using our *call to consciousness* (Ivey, Ivey, &
Simek-Morgan 1993), mental health professionals must systematically tackle the
insidious and systemic issues that have created the social ills and the state of mental unhealthiness in communities of color.

It is a call for social justice, but not without drawbacks. We must remember
that social justice, like culture and like the feminist, multicultural, civil rights,
and any other social movements, is organic, complex, and dynamic—interspersed
with conflict and compromise, nasty divisions, strong alliances, and successes and
defeats. It is not an easy solution to the injustices, inequities, and disparities among
women and people of color, but it is a beginning.

SAY IT LOUD: I'M BLACK AND I'M PROUD

Social Justice and African Americans

> We have also come to this hallowed spot to remind America of the fierce urgency of now. This is no time to
> engage in the luxury of cooling off or to take the tranquilizing drug of gradualism. Now is the time to make

real the promises of democracy. Now is the time to rise from the dark and desolate valley of segregation to the sunlit path of racial justice. Now is the time to lift our nation from the quick sands of racial injustice to the solid rock of brotherhood. Now is the time to make justice a reality for all of God's children.

—Martin Luther King Jr. (1968)

Social injustices come with many nicknames such as discrimination, racism, sexism, classism, inequalities, inequities, disparities, gaps (e.g., in educational achievement), biases, and marginality. All of these have been applicable to the historical and current profile and status of Black and African American people in the United States. Beginning with slavery, African Americans have endured nearly 4 centuries of documented social injustices launched against them.

Unfortunately, these social injustices have continued into the 21st century. These injustices have been a part of the fabric of every major social institution in the United States, namely, the legal, financial, educational, clergy-based, corporate, health, mass media, political, criminal justice, and even mental health systems. This means that as we move toward a more social justice–based society, African Americans have not achieved equity in terms of opportunities, allocation of resources, criminal justice treatment, civil rights, civic engagement, or even respect for their viewpoints.

The Status of Blacks and African Americans

I remember the first time I had to go to juvenile court and plead on behalf of a White child when most of the children up there were Black. I felt, here I am, having to stand up for this White child who the judge was willing to do her best by her, when she and other White judges were sending all these other children to detention and on to jail. I really had strong feelings about that; basically, my training had been primarily to deal with White people. All my training and all of my brainwashing.

—Joshua

It seems that African Americans, along with other groups of color, are up against systems that are innately unjust and, in addition, rationalize, justify, and even legalize those social injustices, and ignore and disrespect their cultural values, traditions, and differences. Since Dr. King on August 28, 1963, delivered his "I Have a Dream" speech on the steps of our nation's capital in Washington, DC, African Americans, though they have made some major gains, have continued to struggle for social justice. Collectively, when compared to children from other racial groups, African Americans are struggling to come up, catch up, and keep up. This is unconscionable and unacceptable in a 21st-century developed nation, especially one that purports to value and ensure, through its constitution, equality, equity, opportunity, and justice for all.

Politics and Bottom-Up Advocacy   For several decades, violence has dominated headlines in newspapers in major cities across the country, such as the one in Chicago that read, "Since September, Over 20 High School Student Murders in Chicago; 18 by Gunfire." This rash of violence has ignited a sense of urgency in teachers, public school officials, parents, politicians, clergy, community-based organizations, and even teenagers to take to the streets of Chicago and demand that lawmakers do something to end the killings, especially to enact and enforce stricter gun control laws. It is a political issue for African Americans.

Today violence is rampant in urban areas. The criminal justice system has created an underclass of people who are not employable and therefore have no alternative to street violence. The solution is complex, and as such, it requires political intervention and a village approach. We have to reach out to lawmakers to create a plan and implement it, even if a vast number of African Americans believe that the government is crooked and cannot be trusted.

Until recently, with the election of Barack Obama, African Americans have not made substantial upward movement in the political arena. Aside from political protests (e.g., the civil rights movement), African Americans have been structurally excluded from the political arenas as they were from other arenas; they were not only excluded but also legally denied rights during slavery and following the Civil War, such as voting rights and the right to hold office. Even after Blacks got the legal right to vote, they were often violently prevented from exercising those rights and confined to offices with minimal political clout for many years.

Similar to community-organizing models for working with African American communities, political social justice and advocacy initiatives must embrace a village approach inclusive of indigenous systems such as clergy-based institutions, spiritual advisors, elders, and community leaders. A grassroots, bottom-up plan is needed, especially for the violence. To be effective, social justice initiatives must incorporate community-level and street-level outreach, public education, community mobilization, faith leader involvement, and local politicians. These initiatives must rely heavily on education, conflict resolution, and cooperation among these entities.

Education   In pre-K–12 education, the achievement gap has been pervasive, insidious, and widening for African Americans. African American children, males in particular, are overly represented in special education and underrepresented in gifted and talented and advanced placement programs.

Also, inequities are evident in the extent to which African Americans have access to the same types of educational opportunities, use these opportunities, and achieve levels of performance in school. Information on various aspects of the educational experiences of African American students, such as their progress through school, academic performance, access to computers and the Internet, and participation in extracurricular activities, provides some indication of the extent to which equity in education for African American students has or has not been achieved. Further evidence of educational inequities can be found in access to technology and to the Internet, the quality of teachers, and the offerings of extracurricular activities at their schools. Access to the Internet and use of technology are tied to the academic performance of students and play a critical role in socioeconomic and racial inequities for African American students.

Another factor bearing on educational equity is the devastating effects of the disproportionally high rates of incarceration of African American men and women, who are sentenced to prisons as opposed to enrolling in institutions of higher education. Since 1985, incarceration rates for African American men were growing at a faster rate than their college enrollment rates (Butterfield, 2002). In the 1990s and early 21st century, there was just about one third more African American men locked up in jails and prisons than there were African American men in college (Butterfield, 2002). For example, in 2002, approximately 791,000 African American men were in prisons and jails compared to approximately 603,000 African American men in higher education (Butterfield, 2002).

Health   Another example of social injustice for African Americans is the area of health disparities. The issue of racial and ethnic health disparities is one of the most pressing problems plaguing the U.S. health care system. Health disparities are twofold: disparities in health care and disparities in health. *Health care disparities* refer to differences existing among distinct populations groups in health care access, coverage, and quality of care, including differences in preventive, diagnostic, and treatment services. *Health disparities* refer to the differences and inequities between two or more groups in health outcomes and in the incidence, the prevalence, the screening, the diagnosis, the quality of treatment, and bearing the burden of diseases; disability; mortality or injury; and life expectancy. In general, these disparities are viewed as a burden that is experienced by specific marginalized groups such as African Americans.

In clearer words, there are major disparities in the burdens of illness and death experienced by Hispanic/Latino Americans, Asian Americans and Pacific Islanders, American Indians and Alaska Natives, and Blacks and African Americans as compared to the entire U.S. population (Institute of Medicine, 2002, 2004). Health disparities also include the affordability of health care, such as insurance, managed care, Medicare, and Medicaid; access to health care; and the lack of medical professionals of color.

For instance, there are major health disparities existing within the African American community. African Americans have one of the highest mortality rates for heart disease, stroke, and diabetes of any group (Heckler, 1985). In terms of gender and ethnicity, African American males have higher rates of lung cancer than both European American and Hispanic males. Similarly, African American females, who experience a lower incidence of breast cancer than other ethnic groups, have a higher death rate from this disease.

Moreover, African Americans make up 50% of all AIDS cases reported in the United States, reaching near-epidemic levels in males with 63 AIDS cases per 100,000 people (CDC, 2005), yet, according to the U.S. Census Bureau (2000b), African Americans constitute only 12% of the U.S. population. An even more major health disparity is that African Americans, in contrast to other racial groups who have AIDS, die younger.

Mental Health   A mental health profile of Blacks and African American mimics their health profile. Mental health injustices are as major as the social ills within the African American community. Though not to the same degree or with the same immediacy as health disparities, mental health disparities also involve life-and-death issues and include issues related to access, such as cultural barriers, transportation, and the affordability issues of lack of insurance and money, unemployment, under-employment, managed care, and Medicare and Medicaid. Inequities and disparities are also related to quality of care (culturally appropriate screening, treatment, and diagnosis, and the incidence and prevalence of mental disorders) and treatment (theory, strategies, and treatment plans).

Last, but not least, mental health care and services are becoming more cul-turally sensitive, responsive, and ethical in addressing the mental health needs of people of color. In spite of this, it remains a social institution that operates within a system that has been historically racist, discriminative, oppressive, and even harmful to African Americans. As a result of the multicultural move-ment, there has been substantive progress in providing mental health services for African Americans and other groups of color. Yet, African Americans are still facing major social ills and have not found effective mental health care, but instead have found themselves victimized further by systemic and insidious men-tal health disparities.

Social Justice Initiatives for African Americans

I remember when I was in Colorado one time with this Jewish person or Hebrew person, and he asked me, "Why do you want to be called an African American?" I said, "I'm not Jewish, but I am Christian. I can tell you your history and your people. I can tell you the day and year Israel became a nation. But, I can't tell you the day or year not one African country became a nation. You understand? So, when we say African American, we are trying to teach our people more about ourselves. But all our lives, we've been taught about you. When I was raised up in school, the history I was taught was your history, the White history."

—Joshua

Social justice initiatives for modern-day African Americans have taken multiple platforms, beginning with the civil rights and Black movements of the 1960s and 1970s and Dr. Martin Luther King's stance as a drum major for justice. During that era, there were many drum majors—Black, White, and other racial groups—who took to the streets to protest the treatment of Black people and others who were being discriminated against.

Rosa Parks, for example, along with other civil rights leaders, helped to stage a bus boycott in Montgomery, Alabama (by having Rosa refuse to give up her seat on a public bus for a White man), that sparked the beginning of the civil rights move-ment. This well-organized movement played out on every platform in the United States in an effort to protest the conditions and abuse (rape, beatings, peonage, and murder) of Black people. It can certainly be categorized as a major social justice initiative on behalf of African Americans.

In more recent times, many organizations and indigenous systems exist within the African American community such as the Southern Christian Leadership Conference (SCLC), National Association for the Advancement of Colored People (NAACP), Divine Nine (Black Greek-lettered organizations), 100 Black Men of America, and National Coalition of 100 Black Women. These groups have strong missions statements that speak to empowering African Americans and eliminating the social injustices that have hindered their progress.

In academe, Black and African American scholars from many different disciplines have attempted to bring attention to the plight of Black people. For example, Kunjufu (1982, 1985, 1987), an educational consultant, through a series of books titled *Countering the Conspiracy to Destroy Black Boys* and other writings, has taken a more radical approach to rectify the dismal educational status for Black boys. Further, in various disciplines in higher education, scholars such as Hilliard (1976), McAdoo (2002), Staples (1994), Billingsley (1993), Asante (2003), and hooks (1991) have vigorously defended Black males.

Mental Health

Until the counseling profession is indicative of the people it wants to counsel, it is going to be lopsided and warped, or skewed. It is hard to balance. We have problems dealing with one another. As I've related in this session, about my experience here at this school. I wonder, "How are they going to counsel people of color when they are having a hard time teaching or supervising them?"

—Joshua

In the field of mental health, several African American clinical psychologists, counseling psychologists, and licensed professional counselor (LPCs) are social justice advocates. For example, distinguished and renowned activists and Afrocentric scholars such as Akbar (1991) have written extensively on the conditions of African Americans and other people of color.

Despite the scholarly work, paradigm shift, and information added to the knowledge base in multicultural counseling, we still have a long way to go. Some African American scholars have called for an African-centered or Afrocentric (Asante, 2003) framework when working with African Americans, specifically in mental health (Parham, 2002; Parham & Caldwell, 2006; Thompson Sanders, Bazile, & Akbar, 2004).

The African American Clients' Social Justice Story

Given the 400 years of slavery and the continued social injustice experienced by African Americans, the African American clients were realistic, optimistic, and, to a larger degree, hopeful about the status of social justice in African American life. Shawn commented, "I see people as having good and evil in them; there is a spirit within a person, and that spirit within people allows them to do good or evil."

Joshua commented, "Being an African American, we have been taught about the other cultures. I have traveled and have gone to workshops all over the country."

Both Shawn and Joshua were products of the South and knew firsthand of the social injustices that existed and the subtleness of it that continues to exist. Joshua recalled this incident during the interview:

A White pastoral friend who pastors one of the largest Presbyterian churches in the Memphis area, we actually met and became friends following a statement he made that I took high offense to during a racial seminar where a group of area ministers met at different churches to deal with the issue of race.

And it was in a group setting, and we had facilitators where we actually dealt with one another.

In the session where we were paired together, he stated that in order for Black people to integrate with White people, we [Black people] must be willing to put up with the prejudices that White people have against us. When I took great exception to that, then he reversed it and said White people have to put up with prejudices we have against them. I told him, my prejudice against you may be that you are rich and you have the power and that kind of prejudice will have little effect on you. Your prejudice against me may be thinking that I am a thief, a rapist, shiftless, no good, and that may have a great effect on me.

For example, you may perceive me to be a snake when I am only an earthworm, and you may kill me because you think I am a snake when I am really maybe the thing that will bring you good. I said, "Don't kill me just because I am an earthworm and you think I am a snake and you don't know me." That's how we established this relationship.

To Joshua, as an African American and a minister, breaking down racial barriers was shared; thus, it was also his responsibility. He commented in the interview,

Being in Promise Keepers, an organization who helps men break down racial barriers, to be able to help one another, and be accountable to one another, has helped me become the god-like type of man that we are all supposed to be.

Last, Joshua also viewed social justice as a way of life and a natural form of love for your neighbor emanating from the natural divine order of God. He said,

My first vision is God, then family, then neighbor, and then self. You have to be able to put everything in focus and the proper orientation. I can't focus on God without focusing on my neighbor. If I don't love my neighbor, I don't love God; If I don't love my family, I don't love God.

Shawn, like Joshua, sourced her energy from God and her fellowship with the church. Shawn reported, "I have the church and a reliance on God. The family is a support system as well as the church."

Shawn and Joshua saw education as a vehicle of social change. According to Shawn,

After education, then the application of that education is needed. The bigger piece for me is "How do we get that information from the university/college to the mall, the play group, the church, the realtor's office, and the bank? How do those who are educated use their power to become agents of change?"

Joshua forcefully declared,

Until we have African Americans who are in assistance instead of being in training, where they can impart this information, then it's going to be hard for people who are not African American writing the textbooks to bring about change without having the experience needed to relate to African Americans.

Conversely, Shawn felt that it was people's (regardless of race) resistance and fear of change that would prevent progress among people from different racial and ethnic groups, in contrast to Joshua, who uses his counseling skills to evoke change in his community through change in the family structure. Shawn reported, "Race relations, I don't see them as getting better. People are afraid to look at themselves and change some things because they are comfortable with things a certain way."

Conclusions

In conclusion, for the African American clients, their experiences of social injustices are generational and can be traced back to their ancestors' slavery experiences. They each talk about growing up steeped in discrimination and racism and share stories of these experiences. Yet, for them, changing systemic racism and having the tools needed for social justice begin with their untiring faith in God, strong family ties, and grounded religious upbringing.

Implications

Theory Implications   Although there is not an urgency to throw out the baby (traditional theories) with the bath water, there is a need, however, to have more culture-centered theoretical approaches such as the Afrocentric theory advocated by Akbar (1979) that is the basis of Black personality. There is also a need to draw from other frameworks such as critical pedagogy, critical race theory, and other revolutionary political movements for understanding the effects of race, racism, and racial bias on African Americans' mental health and linking it to mental illnesses. This also includes fields and movements such as the revolutionary, military, and political pedagogical approaches of Paulo Freire, Ernesto "Che" Guevara, and Don Pedro Albizú Campos that Torres-Rivera, Phan, Garrett, and D'Andrea (2005) suggested for working with Hispanic clients.

Some mental health scholars (Parham, 2002; Parham & Caldwell, 2006; Parham, White, & Ajamu, 2000; Thompson Sanders et al., 2004) are calling for an African-centered theoretical approach for working with Black and African American clients. Afrocentrism, as opposed to Eurocentrism, is more grounded in the traditions, culture, and worldviews of people of African descent. As mentioned previously, an Afrocentric theory takes into consideration a more collectivistic viewpoint, one that embraces the collective thought and unity of its people. It is systemic in that it connects systems to subsystems such as politics in the Black church. It ties extended families, Black churches, and other indigenous systems such as barber shops and beauty salons within the African American community to the schools in the community. Thus, to pluck away at the social injustices, there is a need to augment the extant mental health theories with those that address the massive social hurts and abuses plaguing the mental health of not only African Americans but also the African American community. Last, resiliency theory is needed in order to better understand how a people could endure nearly 4 centuries of abuse and still rise.

Practice Implications   A social justice approach to mental health counseling with African Americans offers implications for mental health practitioners through the need for strategies and techniques that provide an understanding of the history and discriminative practices undergirding the social conditions and the Black experience, and how all of this adversely affects the mental health of African Americans. It also calls for culturally grounded techniques and strategies such as multicultural genograms, and maybe incorporating hip-hop. In essence, it calls for therapy that integrates advocacy, systemic change, and possibly radicalism into counseling work.

A social justice approach implies that mental health clinicians working with African American clients must first examine their own perceptions, values, stereotypes, and biases toward Black people. This means that mental health professionals must ensure that African American clients are not victimized further in counseling, namely, being the victims of counselors' biases and those with biased, racist, and even naïve viewpoints about African American clients or their experiences. Perhaps, it may require that counselors be extra-careful not to make snap judgments about the conditions and systemic racism relating to African Americans trapped in systems (e.g., the criminal justice, penal, welfare, and child protective service systems) and how these experiences play out in the counseling relationship.

Last, it implies that counselors may have to be a lot more uncomfortable than they are now and make some major adjustments to how they practice. That may force mental health professionals to take off the business shoes and suits and come to the *hood*, that is, come out to the African American communities and do some community-based, indigenous-type counseling. Thus, for both traditional and acculturated African Americans, an Afrocentric approach should be considered.

Methods Implications   To investigate the social justice and social injustice in the African American community, more qualitative studies are needed, including phenomenological studies and nontraditional qualitative methods, specifically participatory methods such as participatory inquiry, narrative inquiry, storytelling, performance ethnography, autoethnography, and oral histories. These approaches are more cultural paradigms that allow for African Americans' voices to be heard.

Implications for the Profession   Social justice for the mental health profession is related to what Sue, Ivey, and Pedersen (1996) referred to as *a call to consciousness*. The profession must acknowledge its part in the historical abuse to African Americans, and come to understand how it operates from a Eurocentric position of power, that is, privilege. It must be willing to come down from the pedestal of resistance to change, especially in the areas relating to research and scholarship. It can begin by embracing a grounded Afrocentric paradigm and worldviews as well as methodologies that are nontraditional and less acceptable as scholarly and publishable.

Closely related to this is the need to make more concerted efforts to grow, recruit, and retain African American mental health scholars, practitioners, educators, and researchers, and these should not be carbon copies from a White,

Eurocentric template. Last, as a profession, mental health needs a strategic plan to address the mental health disparities and inequities for African American clients specific to the affordability and accessibility of mental health care.

Implications for Future Research   Social justice implies knowledge of social injustices. Although there are tons and tons of research on social injustices in the African American community, there is very little on social injustices in the mental health field against African Americans. We do know, however, that African Americans, like other groups of color, are not faring well in counseling. Thus, there is a need for major quantitative (including large-scale) studies conducted in mental health in order to flush out where the social injustices lie, especially in the diagnosis and treatment of mental health disorders.

Likewise, more culturally capable qualitative studies that will capture the experiences of African Americans in relationship to experiences of being Black in the United States are needed. We really need a close-up snapshot of how this affects their individual and collective mental health. Therefore, there needs to more research on developing new qualitative and quantitative techniques, methods, and instruments that can measure their experiences and those of other groups of color.

DEADLY SILENCE: SOCIAL JUSTICE AND ASIAN POPULATIONS

> There is a silence that cannot speak.
> There is a silence that will not speak.
>
> —Joy Kogawa (1994)

As mentioned in Chapter 5, Asian American populations have been unjustly labeled the *model minority* ethnic group. Thus, social justice efforts for Asians populations begin with the mischaracterization of Asians as model minorities. Characterizing and stereotyping Asians as ideal and exemplary have legitimized social injustices and racial disparities and inequities existing in the Asian community. To some degree, the myth has kept those Asian groups on the bottom from receiving the support they need in health, education, and mental health. The myth has silenced the abuse, disparities, inequities, and injustices experienced by so many Asian Americans and other groups of color. In short, the myth itself is oppressive.

The term *model minority* was introduced by elite, privileged Whites during the civil rights and feminist eras of the 1960s and beyond as a tool to muffle the cries of societal injustices against other groups, especially people of color (and, more specifically, Black people). It was during this era that major protests such as civil rights marches and strikes against the injustices and racism Black people were experiencing were used.

The Asians were proof that good American values (sacrifice, good education, hard work, personal initiative, and dedication to family) led to success. This implies by default that the oppressive conditions of African Americans were linked to their lack of values such as hard work and personal initiative rather than the 3 centuries of slavery and discrimination that they had experienced.

Placing Asians on a pedestal, for other people of color to see, provided proof that the impoverished conditions of poor people and people of color were their fault, as if to say, "After all, look at the exemplary accomplishments that Asians have made; if they can do it, why can't the rest of you?" Fundamentally, this *model minority* image became a political weapon that positioned Asians against Black people and other groups of color.

Yu (2006) believed this image of Asians being the model minority was, and continues to be, a device of political control, one that misrepresents equal opportunity in the United States while minimizing racism and other inequities and structural problems that afflict Asians and other groups of color. To all intents and purposes, it overlooks and justifies historical abuses and the modern racism, inequities, and social injustices in the United States. It was what Malcolm X referred to as "blaming the victim."

In actuality, this stereotypical image of Asians has major ramifications for social policy, education, school reform, and the health and mental health of Asians and other groups of color. It also affects race relations between White Americans and Americans of color, and among groups of color.

Notwithstanding the mythical image, many urban, inner-city Asian communities are plagued with social ills such as hate crimes, gang violence, drugs, exploitation from other Asians, and poor housing. Asians, especially Asian immigrants, are exploited, unemployed, underemployed, and uneducated; lack English language proficiency skills; and lack medical care.

Social justice issues for Asians are diverse, complex, and broad. It is with the population of mainly immigrants and refugees from developing Asian countries (and, more recently, those from Arab countries) that major inequities and discrimination occur. Disparities occur in nearly every domain of Asian life, including politics, education, health, and mental health.

Education

The most widespread disparities and social injustices for East Asians, especially in pigeonholing Asians as the high-achieving model minority, are in education. The U.S. Censuses of 1990 and 2000 (U.S. Census Bureau, 1990b, 2000a) showed that not all Asian groups are academically successful. Further, Asians from poorer, developing nations (Cambodians, Hmongs, Laotians, and Vietnamese) ranked far below the national average in education. Because of the "super-achiever" label, Asians have been unduly burdened with mythical expectations, but those in need of academic assistance are often overlooked or denied those services.

In addition to the stress to live up to society's expectation of academic excellence, Asian students (pre-K–12 and college level) are also weighed down with cultural and familial expectations to succeed. Typically, Asian cultures value education and high academic achievement for their children. Education attainment, especially for Asians from East and South Asian countries, is directly tied to the family's integrity, honor, and prestige, whereas low achievement brings shame. As a result, their identities, self-esteem, and mental health are adversely affected.

Education social justice initiatives for Asians have to be systemic. This includes attacking the toxicity of the model minority myth and addressing the individual academic and cultural needs of Asian students at all levels of education. It is also means addressing the deplorable conditions of the schools that inner-city Asian and poor other students of color attend.

It is also important to understand how the No Child Left Behind Act (2001) and other educational reforms (such as vouchers) promote social injustice and educational inequities for poor children and children of color, and we must work to change those policies and laws that oppress. These types of reforms and social conditions that oppress their academic performance disadvantage not only Asian students but also all children, in particular children of color and children from impoverished backgrounds. In short, there is a need for national advocacy for educational reform that is equitable, nonracist, nonsexist, and nondiscriminatory, and that genuinely assures the academic success of all children, not only those who score high on standardized tests, as No Child Left Behind mandates.

More importantly, education, like charity, begins at home. Therefore, teachers, schools, school districts, cities, and states are responsible for their students and are obligated to make sure none of their students are being left behind. Social justice means making sure Asian students and other students in urban schools have the educational resources they need to succeed in school. It means that those resources should be available and equitable for all children.

Mental Health

The counseling movement is a middle-class White movement. How do Asians identify with a movement like that?

—Mai Li

Ah, the doctoral program was very painful, but also very crucial too. I felt very scared and almost void. I was the most silent person in the class. I didn't know what to do.

—Wai

Mental illness is an alarming problem in many Asian communities. For instance, Asian refugees (such as Vietnamese and Cambodians) may experience severe trauma resulting from war or conflicts and during their immigration to the United States. Yet, according to Gwynn et al. (2008), Asians have the lowest rates of utilization of mental health services of all ethnic groups.

The complexity of mental health for Asians is another problem. Due to cultural factors, mental disorders are often manifested somatically and are difficult to identify and diagnose. Like other groups, there are culture-specific health diagnoses, and health care for the poor is unaffordable. There are mental disorders emanating from being exposed to social conditions such as racism, violence, and poverty.

In addition to the aforementioned problems, Asians, who are less likely to seek professional help, are under a lot of stress to live up to the high-achiever stereotype. Consistent with the high-achieving theme, Asian children are under intense pressure to succeed in school, which can cause intergenerational conflicts and psychological difficulties for them. This can lead to test anxiety, social isolation, and impaired self-esteem because of their mediocre or good, rather than outstanding or excellent, school performance.

The communication barrier, along with acculturation and generational differences between first-generation Asian language–speaking parents and their predominantly English-speaking children, can cause stress for parents and children. Mental health professionals need to be aware of those stressors and how they impact Asian clients' mental health.

Additionally, social anxiety, social phobias, depression, and trauma-related disorders occur at high rates within the Asian American community, and the myth of the model minority is a contributing factor. Suicide rates are also increasing for elderly Asians and Asian women in the Unites States and in Asian countries. Ironically, Asians rarely get the help they need because mental health treatment is unaffordable and stigmatized; seeking help outside of the family is frowned on in most Asian cultures. Therefore, we need more Asian therapists from the different Asian cultures who understand the distinct subcultures. Last, the mental health profession must continue to seek nontraditional and indigenous ways to serve this population.

Socioeconomics

The *model minority* stereotype contributes to the perception that the socioeconomic status of Asians was better than that of all U.S. ethnic groups, and this disadvantages that large number of Asians whose income falls way below the U.S. poverty line. In fact, there are just as many Asians at the bottom as there are at the top of the income range.

Earlier studies that examined the combined income and level of education data of all Asian groups found that Asians were doing better (higher incomes and higher degrees earned) than all other ethnic and racial groups, including Whites. However, findings from later studies on Asian socioeconomic status showed quite the reverse. That is, more Asians were living in poverty than White Americans, and Asians who had the same level of education were making a lot less money than White Americans with the same level of education (Suzuki, 2002).

Further, data show that Asians continue to experience inequities and injustices in income and socioeconomics (Cabezas & Kawaguchi, 1988; Chan, 1989; Koo, 2001; Lee, 1998; Tang, 1993). This means that the model minority is also a victim of social injustice.

The Asian Clients' Social Justice Story

Like the African American clients, from a social justice perspective, the Asian clients had personally felt the pain of discrimination and were aware of the injustices that other groups experienced. Mai Li commented, "I grew up with different colors, and I never even noticed those colors until I was bigger."

Both Mai Li and Wai remained doubtful of any immediate change to the existing discrimination and social injustices that exist in the world. Mai Li commented, "It became apparent that colors divided people and governmental policies. And I became very sad." Wai commented, "People are becoming more and more outcome and materialistic oriented, but I value the growing process, relationship, and caring for each other." Also, like the African American clients, the Asian clients viewed social justice as a lonesome uphill battle. Wai reported, "I feel lonely and like fighting my battle all by myself."

Regardless of the slow progress toward equity for women and people of color, Wai and Mai Li remained hopeful and grounded in their love of people. Mai Li commented, "I believe in the dignity of persons, regardless of gender, sex, race, and so on." Wai commented,

> I have had broad experiences, and I like to be open to them even though my prejudices or biases may sometimes sneak out, but still, my attitude is open to diversity. I may be highly prejudiced about the way you dress, talk, walk, without me noticing it, but my intent is good.

Conclusions   In conclusion, for the Asian clients, although in retrospect they see inequities and disparities existing in their communities, their childhood experiences, for the most part, sheltered them from the realities of social injustices. Both of them felt discrimination in the United States because of their language and accents. They both were candid about their own human tendencies toward biases and prejudice against others who are different. Yet, their love of people and openness to diversity far outweigh those tendencies to harm others and set the stage for an approach to social justice.

Implications

Theory Implications   Asians are not as high risk for most of the psychiatric disorders that are common in the United States, although they may experience what the *Diagnostic and Statistical Manual of Mental Disorders*, 4th edition (DSM-IV), classifies as *culture-bound syndromes* such as neurasthenia and *hwa-byung*, which has symptoms similar to those of depression (American Psychiatric Association, 1994). Instead, Asians tend to present with somatic symptoms. Therefore, more cultural-bound theories are needed that can describe and explain mental disorders in those cultures. We especially need theories that can be templates for both somatic and psychological symptoms.

Thus, there is a need for a closer partnership between medical professionals and mental health professionals in discovering cross-over theories (both mental health and medical). There is also a call for theories that can function as frameworks to address the effects of achievement pressures to succeed in the United States on the manifestations of depression, suicide, and culture-bound mental disorders in Asians.

Practice Implications   Implications for clinical practice for Asians are centered on Asians' utilization of counseling services, in particular their help-seeking behaviors. Traditional Asians tend to keep their personal problems to themselves or within their family. Also, Asians do not seek mental health services for other reasons such as affordability, stigma, language barriers, and unsuccessful counseling outcomes.

The facts that Asians have an abundance of mental health issues and challenges and Asian Americans have the least contact with mental health services are definitive reasons to transform counseling to fulfill the needs of the Asian community. Thus, it is important to get those high-need individuals and others in need of mental health services into counseling. Equally important is to create a safe, confidential environment that ensures honor and respect for their culture. There is a need to grow more Asian mental health professionals and enlist their help in finding creative ways to penetrate the fear and feelings of dishonor associated with Asians seeking mental health services. Last, assuring social justice implies discovering and even crafting nontraditional, grassroots settings—the "coffee-like counseling" that Mai Li, the female Asian counselor, described, where those Asians most in need of help can come and feel safe.

Method

For Asian populations, large-scale studies on the different Asian groups are desired, especially for those from developing and poor countries. Equally important is to use or create methods that are extremely sensitive to the Asians' view of honor. For culturally traditional Arab and Muslim clients, there is a need to find not only nontraditional (in the mental health field) methods that factor in their traditions, language, and history but also methods that respect their religious beliefs and practices and capture their different voices and experiences.

Profession

Asians, with their great diversity, experience much stereotyping and lumping together, and challenge the mental health profession's sense of social justice the most. What works for one traditional Asian group may not work for another. Thus, it is important to be knowledgeable about clients' country of origin and, for some, their religion, their honor, their immigration status, as well as their presenting issue. It means we begin by closely examining our stereotypes and expectations of this group, especially any group from East Asian countries. In other words, we need to eliminate those myths and stereotypes within the mental health field first.

Research

Further research is needed to identify *culture-bound syndromes* found in the 40-plus countries in Asia. Research is needed to determine whether there are any negative effects of mental health professionals' view of Asians as high achievers and the model minority on their counseling outcomes. More mental health research is needed on Arabs as Asians and their social injustices, especially in mental health theory and practice.

Summary

The *model minority* is a myth. Asians are discriminated against just as much as other people of color. There are major social stressors within the Asian community that adversely affect Asians, mostly Asian immigrants, who need to come to the forefront. There are also a lot of societal stressors resulting from their experiences as racially and ethnically different people and as immigrants, and from the poverty, violence, and other social ills existing within their communities. This is on top of the pressure to live up to an American-created stereotype that demands a standard of excellence for Asians while denying equality to those who surpass this standard.

There are also heavy-duty issues, both historical and contemporary, threatening the same Asian groups and the Asian community's mental health. Thus, to attack the social injustices and the major inequities present in those Asian communities, mental health professionals must continue with proven strategies and techniques that work with Asian clients and simultaneously search for new ones that are culturally grounded and sensitive.

However, to really get at the systemic insidious injustices afflicting Asian Americans, mental health professionals will have to do something different— something radical, revolutionary, and possibly out of their comfort zone. Silence is not an option. Being silent about the hate crimes, racism, disparities, and inequities for Asian Americans is an acquisition of injustice and a blatant contradiction to the notion of social justice.

BEING THE CHANGE YOU WANT TO SEE IN THE WORLD: SOCIAL JUSTICE WITH LATINOS

If you're outraged at conditions, then you can't possibly be free or happy until you devote all your time to changing them and do nothing but that. But you can't change anything if you want to hold onto a good job, a good way of life, and avoid sacrifice.

—César Chávez (Levy & Ross, 2007, p. 335)

Counseling Beyond the Office With Hispanics and Latinos

The counseling profession needs to get serious about serving people of color.

—Alexias

Understanding social justice in specific populations requires a complete understanding of the population itself. This overview examines social justice issues in relation to the Latino population. Social justice in Latino populations is as complicated as the very definition of *Latino* itself. Torres-Rivera and colleagues (2005) defined *Latino* as a cultural definition of people of Latino or Hispanic descent in the United States. It was defined by the people themselves to capture the empowered politics, music and arts, and heritage of this population. However, even that term is far too broad and misses the group's unique complexity. Latinos include Mexican, Puerto Rican, Cuban, Dominican, Central American, and South American populations, with Mexican and Puerto Rican people constituting 75% of the population subgroups (U.S. Census Bureau, 2006).

The Latino population is diverse; thus, efforts for social justice and advocacy should reflect that diversity. According to the U.S. Census Bureau (2006), Cuban Latinos receive far different political and economic advantages than do immigrants from Central America and Mexico. Cubans have reached comparable economic levels to the larger U.S. population within 2 decades of immigration. Other Latino populations are unable to make similar strides after hundreds of years. Therefore, advocacy and social justice issues may differ, even between subgroups. This further adds to the complexity of the issue.

Latinos in Western society have a rich tradition of music, food, art, theater, and many other cultural aspects. However, the realities of this population as an underrepresented group are still evident. Many Latinos have been unable to escape the trappings of poverty, incarceration, educational limitation, and political disenfranchisement.

Socioeconomically, 21% of all Latino households are below the poverty level. More than 87% of all Latinos are employed in service-, support-, or labor-related jobs. Although there are an equal number of Latino men and women in the United States, the unemployment rate for Latino men is 12.2% versus 9.8% for Latina women and 5.4% for non-Latino men (Torres-Rivera, Wilbur, Phan, Maddux, & Roberts-Wilbur, 2004).

These data are not startling to most counselors who work with clients of diverse cultures. This type of systemic discrimination requires that counselors move beyond simply treating clients for mental health issues to moving forward by speaking out for and challenging a social system that limits access for certain individuals.

Issues for Consideration

The major issues facing Latinos are immigration policy, political challenges, economic status, and health care. Before addressing the major issues within the social justice realm, it is important first to recognize the role that traditional Latino values may play in social justice issues. Claudio (1998) from the Council on Foundations asserted that Latino families pass on to their children a sense of allegiance to religious and national traditions. Three key traditions are family, church, and mutual assistance associations. Therefore, mental health professionals or government agencies may be met with understandable skepticism.

Politics Latinos have long been active in the political realm. Most notably, César Chávez advocated for the rights of migrant farm workers. These advocacies led to a revolution in Latino politics, firmly placing Latinos at the political table when it came to discussions of public policy. Political influence is an avenue for reform, but it is difficult to change long-held and ingrained beliefs. To do this, Latinos must begin to capitalize on their growing population to influence public policy.

By the year 2050, Latinos will make up more than 40% of the U.S. population (U.S. Census Bureau, 2000b), and Texas and Arizona are supposed to be majority Hispanic by 2050. Increased population and voting power result in gained political influence. In addressing Hispanics attitudes toward public policy, Branton (2007) wrote that Hispanic voter participation increased 50% between the 1996 and 2000 presidential elections. Although the overall percentage was only 7% of the total votes cast in the 2000 election, Hispanics voting increased from only 4% in 1996, and this is reflected in the number of Hispanic elected officials. Further, according to the National Association of Latino Elected and Appointed Officials Community Investment Network (2002), which credits its inception to the dramatic increase in Latino elected leaders, in 1984 there were 3,128 Latino elected officials, and as of June 2002 there were 4,464.

Hispanics should begin the shift in political importance in the same way they have tackled issues from workers' rights to improving education: by beginning at a grassroots level. Given the Hispanic tradition of strong family and community involvement, organizing local, state, and then federal representatives for their issues is critical.

Economics   Although the number of Latinos in the workforce has increased over the past few years, their wages have decreased because of an increase in migrant workers saturating the market. The Pew Hispanic Center (R. Kochhar, 2006) published a report stating that the latest economic slowdown has had a disproportionate impact on Latino workers:

> From a historic low in late 2006, the unemployment rate for Latinos rose sharply in 2007 and currently stands well above the rate for non-Latinos. Immigrant Hispanics, especially Mexicans and recent arrivals, have been hurt the most by the slump in the construction industry. (p. i)

In an examination of Latino economic injustice, Jost, Pelham, Sheldon, and Sullivan (2003) asserted that members of disadvantaged groups often support the social networks and status quo to an even greater degree than members of advantaged groups do. They likened this hypothesis to system justification theory, stating that "people are motivated to defend, justify, and uphold the status quo, sometimes at the expense of personal and collective interests and esteem" (Jost et al., 2003, p. 14).

Advocates for Latino economic advantages should stress that the status quo has not worked for Latinos and that change to the system is the only way to bring about a more positive outcome. The simple principles of cognitive behavioral therapy suggest if a behavior is maladaptive, the focus should be to change the behavior. Therefore, if Latinos are subscribing to a social framework that is historically and systemically disadvantageous for them, the only recourse is to change the system.

Health   Health care should be looked at as the quiet storm for social justice advocates involved in Latino issues. In the book *Promoting Health in Multicultural Populations*, Robert M. Huff and Michael Kline (1999) addressed the challenges of Latino health issues, stating that the

> National Council of La Raza (NCLR) and the California State University, Long Beach (CSULB) Center for Latino Community Health, Evaluation, and Leadership Training found that Latinos are at a disproportionately high risk for depression and other conditions associated with mental illness. (p. 5)

Beyond mental illness lies a global obesity challenge, which affects Latinos at an alarming rate. Goel, McCarty, Phillips, and Wee (2004) found that the high occurrence of obesity has produced a major burden of obesity-related illnesses. In the year 2000, overweight and obesity accounted for nearly 17% of all deaths in the United States, a mortality rate surpassed only by that of tobacco use. To combat this, the Centers for Disease Control and Prevention have asserted that poor diet and lack of physical activity are responsible for the high rates of death from complications related to being overweight. Therefore, advocates should work with federal, state, and local organizations to promote guidelines recommending obesity prevention through the promotion of exercise and healthy diet.

Evidence suggests significant racial and ethnic differences in the prevalence of obesity and susceptibility to obesity-related illnesses, particularly among individuals who are Black, Latino, and Asian, relative to Whites (Goel et al., 2004). This assertion is reinforced by the findings of Bowie, Juon, Rodriguez, and Cho (2007) when examining health-related issues in California:

> High rates of overweight and obesity among Mexicans and Central Americans in California indicate the need for a wide variety of effective weight-loss interventions targeting these populations, and the differences we found in the factors associated with overweight and obesity may suggest the need for unique intervention strategies for different Hispanic subgroups (p. 1)

Furthermore, immigrants face more barriers to quality health care and are less likely to receive preventive health care than persons born in the United States. One possible reason for this is that Latinos are less likely to discuss diet and exercise with doctors.

Access to health care is a national problem, but it most notably affects lower-income Americans. The 1996 federal welfare reform law, the Personal Responsibility and Work Opportunity Reconciliation Act (PRWORA), restricted the Medicaid eligibility of immigrants, so those admitted to the United States after August 1996 cannot receive coverage, except for emergencies, in their first 5 years in the country (Ku & Matani, 2001). Access to health care is not only a problem for immigrants. Ku and Matani examined Hispanic access to health care even further. They stated that even after immigration status was controlled for Hispanics, they were getting less medical care, with both citizen and noncitizen Latinos having poorer access to care than non-Hispanic White populations.

The Latino Clients' Social Justice Story

Alexias, like Shawn and Joshua (the African American clients), grew up in the United States during an era when people of color were denied rights and freedom, and people fought and died so that they could have their unalienable rights. Alexias commented,

> I see a lot of changes since the time I was growing up, in terms of equality and opportunities. At one time it was more obvious in terms of denying us opportunities in terms of getting equal education, to get equal employment, equal representation. It seems that we've made some changes there, and people have sacrificed for us, such as Martin Luther King, the Kennedys, even Johnson, some of those people.

In contrast, Angelica, though coming from primarily a Western view, grew up outside of the United States in Uruguay, one of the most politically and economically stable countries in South America. She also traveled extensively throughout the world.

Alexias also personally and in his professional work in mental health experienced the ugliness of social injustices. He reported,

> In my perspective, I have always perceived and experienced some form of prejudice, racism, or discrimination; not from everyone I meet or work with but in my years of counseling and experiencing life in general, discrimination and prejudice seems to raise its ugly head now and then.

Alexias remains hopeful and loyal not only to this country but also to the people of the United States and the discipline of counseling:

> When I was growing up in the 1960s in school and learning how our government worked, I was taught that the government was by the people and for the people, and of the people, and the politicians were servants of the people. Now it's reverse and the people are servants of the politicians. We the people have to take that back. Most of all vote, we have to utilize that right, we have to vote and try to make it fair for all people.

Angelica, in reflecting on her experience with people who are culturally different, like Woodro the male American Indian client said she embraces, celebrates, and rejoices in her and others' differences. She commented,

> It's something that cannot be denied. It's everywhere. It's around. It's who I am. I mean, it's everything that surrounds me. It's part of life. It's enriching! I see myself as a richer, better person because I am more bicultural now in my culture as opposed to being monocultural years ago when I was more part of one culture.

Conclusion

The Latino clients speak the same language, but with different dialects and from different cultural backgrounds and experiences that have resulted in two vastly different worldviews. Angelica came from a working-class family and stable home environment, and from a country that was politically and economically sound. Her travels throughout the world allowed her to make great friends and to be invited to partake and nibble off of the best of each culture.

On the contrary, Alexias is the first-generation son of uneducated Mexican migrant farmers. His parents had to work day and night in order to survive and to feed their children. Alexias is the first of his family to get a college degree. His childhood was a byproduct of indigenous people with a territorial and violent history with the United States. He, like Angelica, has traveled the world, but from the position of being an American soldier. He visited war-torn countries and saw firsthand the devastation and disparities in developing nations. Yet, like the African American, Asian, and American Indian clients, the hope that comes from spiritual strength fills Alexias with a love of humanity and what is right and just, and arms him with a silent commitment to social justice.

Implications

Social justice and advocacy by counselors help give a voice to underrepresented populations. Famed American historian and author David McCullough (on Rose, 2008) once stated that humanity is evident not only in our failings but also, rather, in our enormous ability to achieve and do great things. It is our ability to transcend that helps to fully capture the power of the human spirit. As counselors, our duty is to transcend or go beyond and speak for those whose voice is unheard.

As discussed earlier in this overview, advocacy may be understood as the protection and advancement of the rights of people of color. As it relates to mental health, advocacy is speaking up or taking action on behalf of our clients (American Counseling Association, 2005). As counselors, it is our charge to work with individuals and help change behaviors. But, social and political issues influence behavior that is outside of the individual's control. A counselor finds himself or herself in a position of advocacy when all other avenues of help for the client are exhausted, and yet there is still more that can be done.

Practice Implications   First and foremost, practitioners should work to instill within Latinos a proud sense of heritage and respect for family. Counselors should work to set up strong community networks of social service workers who are able to communicate well with Latinos. Mental health professionals should adhere to the propositions of multicultural counseling and therapy (MCT) when working with Hispanic clients.

Immigration policy implications for practice may be to work with the clients to identify all the ways their contributions can help make this country great. By knowing that rights differ based on legal status, a counselor could work to connect clients to social workers who may help them take full advantage of what rights are available.

Theory Implications   Given the immigration status and changing demographics of Latinos, there is a need for more revolutionary and radical theories. Because of the multiple dialects existing in the Hispanic population and the language barriers resulting from them, there is a need to combine counseling and linguistic theories. There is also a demand for frameworks that can serve as lenses to examine the effects of immigration pressures on the manifestations of depression, stress, and familiar problems.

Implication for Methods   Last, there is a need to search out and utilize both quantitative and qualitative research theoretical orientations (e.g., phenomenological) that explore the social reality of Hispanics, including immigrants from U.S. territories such as Puerto Rico. This includes other nonconventional narratives, oral histories, archival research, and interviews.

There is also a need for more quantitative data using nontraditional methods and statistical techniques. Last, though no easy feat, there is a need for large-scale studies of social justice issues for Hispanic immigrants.

Implications for Research   There is a need for qualitative research on the immigrant populations, especially on how the United States, on the one hand, relies heavily on them as a labor pool and, on the other hand, exploits them. Also, more research on the role that language plays in the oppression of Hispanics is necessary. More research is needed on Hispanic citizens who experience discrimination solely on the assumption that they are immigrants. Last, there is need for more research on those Mexican American citizens who live in states (Texas, California, and New Mexico) where their ancestors lived when the states belonged to Mexico and Spain.

Implications for the Profession   This section on Hispanics has touched on some of the challenges facing Hispanics involving political challenges. From a social justice perspective, the role of mental health professionals is to work with the clients and represent them within the political system to promote change helping underrepresented populations. From an advocacy perspective, mental health professionals should organize political action committees and support candidates for public office who represent their views. This takes people and resources. Promoting higher education and assisting clients in finding funding for education have great potential.

The final major social justice implication involves the role of health care. Both access and information about a healthy lifestyle are critical. When a large percentage (90%) of Hispanics works in service-type jobs, access to health care is restricted. Thus, mental health professionals can advocate on behalf of access to affordable health care coverage or insurance. Also of importance is promoting a healthy lifestyle and wellness due to the high rates of diseases and health issues (obesity, diabetes, and high blood pressure) in the Hispanic community. Other areas for social justice include language barriers, transportation, and affordable health and mental health services.

THE GREAT UNDERTAKING: SOCIAL JUSTICE FOR NATIVE AMERICANS

I have seen that in any great undertaking it is not enough for a man to depend simply upon himself.

—Lone Man (Isna-la-wica), Teton Sioux (quoted in Legends of America, 2003–2010, p. 1)

Social justice for Native Americans has a different political and social flavor inasmuch as Native tribes consider themselves sovereign nations within the United States. This standing does not mean that the U.S. government has not interfered with Native American policies or ways of life. Throughout history, and still today, Native Americans have had their land, children, culture, and customs forcibly taken away from them, and they have been forced to assimilate to the dominant European American culture. In addition, specific groups, particularly Alaska Natives, Hawaiian Natives, and Pacific Islanders, have had to fight for recognition from the U.S. government to be recognized as Native Americans, which gives them the benefits and recognition that they historically deserve. The Native American Programs Act of 1974 recognizes these groups as Native Americans and provides funding and programs that increase social and economic independence.

Awareness and knowledge of historical and current oppression faced by Native Americans comprise the first step toward working for social justice. For example, Native children have historically been removed from their homes and placed predominantly with White families in foster care and adoption situations. Some removals have stemmed from ignorance of Native customs and traditions or the belief that White families could better raise the children. This resulted in children with a foot in both worlds and acceptance in neither.

To discourage these practices, the U.S. government put into effect the Indian Child Welfare Act (1978), which, among other things, provides for culturally knowledgeable advocates for the children, and if removal is necessary, attempts to place the children in Native homes before placing them in White homes. Mindell, de Haymes, and Francisco (2003) completed a study revealing that even today, and even in areas with a large Native population, social workers have little knowledge of this law and don't follow its tenets. This is an example of how awareness and knowledge could drastically affect the lives of Native American children and families.

Mental Health

Counselors must understand the culture of that particular client and that culture goes beyond the color syndrome.

—Woodro

Another common issue for Native Americans is funding for mental health and substance abuse services. Urban Indians, who are unable to claim or prove tribal membership or who are not close to a reservation, have a particularly difficult time finding accessible and affordable treatment. Another issue is the lack of cultural sensitivity when it comes to common funding sources, such as Medicaid, covering traditional healing methods. Tribal members are understandably suspicious and resentful of a funding source that dictates what would be effective treatment, especially when it does not follow what they believe to be effective.

Awareness and knowledge alone do not constitute social justice. Counselors have a duty to work toward change on many levels, help the oppressed group learn to self-advocate for equality, and address how to deal with the negative effects of inequality, racism, and oppression in the Native client's everyday life.

The American Indian Clients' Social Justice Story

For Woodro and Lioma, like Joshua and Shawn (African American clients) and Alexias (Hispanic client), social justice begins with vivid memories of heart-rending stories from their professional life and childhood of discrimination and social injustices. Lioma reported,

> The one thing that I remember about ethnicity and being exposed to it was when we moved back to the country and I went to a very rural, country school. There was an African American male administrator's family moving into the area, because we had a big conservation area, and he was one of the administrators that was going to be moving in. When they came to see the school, White parents in the community came around to say, "We are not having you in our school." This must have been about '73 or '74. There were only two Indian families in the school: my family and one other family.
>
> I can remember standing behind a group of kids where we were watching and listening to these parents in the parking lot and thinking, "This isn't fair. Why are they doing this to them, and yet, they don't care that we are here?" It gave me a feeling of being less than the mainstream, than the dominant group. And to my knowledge, in 1997, that school was still White, and there were no Indian families there.

Woodro reported,

> I'm on the advisory board for the American Association of University Women (AAUW) to get an understanding of the experience of being minority. I go to the AAUW meetings, and their diversity is very limited. For example, I went and there were White feminists with maybe three males on the committee: one Black and myself, an American Indian, and another male who was in the meeting who didn't make much of an impression on me, because he was White.
>
> My experience was as a minority male saying to them, "You know, you haven't experienced it all that badly. You're part of the system." What I am seeing substituted in academia and the private sector, too, are White females become the legal response to affirmative action—making females a minority in that sense.

For Lioma and Woodro, like the Asian clients, Wai and Mai Li, change, flexibility, and openness to change are critical to making counseling work and to eliminating social injustice. Lioma commented, "Counseling works for anyone who is willing to change. Not necessarily change, but willing to be open to their own potential." Woodro commented,

> I know when to act White, and I can even act Black if I have to. I could even act East Asian when I have to—because there are certain behaviors that I would incorporate. Respect, I guess, is what you do. I wasn't trying to emulate anyone. I was just trying to get along in this world. Adapt: "When in Rome, you do as the Romans do."

Last, Woodro came to understand the personal aspect of social justice and admits his own shortcoming to doing something to eliminate social injustices in and outside of counseling situations. Woodro reported, "From a social justice perspective, I know there have been things that I have failed to do, even as a counselor, with people I've worked with in the past, and I'm not doing it now."

Conclusion

The Native American clients have had to give up a lot, including their culture, language, and country, in order to *arrive*. They are keenly aware of the politics, socioeconomics, educational status, health and mental health issues, disparities in their lands, and struggles of their people. Yet, remarkably, they are not bitter, but like all the participants of color, they are upbeat, committed to social justice, and hopeful about leveling the playing field, and they believe strongly that counseling is one vehicle to accomplish equity and a balance.

Implications

Theory Implications   Like African Americans, Asian Americans, and Hispanic Americans, Native Americans benefit from culture-centered treatment approaches that consider environment and cultural beliefs and values in a counseling context. In addition to this generality, a strengths-based approach helps the counselor and client focus on what is working for the client and what to build on.

Critical race theory (CRT) is a commonly utilized theory in counseling and education that assumes the insidious presence of racism and differences in the experiences of racism within and between ethnic groups. The theory was initially constructed with a Black–White division in mind, so it has been expanded to be more specific to different ethnic groups. Brayboy (2006) constructed tribal critical race theory (TribalCrit), which follows the basic tenets of CRT but focuses on the Native American experience. Like CRT, TribalCrit espouses the belief that narratives and storytelling constitute a valid form of research and theory. TribalCrit considers the effects of U.S. policies toward indigenous people; the desire for "tribal sovereignty, tribal autonomy, self-determination, and self-identification" (Brayboy, 2006, p. 429); and indigenous lenses through which counselors and educators can consider their Native clients and students. In addition, this theory posits that colonization is endemic to society and results in forced assimilation. This brief summary of TribalCrit is not intended to be comprehensive, and the interested reader is encouraged to read Brayboy (2006) for further details and implications.

An additional counseling approach that takes both historical and contemporary trauma into consideration is colonial trauma response (CTR; Evans-Campbell & Walters, 2006). This approach, which is unique for considering the impact of colonization, links the effects of current-day traumatic events like overt racism and oppression to collective historical traumatic events. Evans-Campbell (2008) discussed how the effects of historical trauma from events like child removal from homes and the loss of many community members can have an intergenerational effect that links to the social injustices experienced by Native Americans today. This approach also provides an explanation as to why the injustices of the past are still relevant generations later.

Practice Implications   When discussing practice implications, the need for knowledge once again reveals itself. Learning about the worldviews, traditions, and cultural values of Native Americans is imperative, as is realizing that there will be differences among the many tribes. Counselors must also not forget about Native populations who receive less scholarly and governmental attention, such as Hawaiian Natives and American Pacific Islanders. Also, with about 87% of Native Americans living in urban areas instead of on reservations (U.S. Census Bureau, 2002), the informed reader should be aware that there is a difference between urban Indian culture and culture on the reservation, which once again stresses the importance of hearing about the client's lived experiences. These experiences reveal to us the context of the clients' lives, surroundings, and resources, helping us to provide more culturally sensitive treatment.

Another area in which knowledge is essential is government policies such as the Indian Child Welfare Act, which should guide the treatment and placement of American Indian children. Related to policies is the issue of funding. Tribes that receive government funding must follow the dictates put forth by the government, whereas tribes that do not receive this funding have greater freedom. This government intervention or lack thereof will often lead to differences in treatment of which the counselor should be aware.

A program studied by Friedsam, Haug, and Rust (2003) provided *tribal benefits counselors*, who worked in clinics on the reservations to help the community members with applications for Medicaid, documentation, and advocacy issues such as appeals. These benefits counselors consisted of tribe members who were highly trained to deal with the intricacies of Medicaid. By providing people who were on the inside, knowledgeable about federal programs, willing to meet the families where they were, and willing to advocate, Medicaid enrollment and therefore medical and mental health services increased drastically. This is a model of service that counselors would be wise to learn from.

Method Implications   Just as it is needed with the other underrepresented cultural groups, research that truly reflects the lives, experiences, and needs of Native American people is needed. Following the ideals put forth by critical race theory and tribal critical race theory, the research should consist of the voices of the Native people and their stories to help guide theory and practice. Nixon, Kayo, Jones-Saumty, Philips, and Tivis (2007) agreed that nontraditional research methods are generally called for and suggest that to get a truer picture, research should be conducted in an authentic setting, such as on the reservation or in schools.

Data collection disparities have been noted by Arzubiaga, Artiles, King, and Harris-Murri (2008) that make accurate and consistent research on usage and effectiveness of treatment an impossibility. They pointed out that different agencies and institutions have different ways of keeping data that make comparisons inaccurate. To remedy this situation, they encouraged collaboration among individuals, agencies, and institutions. Arzubiaga et al. also cautioned that researchers must watch for bias in data collection because data collection is grounded in cultural assumptions, traditions, and values. In the Native American culture, silence and nonverbal communication are valued over verbosity, which may affect the way researchers record and interpret behavior. Another example is rating on-task behavior versus off-task behavior, which may look different in various cultures.

Implications for the Profession

Working with tribes is a significant way to learn about effective treatment and research methods. This doesn't mean that the tribes are merely consulted in treatment and research matters, but that they are "engaged as full and equal stakeholders at every stage" (Mindell et al., 2003, p. 215). To do any less is to continue the tradition of the dominant culture's superiority and oppression. Tribal representatives and leaders should take key roles in planning services and policies that will affect Native American clients. Once again, counselors and researchers should be aware that one tribe does not represent the whole Native American population.

In addition, the counseling profession as a whole has the obligation to recruit and support more counselors, researchers, and educators of color. Rogers and Molina (2006) have suggested that the presence of faculty of color at the university, mentorship programs, faculty–student collaboration on research, and an environment supportive of diversity would be encouraging recruitment tools for postsecondary institutions. The fact that to gain diversity one must have diversity, and to have diversity one must gain diversity, is not lost on us, so a supportive environment and mentoring may be the best start in the absence of already established diversity.

Implications for Future Research

A dearth of quality research is noted for Native American populations, especially Hawaiian Natives and American Pacific Islanders, who are often simply not considered when Native Americans are studied. In fact, it was not until 1974 that the Native American Programs Act was amended to include native Hawaiians. This smoothed the way for native Hawaiians to become eligible for some, but not all, federal assistance programs originally intended for American Indians.

This lack of research leaves the counseling and education professions at a loss and is a disservice to the diverse Native American tribes. Relevant and authentic research is needed to learn more about the issues facing the Native American population. Having more Native American researchers or "insiders" who assist the researchers and give them an "in" to the tribe would work toward this goal. Also, expanding our ideas of what legitimate research looks like to include narratives of the people and culture we are studying would further the cause. Finally, being aware of cultural bias in interpreting data would make our research more true to the culture we are studying.

Recommendations

It is apparent that without knowledge of a group's history and current treatment, a counselor cannot effectively advocate for that group and work against oppression; therefore, counselors should educate themselves about Native American history, policies instated by the U.S. government, culture, and traditions. In addition, the field should strive toward more effective research methods that consider Native Americans' lived experiences and accurate data collection. Finally, counselors should strive to truly work with tribal leaders and representatives as equal stakeholders who have the key to understanding and improving treatment for Native Americans.

AGAINST THE WIND: SOCIAL JUSTICE WITH WOMEN

Because I am a woman, I must make unusual efforts to succeed. If I fail, no one will say, "She doesn't have what it takes." They will say, "Women don't have what it takes."

—Clare Boothe Luce

People call me a feminist whenever I express sentiments that differentiate me from a doormat or a prostitute.

—Rebecca West

From the beginning of civilization, sexism has been the most pervasive *ism* of all. Ever since recorded history, there have been written and well-documented accounts of the abuse that women have suffered at the hands of men and patriarchal systems (e.g., familiar, social, political, and religious). Women have suffered the longest, most pervasive, and most violent and insidious forms of social injustices, surpassing even the discrimination and abuse experiences of people of color.

Perhaps even in ancient times—and at least in biblical times, from the time when Eve received eternal punishment for feeding Adam the proverbial fruit from the tree of life—globally women have been viewed as subservient and treated as lower- and second-class world citizens. As a result of Eve's misdeed (leading Adam to the trough), say the Christians, the race of females is, in essence, forever relegated to the back of the bus (as Rosa Parks and other Blacks were until the 1960s).

As a group, women are more educated, more politically involved, and have more rights, yet they continue to fight an upstream battle—against the wind. American women (especially women of color) have not fared much better than women have globally (even in developing nations). For example, African American women are one of the largest groups of victims of HIV/AIDS (Centers for Disease Control and Prevention, 2005), which is comparable to the incidence of HIV in women in some developing nations (e.g., Vietnam and Cambodia). As stated in Chapter 7, American women are barely one generation past an era in U.S. history when those committing violence against women (especially men) had carte blanche. Thus women, similarly to groups of color, have in the past, as they do today, occupied a minority status.

Also, similar to people of color, women are up in arms with systems that are intrinsically unjust. Entrenched systems have often justified, legitimized, and even legalized those injustices, while virtually ignoring the plight of women. These systems disrespect feminist paradigms and epistemologies, and the cultural values, traditions, and differences existing among women.

The Status of American Women

It's a male and female thing. Back home, male superiority is always in the news. Emotionally, I struggle with that from time to time. I am a woman minority.

—Mai Li

Unlike with groups of color, to oppress women and deny them their basic rights means to oppress and deny rights to half of humanity. Most importantly, when we oppress people, we lose important and valuable resources and the contributions those individuals can make to our society. Thus, for a society to oppress its women means that society loses half of its resources, potential, and power.

As an incentive for African American men to cease the sexism, Black feminists have appealed to Black men's own liberation. That is to say, Black men's consciousness should be raised so that they come to realize that men's freedom and survival are integrally, intimately, and eternally linked to the freedom of Black women. Likewise, men's and women's survival, regardless of cultural and ethnic backgrounds, are tied together.

Historically, countries flourish where women enjoy equity and equality. In contrast, nations that oppress and deny basic freedoms to their women are not as prosperous. Thus, the more progress women make, the more substantial progress their countries make. Even with that knowledge in mind, social justice (safety, equality, and equity) for women is still lacking even in developed nations. In fact, violence against women has not ended, even in developed nations such as the United Sates. In particular, violence and rape, grave manifestations of discrimination against women, are still omnipresent, especially in the home and in the workplace.

Education Equity for Girls and Women

In pre-K–12 and higher education, the achievement gap between females, particularly White females, and males has been closing, and in some instances it has been eliminated. In fact, in those earlier grades, females tend to outperform males. This gain does not hold true for females of color, especially those from economically poor backgrounds and those attending low-performing schools.

Nevertheless, notwithstanding the gains females have made in education, gender inequities have not been eliminated. As an example, blatant inequities continue in the underrepresentation of women in graduate and professional degree programs and in certain fields, mainly science, technology, engineering, and mathematics.

Gender equity in education for women can also be measured in their academic progress, their academic performance, the quality of the educational programs in which they are enrolled, their access to technology, and their level and type of participation in extracurricular activities. For example, in 1972, Title IX, a federal law prohibiting all forms of gender discrimination in federally funded education, including athletics, was passed to assure gender equity in high schools and colleges. It, in essence, mandates the right to equal educational opportunity for women and forbids sexual discrimination in areas of education such as admissions, sexual harassment, and pregnant students.

Inexcusably, nearly 4 decades after the passage of this law, sexual discrimination continues; females still do not have equal access to all aspects and areas of education. This includes gender equity in sports (high schools and colleges).

It also follows that inequity for women exists in the workplace, regardless of level of education, in terms of equal access to the same kind of educational opportunities and equal access to jobs and equitable pay. Although gender equity may differ for women of color from different ethnic groups, they tend to be lagging behind White women, White men, and men of color regardless of their level of education, chosen profession, and degree attained and the rigor and quality of schools they attended.

Health

Women, compared to men, seek medical care more frequently, go to the doctor more, and spend more money on medications. Yet there are major disparities and systemic barriers that limit the quality of women's health care such as access to various proven diagnostic procedures and therapies (Grady, Chaput, & Kristof, 2003; Nunez & Robertson, 2003; Weisman & Henderson, 2001). Thus, social inequities exist in women's health both globally and nationally at all levels of the developmental curve. Again, these disparities are multiplied for women of color, women from developing nations, and women who are poor to the point of it being, at the basic level, a human rights issue.

Similar to gender equity in education, realizing gender equity in health means eliminating health disparities between men and women. It means we need a Title IX–type law in health to flush out health inequities, prohibit all forms of gender discrimination in health care services and programs, and mandate that equity measures be put in place.

In terms of addressing gender disparities in health, it is important to realize how interwoven health social injustices are in the fabric of our society. As such, social injustices have to be unraveled and tackled in segments.

Sexism is not just a woman's issue, and women's health care is not just a woman's issue. Rather, women health's care is a public issue. Gender health disparities, like women's health care, is both complex and challenging and requires the combined efforts of the public, that is, researchers, practitioners from multiple health fields, providers, policy makers, and women's interest groups—a multidisciplinary approach (Correa-de-Araujo, 2004).

Women health care inequities range from reproductive health risks such as those related to fertility, lactation, and pregnancies to those that are developmental. Inequities also include those factors that indirectly affect women's health status such as encountering racism, sexism, and sexual harassment; less access to education, employment, and income than men; and less leisure time than men.

For women of color, health disparities are compounded in health-related matters such as access to information, incidence and prevalence of certain diseases, screening, diagnosis, early detection, life expectancy, and quality of treatment. For example, African American women die at a faster rate from breast cancer than do White women, even though White women contract the disease at a much higher rate. This means that, for women of color, health injustices often involve life or death.

Inequities also include health needs for women that may differ from those of men and women's needs taking a backseat to those of men. They include women's behavior such as placing the needs of their children and families before their own health, particularly when a lack of income and time is not a major factor. Last, women in the health field tend to work in jobs that pay less and have less influence in decision making, policy change, curriculum and training, research training, and what get researched. Thus, social justice strategies aimed at systemic change have to be carefully crafted to address each area of health disparity in isolation.

Mental Health

To begin this section on mental health, it is important to note that there are virtually no differences in major clinical psychiatric and mental health disorders between males and females. According to the National Institute of Mental Health (1995), there are multiple factors that impact women's mental health, like women's health at different junctures in their lives across the life span. Specifically, there are gender-specific risk factors (gender-based violence, social status and social position, women as caretakers, and poverty) that disproportionately and adversely affect women at various stages on the development curve.

Thus, mental illness and mental health, like gender and race (both a complex mixture of biological, behavioral, and psychosocial variables), are mainly social constructs and ones that are defined by each culture. Yet, of all the demographic variables, gender is a critical determinant and the single best predictor of mental health (and, conversely, mental illness) and risk for different types of mental disorders.

As previously stated, historically and globally, gender determines power, and with few exceptions, power has always been with men. Gender, in essence, determines the power differential that men and women have over financial, decision-making, and policy-making determinants of their mental health and lives that sequentially affect the diagnosis, treatment, research, and delivery of mental health services.

Ultimately, gender, gender roles, and the abuse that results from the imbalance and misuse of power expose women to environmental factors that place their mental health at risk, such as by causing depression. These also can lead to mental health disorders that may differ in clinical features, risk factors, and incidence from similar disorders in males and be more prevalent in females than in males, such as anxiety and depressive and eating disorders. These are disorders, conditions, and behaviors that transcend women's reproductive health, although the social impact of mental disorders falls disproportionately on women during the childbearing and childrearing years. Gender, along with ethnicity and race, also influences help-seeking behaviors and gender stereotyping.

Social Justice Initiatives for Women

Sustaining social justice initiatives for women's health begins with balancing the power. More realistically, at least in mental health, it means overhauling a traditional patriarchal system in productive ways that change how health care is delivered to women. It means flushing out the social injustices that virtually guarantee that women in general, poor women, and specifically women of color will not have access to high-quality care, are likely to receive inferior health care, and will die at faster rates. These mean that *everyone* has a major stake in keeping women healthy.

Thus, social justice solutions are as challenging and complex as health care for women; they require bringing to the table all the major stakeholders (men, researchers, providers, policy makers, special interest groups, nations, and feminists) with a multidisciplinary team of health care professionals. In the spirit of feminism, the coordinated effort should be one that is egalitarian, collaborative, empowering, and inclusive.

Ultimately and from a feminist perspective, achieving social justice in the mental health care of women means leveling the playing field where women of all races and socioeconomic backgrounds, all over the world, have equal access to quality schools and safe environments (home, workplaces, and residences). It means eliminating mental health risk factors by fighting to eliminate all forms of oppression (sexism, racism, ableism, heterosexism, ageism, and capitalism) that harm not only women but also men.

Implications

Theory Implications   Feminism and feminist approaches are naturally grounded in social justice. These theories have invaded every major field of study. There are established feminist theories; they just need to be respected, taught, and integrated into classroom teaching at all levels of education, especially in pre-K–12 education. So not having effective theories for women's issues is no longer an excuse; mental health professionals, practitioners, educators, and researchers need only avail themselves of them.

It is also necessary to know and understand how to apply non-White feminist theories such as Black feminism, womanism, multiracial feminism, and other feminist approaches from women of color to our curricula and teachings so that we can address issues that are unique to women of color and women from an identifiable ethnic group. There is a need for mental health professionals to have knowledge of even the more radical theories such as critical feminist theory and revolutionary Black feminist theory. In short, mental health professionals need to be armed with culture-specific feminist and womanist theories to view women and women's issues regardless of their cultural background.

Practice Implications   A social justice approach to mental health counseling for women with implications for mental health practitioners begins with the need to eliminate sexism in mental health. Mental health social justice requires mental health practitioners to use strategies that incorporate the history and discriminatory practices against women, especially the power differential of men and women. It also calls for feminist and culturally grounded techniques and strategies that factor in women's multiple identities.

In essence, women's social justice, like social justice for groups of color, calls for therapy that is egalitarian and simultaneously integrates social justice, systemic change, and possibly extremism into counseling work with women. From a practical perspective, social justice for women's mental health means that in counseling, the woman's identity is kept intact. *Social justice* implies that women in general and those from different cultural backgrounds are not revictimized in therapy due to mental health professionals' biases that are sexist, racist, or both, but rather they receive effective counseling and successful counseling outcomes that take into consideration not only their mental health issues and disorders, but also their gender, ethnicity, race, and other identities.

Social justice also implies that mental health professionals (both male and female) know how their gender affects females in counseling situations. This includes the gender biases of their female clients as well as their own biases.

Methods Implications   Although feminist research includes multiple research methods and is not confined to a single set of research methods or guidelines, there are multiple feminist methodologies and methods. Thus, from a social justice perspective, there is a broader scope of research conducted on women that should embrace and use methods and methodologies that take into consideration their gender and privilege, minimize any power differential, and avoid exploiting and victimizing women. There is a need to seek and use quantitative and qualitative techniques, and research theoretical orientations (e.g., performing ethnography and case histories) that explore the social reality of women's experiences and problems. This includes more nontraditional methods such as performance ethnography.

Implications for the Profession   In many ways, women's issues have made more headway and impact than those of people of color—or, at least, they are more visible and recognizable. When digging deeper, however, sexism is spreading. For example, women continue to be sexually harassed and sexually exploited in counseling and psychotherapy relationships with men. Clearly, gender equity and social justice are not achieved in mental health.

Implications for Future Research   Social justice initiatives in research for women call for more women researchers, in essence more insiders in all the aforementioned areas (education, health, and mental health). They require more nontraditional feminist and culture-specific paradigms and methodologies. There is a need for newer, more daring, radical, and revolutionary approaches that can eradicate the deep-seated, insidious, violent, and deadly behaviors against women (including calling for the elimination of racism, because racism, itself, is an act of violence).

There must be more women researchers who have the power to affect policy change and decision making in determining large-scale studies on women's issues. There must be more female researchers in those same positions. Likewise, male feminist researchers who are committed to conducting research on women's equity issues are crucial. Last, there needs to be an organized, multidisciplinary team approach of all disciplines coming together to conduct research, share findings, and make recommendations for liberating the other half of humanity.

Summary

Today, following decades of challenge, evolution, and growth, American women (women of color to a lesser extent than White women) have made huge, momentous strides in gaining their inalienable rights of life, liberty, and the pursuit of happiness, though the ideals of equality, equity, and social justice are not yet things of the past. Women have won major battles such as the right to vote, the right to choose, the right to an education, and even the right to work in an environment free of hostility and sexual harassment. We have not yet won the battle of social justice. We still have a very long way to go.

Women, like the lyrics of Seger's (1980) song, have been running against the wind. For women, social justice issues such as poverty, violence, trafficking, welfare, and pay equity remain ubiquitous. In too many instances and for far too long, women's struggle for equity and social justice has been an uphill battle that has not yet been won.

As old times have left and new times have come, despite the progress women have made, women remain oppressed along with societal mind-sets and tendencies to lionize and worship men while maligning and oppressing women. In many ways, second-wave feminists have taken this quest for social justice for women as far as we can. It is up to us to pass the baton on to younger women and men (X'ers and Millennials) and third-wave feminists (Baumgardner & Richards, 2000).

The words at the end of Seger's (1980) song characterize the current status of women, their strife, and their striving for social justice. The song ends with the following words:

> I'm still runnin' against the wind
> Well I'm older now and still runnin'
> Against the wind.

Conclusion

The term *social justice* was never spoken by any of the clients, yet it was an integral part of nearly every conversation and of every fiber of their being. Across the board, these clients of color had a strong personal and collective sense of purpose and spirituality that overshadowed any negativity associated with their personal experiences of social injustices and propelled them forward posthaste to change the conditions of their people and others (including their clients) who are oppressed.

Social injustices were unevenly distributed among these clients in terms of ethnicity and race, gender, and country of origin. For these clients of color, social justice was more painful and salient for female clients than male clients, for older clients than younger clients, and for those clients of color born and raised in the United States as opposed to those born and raised in other countries. Nevertheless, their passion for social justice, like their passion for the art of healing, shone through brightly. Despite the massive disparities and inequities existing in their professional disciplines and their communities, countries, and personal lives, they remain hopeful.

RETRIBUTIVE SOCIAL JUSTICE: THE ART OF FORGIVENESS

Although research on retributions, reparations, and forgiveness is relatively new in the field of mental health, it has been more entrenched in other fields such as theology, law, business, and philosophy. Changes occurring in those fields are centered, for example, on retributive justice for victims in the law field. In the business field, recently researchers have focused on forgiveness relating to workplace relationships, especially those that resulted in lawsuits and violence (Aquino, Grover, Goldman, & Folger, 2003). On the other side of the coin, philosophy and theology scholars are debating the ethical, moral, and virtuous nature of forgiveness (punishment, repentance, atonement, and unconditional love) and how it is viewed within different religious traditions.

In the mental health field, psychology researchers, in particular, have conducted descriptive empirical studies relating forgiveness benefits to health (Witvliet, Ludwig, & van der Laan, 2001) and mental health (Coyle & Enright, 1997). Yet, regardless of the field of study or the focus of the research, apologies, forgiveness, retribution, and restitution can be effective in the lives of those who have suffered massive and historical abuses. Thus, these acts can be social justice tools.

CONCLUSION

The discourse on the inequities, discrimination, and social injustice experiences of groups of color and women, discussed in Chapters 3 through 7 have given numerous accounts of social injustices against Blacks and African Americans, Native Americans, Asian Americans, Latinos, and women. Suggestions for social justice initiatives have been provided, and the need for a radical revolutionary change has been implied.

We know from research conversations in and among multiple disciplines that forgiveness is a powerful and benevolent tool. It can be valuable, moral, ethical, and virtuous, and it has the ability to avert wars, divorces, family breakups, lawsuits, and even executions. From a mental health and health perspective, forgiveness can reduce health risks, foster resilience, and have the power of healing. From the research, we know that the definition, topic, cost, application, and benefits of forgiveness are controversial and challenging.

In spite of the challenge and controversy surrounding forgiveness, from a social justice perspective, for people of color, forgiveness should be a conscious cultural decision to let go of past misdeeds and abuses as an act of healing that benefits them as victims as opposed to a system that continues the abuse. Thus, one possible formula for reducing the pain of social injustice for women and people of color is for the offenders (and, for us, the mental health field) to offer public acknowledgments of the wrongdoing (as an expression of remorse), apologize, and make reparations.

Even if apologies are not forthcoming, people of color must forgive: They must let go of the bitterness, vengeance, and hatred, but not forget or easily trust, and yet hold the mental health field and society accountable. Thus, forgiveness is not a mere turning of the other cheek, nor is there a need for an eye for an eye. Rather, it is a selfless, life-infusing gift of mercy, kindness, and goodness given by women and people of color to themselves as a balm for their own pain and suffering.

10

Engendering Hope
Reconciliation and the Power of Forgiveness

*T*his chapter concludes with the implications for practice, theory, and methods for the profession and future research as well as comprehensive recommendations for the mental health and higher education programs that focus on training mental health practitioners, scholars, and educators to meet the mental health needs of people of color. A special emphasis is placed on these recommendations as they relate to each chapter theme. Additionally, this chapter will discuss areas of needed research as they relate not only to these ethnic and racial groups but also to gender and the massive intragroup differences. The chapter also includes a discussion of the impact of the racism, sexism, and bias of academic and training programs that exist within higher education institutions and their relative impact on the admittance of people of color into mental health services and their experiences.

The chapter begins with a summary of the significant results and draws conclusions about people of color's experiences with mental health services through these participants' personal and professional perceptions and experiences with counseling psychotherapeutic services (as both clients and counselors). This chapter offers ways that my experiences and the experiences of Joshua and Shawn, Wai and Mai Li, Woodro and Lioma, and Angelica and Alexias in their roles as clients and counselors of color can inform methods, theory, practice, research, multicultural counseling, the counseling profession, and future research. In Chapter 9, my coauthors and I offered implications for and recommendations on social justice issues and explain ways that this research can inform researchers, theorists, and practitioners in the areas of advocacy and social justice. Finally, this chapter ends with a call to the mental health profession to consider issuing an apology for the mistreatment and injustice that women and people of color have experienced in mental health.

175

The heartfelt stories of these counselors of color suggest that in spite of the Eurocentrism and ethnocentrism prevalent in the mental health field and the somewhat grim record of the success of people of color with mental health services, the future for clients of color in counseling is hopeful. The stories across these four case studies suggest that counselors in cross-cultural or multicultural counseling encounters must be equipped with culturally specific knowledge of the client's culture. This is consistent with multicultural counseling and therapy (MCT) theory (Sue, Ivey, & Pedersen, 1996) and the multicultural counseling competencies that Sue, Arredondo, and McDavis set forth in 1992.

Second, counselors must be willing to invest more time in the relationship and rapport-building phase. All of these participants, through their experiences as clients and counselors, have found creative ways to have successful cross-cultural or multicultural counseling experiences for themselves and their culturally diverse clients.

BACKGROUND

As indicated throughout this book, research on the lack of success of people of color with counseling services can be caused by racism, discrimination, access to and affordability of mental health services, language acquisition, ethnicity and racial differences, acculturation, racial identity, and Eurocentric epistemologies and axiology. It is also linked to counselor and client variables such as ethnic and racial biases, level of multicultural competency, diversity and sensitivity training, level of acculturation, and level of racial identity.

As you have read, the mental health field is struggling internally, and desperately, to improve its services to people of color. For example, mental health scholars and practitioners are seeking out-of-the-box ways to transform counseling, such as exploring indigenous methods of healing. Other transformative methods include adopting and adapting multicultural competencies, training, and ethical guidelines to meet the mental health service needs of people of color.

Previous studies have looked at race preference as a predictive variable in cross-cultural counseling studies (Bryson & Cody, 1973; Burrell & Rayder, 1971; Cimbolic, 1972; Constantine, 2001; Jackson & Kirschner, 1973; Stranges & Riccio, 1970; Wade & Bernstein, 1991). It is important here to define *race*, not as biologically determined, but rather as psychologically and socially constructed and—for people of color—legally constructed. Race is an institutionalized phenomenon in bed with an insidious racism, both of which are deeply ingrained in the institutional fabric and structure of American society and the mental health field. Pedersen (1990) wrote that culture is dynamic and complex, and to disregard these two essential components results in bias, racism, and social injustice.

Last, culture is impacted by not only race and ethnicity but also other factors (psychological, economic, and socioeconomic). Contrary to popular opinion, within-group differences exceed solely intergroup differences among all ethnic and racial groups. Although the lines are blurred between the influences of nurture versus nature, greater genetic, social, and cultural variation exists within the populations typically labeled *Hispanic* and *White* than between these populations.

In other words, the color of our faces, the texture of our hair, and the shapes of our noses are not our souls.

RACIAL IDENTITY, ACCULTURATION, AND MULTICULTURAL PERSPECTIVES AND COMPETENCIES

Culture is complex and has been influenced by sociopolitical, historical, socioeconomic, psychosocial, and psychological factors, so race cannot be the only factor to consider when working with culturally different clients. This complexity is, in part, a result of the enormous differences found within each group of color (Herring, 1996). As an example, Native Indians are an extremely diverse group encompassing approximately 530 distinct tribes. Another example would be the heterogeneity found within the Asian population, whose people's country of origin may be any one of many countries, including 14 Arab nations, each with its own distinct culture, traditions, languages, religions, history, and political structures.

METHODOLOGY

The purposes of the earlier study were (a) to gain insight into the experience and perceptions that clients of color have of counseling services; (b) to uncover which factors or variables may contribute to the decisions of clients of color to utilize or not utilize, continue or not continue, or report negative outcomes in counseling services; (c) to identify factors that may contribute to successful and unsuccessful counseling outcomes; and thus (d) to bring more clarity to the existing multicultural, theoretical, and empirical research in regard to people of color.

This study was conducted in five parts: (a) a standardized open-ended interview; (b) an informal conversational interview; (c) administration of the Racial Identity Attitude Scales; (d) a debriefing, including interpretation of the instruments; and (e) interactive follow-up interviews.

INSTRUMENTS

These individuals, based on their racial identification, self-administered one or more of three racial identity instruments: the White Racial Identity Attitude Scale (WRIAS), Black Racial Identity Attitude Scale (BRIAS), and People of Color Racial Identity Attitude Scale (POCRIAS). These instruments were used to identify each participant's stage of racial identity development and to explain some of the intragroup differences found within each ethnic and racial group.

Site and Participant Selection

The site selection criteria for this study referred specifically to the participant and not his or her institution of higher education. Nevertheless, the result was that the final participants were acquiring degrees from counseling programs in land grant and research institutions in Arkansas, Oklahoma, Tennessee, and Texas.

The sample group consisted of eight licensed counselors enrolled in doctoral programs. There were two (a male and a female) from each of the four major groups of color: African American, Asian, Hispanic/Latino, and Native American. All of them resided in the South-Central region of the United States.

Data Collection

This was initially based on a qualitative study using a phenomenological theoretical orientation. It focused on the participants' roles as both client and counselor. It encompassed investigating their relationships, emotions, and cultures (Patton, 1990). Data were collected through videotaping, audiotaping, self-administered instruments, and document collections such as journals and clientele data. There were also electronic, telephone, and, when possible, in-person follow-up and interactive interviews.

Data Analysis

The research questions were addressed by qualitatively analyzing the data collected that described the perceptions that clients of colors had of (a) the utilization or nonutilization of counseling services, (b) negative or positive counseling outcomes, and (c) the decision to continue or to drop out of counseling.

The data were analyzed through the grounded theory approach in order to uncover relevant categories and the relationships among them. I examined the data using models such as the paradigm model (Strauss & Corbin, 1990). Initial coding yielded 19 pages of open codes (two to four pages per participant), which were further reduced to 47 axial codes using the paradigm model. Finally, selective coding yielded 3 categories and 10 subcategories.

DISCUSSION OF SIGNIFICANT RESULTS

Bias

The individuals' preferences for either same-sex or opposite-sex counselors played a key role in the success of their counseling outcomes. The individuals believed that the disproportionate prevalence of poverty in their communities affected their ethnic or racial group's utilization of and continuation in counseling. Last, the individuals' day-to-day life exposure to racial and ethnic biases often trickled down into counseling relationships, tainting their experiences with and perceptions of counseling, counselors, and therapeutic services. This continual and (in some cases lifelong) exposure to racial and ethnic bias created in these clients of color a paranoia and mistrust of Whites and sometimes other culturally different therapists.

Bias is defined as a predisposition, preconception, predilection, partiality, proclivity, bent, prejudice, strong inclination of the mind, or preconceived opinion about something or someone (*Random House Unabridged Dictionary*, 1993, p. 202). Although researchers agree that bias or prejudice should be kept out of the counseling process, others have addressed how client bias may impact initial choice of a counselor, as well as perceptions about the effectiveness of the counseling process.

These aforementioned individuals articulated a gender bias in terms of a personal preference for selecting a counselor. The females leaned toward a preference for a female counselor, whereas the males' gender preference was related more to their ethnic and cultural background. The Asian and Hispanic men preferred male counselors, and the African American and American Indian men sought out female counselors.

A second form of bias that these individuals reported was related to their belief that a disproportionate prevalence of poverty existed within their communities. Poverty becomes a bias in terms of the utilization of counseling services, particularly if counselors are trained that clients usually "continue" or "benefit from" therapy when they see a counselor for a fee. Even with managed care, counseling services can cost anywhere from $20 to $150 an hour, money that people in poverty cannot afford and would not see the benefit of paying for counseling considering that safety and security needs must be met before higher order needs like self-actualization.

Staples (1994) reported that women of color, and particularly African American women, are the majority of individuals representing the American lower socioeconomic status (SES) group. However, cultural differences do exist with regard to numbers of individuals within the ranks of poverty.

Conclusions About Bias   I conclude that the perceptions of clients of color regarding gender, socioeconomic, racial, and ethnic biases, if understood and validated in counseling, can be vehicles to facilitate growth in counseling. The stories of these individuals in this book add some clarity to the multifaceted interaction of gender, class, race, ethnicity, and culture as they relate to clients of color and their perceptions of counseling services.

Credibility

To the individuals in this book, credibility is established by the value of the therapeutic relationship, the competence and skill level of the counselor, internal resources and a willingness to self-examine, and the counselor's display of self-disclosure, genuineness, and being nonjudgmental. I also observed that in their roles as both counselors and clients, the themes of internal strengths, a sense of balance, and self-disclosure were salient ingredients for achieving counselor credibility.

Credibility refers to the client seeing the therapist as an effective and trustworthy helper. Credibility, in terms of empowerment, bonding, and essential qualities, is one of the key components in these individuals' positive experiences of counseling services. According to Sue and Zane (1987), the two types of credibility, achieved and ascribed, are both important factors in achieving credibility among clients of color. *Ascribed credibility* refers to a position that is assigned by others and controlled by factors such as age, expertise, and gender, whereas *achieved credibility* pertains more to counseling and therapeutic skills.

Sue and Zane (1987) further conjectured that underutilization is more a result of lack of ascribed credibility, whereas premature termination is more related to a lack of achieved credibility. Examples of both ascribed and achieved credibility are evident in the stories in this study. For the Asian, Hispanic/Latino, and American Indian individuals, and to a lesser extent the African American ones, ascribed credibility concerning age, experience, and gender was very important. For example, Mai Li, the female Asian participant, commented that she highly respected her therapist because of her extensive experience and age. She added that she was not comfortable with young people. An example of achieved credibility can be found in the following remarks by Lioma, the female American Indian participant:

> I can actually remember sighing, thinking, "This is going to be OK." It was a pretty positive situation. For the counselors and the RN doing the group, I don't think that the skill level was there. They were really in over their heads.

Due to past and continued exposure to racist and discriminatory experiences, African Americans have historically been mistrustful of Whites. Therefore, mistrust of White counselors was a critical factor for the African American individuals. Joshua shared his perception of a racist incident:

> When I came here to this university, which was another great cultural shock because I didn't consider myself a dumb person at all, I took freshman English, and I took it from a White Anglo-Saxon Protestant. We were reading a poem that alluded to the soliloquy in *Macbeth*, where it said, "*Out, out* brief candle." We had gone through all of this in high school. And this poem alluded to this soliloquy. In fact, I think it was called "out, out" or something of that nature.
>
> So the professor said, "Don't do any research on this; I want you to tell me what you think this poem means." So, I knew the soliloquy by heart; it was one of my favorites. Man, I just knew that I got an *A* on this. I wrote it down line for line. I knew what this poem alluded to and everything. I turned my paper in and got it back, and got an *F*. I mean, just a flat-out *F*. I just couldn't believe it. I said, "You mean nothing that I said was correct?" I just couldn't believe it.
>
> So, I confronted the professor. He said, "Well, I told you not to do research on this, and the only way you could know this is that you went and did research." I said, "Look, we took this in high school, we had *Macbeth* in the eleventh grade." He said, "You wouldn't have known the soliloquy if you wouldn't have done research." I said, "I know this by heart." And he asked me to say it, and I quoted it word for word and he changed it from an *F* to a *C*.

Counselor Credibility   Even though all of the individuals in this book clearly wanted their racial and ethnic group affiliation to be recognized, counselor credibility was most important. For the Asian and Hispanic individuals, age, experience, and skill were most important. The American Indian individuals felt that having a counselor with a high skill level and having an older counselor were also preferable, but feeling trust, safety, connectedness, and understanding with the counselor was most essential for a successful outcome in counseling. Lioma commented, "It wasn't a decision-making process. It was just a 'No.' I felt that I was in an unsafe environment and I had a total lack of trust." Woodro commented,

It is the acceptance, the immediate, if you want to call it a connectedness to the counselor or if you want to call it trust. Those kinds of things. If you don't feel that, you can always say, "It's a piss-poor experience, I don't want to do it again."

All of the participants felt that the counselor's self-disclosure, knowledge, and involvement in their culture could expedite this rapport-building phase. In conclusion, when credibility was achieved, these individuals could open up, take a chance, and learn to trust. Parham and Helms (1981) found that when race was examined in conjunction with other variables, though it was important, it did not emerge as the most salient factor in African American students' selection of a counselor. Other factors such as credibility, experience, and stage of racial identity were more important factors in their preference for a counselor.

Culture

Dialoguing   The *dialoguing* category was created from axial codes and emerged from the data as communication that involved patience, real language and conversation, and a genuine and active interest in knowing about the cultural background of clients of color. It took on attributes such as (a) open or good communication, (b) being collaborative with the client, (c) a willingness to talk about cultural differences, (d) speaking their language, (e) a willingness to listen and ask questions, (f) sharing in clients' experiences and fantasies, (g) matching the language and metaphors to those of the client, and (h) communicating at the level of the client and empowering the client with words.

For example, the Asian clients discussed dialoguing as the counselor being patient, taking time to develop trust and create a safe environment for the client. The African American individuals were able to connect with African American clients who spoke and understood their language. Joshua said, "When the client can communicate with the counselor, the experience is very successful. In order for me to identify and communicate with them, I must talk their talk, speak their language."

The persons in this book believed that culture was complex and played an integral role in the success of clients of color in counseling. *Culture* was defined in Chapter 1 as the "totality of manners, customs, and values of a given society, inclusive of its socioeconomic system, political structures, science, religion, education, art, and entertainment" (Wolma, 1989, p. 80) and

as patterns of behaviors that are acquired and transmitted by symbols over time, which become generally shared within a group and are communicated to new members of the group in order to serve as a cognitive guide for future actions. (Kluckholn & Kroeberg, 1952, p. 335)

These counselors believed that it was paramount for counselors to have knowledge of and sensitivity to the client's culture. Equally important was that counselors recognize the massive intragroup differences existing within each ethnic and racial group.

These individuals in their counselor identities also advocated a collaborative approach, which includes tapping indigenous support systems existing within their communities and encouraging increased minority representation in the field of counseling and psychotherapy. A shortage of counselors of color is still a problem in the new millennium, and unfortunately, counseling is still viewed by people of color as a White or Eurocentric endeavor, which operates from a White middle-class value and economic system.

Last, Wai, the Chinese participant stated that counselors are scarce, almost non-existent in China. Therefore, for them as counselors, the critical need is to get more trained, professional counselors. I also observed that these participants used dialoguing with the client as an opportunity to develop trust, achieve credibility, and create a safe environment.

Conclusions About Culture Counselors with intimate knowledge of their clients' cultures comprise one of the cornerstones of success in counseling clients of color. Having knowledge of the clients' cultural background when working with culturally diverse clients is one of the most important components outlined in Sue et al.'s (1996) theory of MCT. However, for the participants in this study, intimate knowledge extends far beyond a counselor's rudimentary knowledge to a more intimate knowledge of their culture. This entails counselors immersing themselves in the minority client's culture, sampling their art, food, music, religion, and so forth. It also involves some awareness of and collaboration with the indigenous support systems in the clients' ethnic and racial community. This more familiar, firsthand knowledge and awareness of, and involvement in, the culturally different client's world provide a strong starting place for counselors and their clients of color to dialogue.

FOCUS ON SUCCESS

The participants all appeared hopeful about the future of clients of color in counseling. Several implications related to the phenomenon emerged out of analysis of the data that appeared to be significant for working with people of color. First, though these participants reported several unsuccessful counseling encounters, unlike many clients of color, they remained steadfast and discovered ways to be empowered by the counseling relationships that were successful.

White Counselors' Success

The participants in this study all reported successful counseling relationships with White counselors. These White counselors' success can be explained in terms of the aforementioned themes of bias, credibility, and culture that emerged from the data. For example, these White counselors were people whom these participants as clients believe were respectful of their cultural background and demonstrated a willingness and skills to help culturally different clients make decisions within their own cultural framework. For example, Alexias, the Hispanic male participant, stated that his White male therapist would ask about his childhood background and use that as a starting point for him to reflect on how his life was and how he wanted his life to be.

In addition, these White counselors did not appear biased toward them because of their minority status. Lioma felt that her male therapists understood her, and she applauded them for being nonjudgmental.

Though some of the participants had a gender preference, there were essential qualities they felt made the counseling relationship successful. All of the participants described their White therapists as older, more experienced, having a high skill level, and being sensitive and safe.

Conclusions About White Counselors' Success   I conclude that the role of culture as it relates to ethnicity and race among clients of color remains very complex. However, for these clients of color, having an experienced, skilled counselor, regardless of race, who is respectful, sensitive, and responsive to their cultural background, was most important.

Timing

Another significant finding critical to the success of clients of color in counseling involves the element of timing. The individuals of all four ethnic and racial groups saw themselves as bilingual, bicultural individuals. Language played an important part in these counselors-as-clients' experiences in counseling encounters. The bilingual (Latina and Asian) participants had to first process either affectively or cognitively in their mother tongue before they could express their feelings or thoughts in English. The U.S. bicultural (African American and American Indian) counselors as clients, who spoke English yet are linguistically different, had to make similar semantic, psycholinguistic translations. For instance, Lioma, the female American Indian participant, said she had to be cautious and think carefully when speaking so that her words would not be misinterpreted.

Similarly, Woodro, the male American Indian participant, said,

> The English language has so many words and semantics that have such an impact on how people are perceived. Trying to choose the right thing to say and maybe not having the words to say them. A lot of times they mistake us for being reticent, or maybe shy, or maybe noncommunicative.

In reference to the African American language and understanding traditional African American people, Joshua, the male African American participant, said, "It really is a second language. You must be able to know where the people are coming from and be able to deal with them where they are."

In addition, in a cross-cultural situation, each of these individuals in their multiple roles as student, counselor, and client did not want to be misunderstood, and therefore felt that they had to choose their words carefully. Also, they expressed the idea that when they were in a situation with someone who did not know their culture, it took more time for them to trust and feel safe.

Conclusions About Timing   Clients of color require more time for many reasons. First, because of historical racial issues (i.e., the relocation experience of American Indians and the forced immigration and slavery experience of African Americans) and cultural differences, clients of color need more time to develop trust and feel safe. Also, for those individuals as clients whose native languages were not English, they felt that they needed extra time to process their thoughts and feelings in their own language first and then translate it to English. Also, based on the cultural, semantic, or dialectal differences of American Indians and African Americans, these counselors as clients also require additional time to process and translate their thoughts and feelings into mainstream English.

Individualistic Versus Collectivistic

There is an apparent paradox in that the participants viewed themselves as unique individuals and also human like everyone else. Research has identified a complex group of variables that differentially characterize individualism and collectivism between and within cultures. Lee and Kelly (1996) defined *individualism* as "characterized by a primary focus on individual goals with a strong orientation toward individual autonomy and independence from within groups" and *collectivism* as "characterized by a primary focus on group goals with a strong orientation toward interpersonal cooperation and in-group interdependence" (p. 254).

Again, the individuals throughout this study strongly identified themselves as unique individuals (both the same as and different from members of other ethnic and racial groups) and human beings just like everyone else. This seeming contradiction may come from a highly individualistic society, which, though sometimes beneficial, has historically used individual differences as tools to discriminate against and judge people. However, other cultures, such as those of Native Americans and Asians, are more collectivistic. American Indians not only are collectivistic but also embrace and celebrate differences. As Woodro, the male American Indian participant, explained, "That's probably what challenges our people because they don't understand cultural diversity. They see being alien—differences are seen as being good." Zhang (1994), a school counselor from the People's Republic of China, after his eighth week at a U.S. university remarked,

> In contemporary China, where submergence of self for the good of the family, community, and country is still valued, and individualism condemned, our beginning counseling practice could fail should we adopt American counseling theories and skills without considerable alteration. (p. 80)

It may not be as important for counselors to categorize clients of color as individualistic or collectivistic, but more fruitful for counselors to be mindful of the interplay of individualism and collectivism in clients of color. Alexias, the male Hispanic participant, concluded, "I guess we are all unique and we are all different," and Pedersen (1997) stated,

An accurate cultural-centered perspective requires us to be "cross-eyed" with one eye always clearly focused on differences and the other eye focused clearly on similarities. In this way, we honor the important cultural differences that give individuals and groups their identity while at the same time celebrating the common ground we share. (p. 28)

Conclusions About Individualism and Collectivism   For these counselors as clients, the foci on the collective whole and self-in-relation are very important. The theme of individualistic versus collectivistic, which for them is emotionally charged, has a sociohistorical political flavor to it. For the U.S.-born individuals in this book, it is well grounded in their oppressive experiences in a country that has a history of intolerance of differences. This means that most people of color have had to develop or redevelop a sense of ethnic and racial pride, and at the same time they have had to fight to be treated as human just like everyone else.

When counseling people of color, counselors need to be sensitive and responsive to the idea that clients of color may come from cultures that have a national, tribal, or collectivistic focus, instead of an individualistic focus. When counseling clients of color, it is important to be aware that individualistic and collectivistic viewpoints quite often coexist.

TAKING COUNSELING TO THE NATIVES

In addition to utilizing natural support systems, counselors may need to be creative or tailor specific techniques to entice traditional, economically marginal clients of color to utilize counseling services. One of the reasons for the underutilization of counseling by some groups of color is because counseling is nonexistent in many non-Western, non-European cultures.

For many other cultures or subculture groups, counseling is viewed as taboo and stigmatized as something you do if you are crazy. Therefore, the participants in this study believe that in many instances, counseling has to be presented in a different format than the office or clinic setting. There is a need to take counseling to the trenches, to the grassroots. As Mai Li, the female Malaysian Chinese participant, said, "To provide that coffee-like kind of counseling." That is, friendship-based counseling or informal kinds of counseling in the form of social activities.

The mental health field will need to change the way counseling is done in order to make progress with clients of color. To reach the more traditional, economically marginalized clients, counselors may have to leave their plush offices and go to where these clients are. They will also have to find safe ways or nonthreatening approaches that are consistent with the cultural values and differences of people of color.

IMPLICATIONS

Consistent with Sue et al.'s (1992) cultural competencies, and Sue et al.'s (1996) MCT theory, the findings from this study suggest that those counselors who are (a) armed with awareness and knowledge of, and skill in working with, clients' cultures; (b) capable of achieving credibility; and (c) aware of their clients' and their own biases will have a better chance at attaining successful outcomes with clients of color. Qualitative, specifically phenomenological, studies that allow for the self-described perceptions and experiences of clients of color with counseling services can add to the current multicultural counseling and psychotherapy literature.

Qualitative studies can also shed light on people of color using, continuing, and having positive outcomes in counseling. And last, these studies can provide interventions, strategies, and techniques for working effectively with people of color.

Theory Implications

The nature of social justice implies a more radical, revolutionary, and cultural theoretical framework. Thus, for African American clients, there is a need to apply more race-based and race-sensitive theories such as critical race theory (Brown, 2008).

Practice Implications

This study offers implications and recommendations for practitioners through the examination of factors affecting clients of color in their underutilization, premature termination, and negative outcomes of counseling services. The voices of the counselors of color in this study shed light on the experiences and perceptions of clients of color regarding counseling services in three areas: bias, credibility, and culture. It also identifies factors that contribute to the success or lack of success of clients of color in counseling services. Last, it brings clarity to existing social justice multicultural research on the utilization of counseling services by these clients.

The findings from this study imply that despite the lack of success of clients of color with counseling services, one must take new and more culture-specific avenues in order to engage more clients of color and to ensure them better success with counseling services. The findings of this study imply that counselors need to be sensitive to the individualistic-collectivistic theme that coexists in the lives of clients of color. Through dialoguing, counselors may be able to better understand these clients' worldviews and empower them to make decisions that are consistent with these worldviews.

The findings further imply that counselors who counsel clients of color must first do some work on having an awareness and understanding of their own values, stereotypes, biases, and beliefs about culturally diverse groups. They need to establish credibility in ways that may at times violate the traditional training. For example, these participants indicated a definite need for counselor self-disclosure, and more time in order to feel safe, build trust, and translate (switch) to and from their first languages.

Methods Implications

To investigate the phenomenon of clients of color using counseling services and to understand the structure and essence of the experiences of groups of color with counseling services in a comprehensive and personal way, I chose phenomenology.

This approach covered the participants' feelings and emotions, relationships, programs, organizations, and cultures, and combinations of these structures. All of these structures are familiar to counselors and consistent with how we do counseling.

Further, phenomenology was an appropriate tool for uncovering the unique and shared experiences of these clients of color. According to Patton (1990, 2002), the essence of the client's experiences is the core meaning mutually understood through a universal shared phenomenon commonly experienced.

In order to obtain the fullest context and depth of the perceptions of the participants in this study, I used video and audio taping. Both qualitative inquiry and quantitative measures were used. In addition, I conducted interviews, made observations of the videotaped interviews, administered instruments, and collected documents. In other words, I used triangulation methods to increase the range, credibility, and trustworthiness of my study.

The voices and experiences of the participants suggested that researchers may need to employ more nontraditional approaches to qualitative research (e.g., narrative therapy), nontraditional data-gathering techniques (e.g., friendship cells), and research tools when investigating the experiences of traditional people of color. Mai Li labeled this "coffee-like kind of counseling," which means that, to be effective, techniques for gathering data in some cultures need to be an indigenous grassroots effort that is culturally grounded in the population being studied.

Implications for the Profession

The findings of this study have far-reaching implications for the profession. First, counseling is a White, middle-class phenomenon. The profession must decide if it really wants to or can afford to include the massive numbers of traditional, economically marginalized people who are not utilizing counseling. On the one hand, counseling is expensive, and this is a reason why a lot of clients of color shun and prematurely discontinue counseling services.

On the other hand, a disproportionate number of people of color are living in poverty. Due to the large numbers of poor people who are affected by devastating social ills, such as violence, HIV/AIDS, drugs and alcohol, teen pregnancy, and so forth, the profession cannot afford to exclude these groups.

Through their voices, these counselors as clients of color have shed light on what affects underutilization, premature termination, and negative outcomes of counseling services for racially marginalized people. For example, Joshua, Shawn, Wai, Mai Li, Yuchen, Woodro, Lioma, Angelica, and Alexias have shared their perceptions and experiences, as both clients and counselors, of the techniques, approaches, and strategies that could be used to fill that void and yield better success with clients of color. As a result, these findings have both augmented and substantiated the existing research on the utilization of counseling services by people of color.

Implications for Future Research

First, to me *diversity* means that everyone has a voice at the table. For the most part, White people's voices are not equally represented in the multicultural conversation. Clearly, there needs to be more research conducted on the massive differences that exist among White and European populations and the discrimination, inequities, disparities, social injustices, and historical abuse against certain subcultures such as Jews, Italians, Irish, poor people, and those who live in rural areas. We need to hear about their perceptions and experiences of hurt and abuse as well as their successes and triumphs with mental health services.

Next, the dismal record of people of color in counseling indicates a need for more knowledge and direction on how to meet the needs of these groups in counseling. Language and conversation, or dialoguing, has a proven track record in counseling as effective tools for counselors to use to access the inner world of the client. Unanimously, the participants said, "If you don't know or understand my culture, let's talk."

Being open to learning about the client's culture, asking and really listening, and getting involved in the community are ways for counselors and the counseling profession to really understand people of color. Qualitative research is a great tool for doing this. It is a means of investigating not only the client's culture but also his or her feelings, relationships, and emotions (Patton, 1990). Qualitative research provides language, conversation, and the real listening involved in learning about different cultures.

RECOMMENDATIONS

The researcher is the instrument in qualitative research. Researchers are members of their own cultures and therefore have a tendency to interpret data from their own cultural, narrowly focused worldview. Accordingly, researchers conducting work on culturally different individual groups should use multiple data methods. They should do several member checks and peer debriefings. The peer debriefings, when possible, should include others from the cultural background under investigation.

From entry to exit, every precaution should be made to understand and respect the cultural values of the participants. Researchers with a Western, European worldview should take steps not to impose, interpret, or make assumptions about groups of color based on their epistemologies and axiology. In this study, I had several follow-up and interactive interviews with the participants. I had peer debriefings with people who share ethnic and racial group affiliations with those of my participants. I made an effort to understand my own epistemological racism. I made every effort to analyze my data incorporating the epistemologies and axiology of my participants' cultural backgrounds.

In addition, I think socioeconomic status in counseling should be closely examined. Because counseling is a middle-class phenomenon, its lack of success with other White subgroups, like rural, poor, and White ethnic groups, needs to be documented and addressed in the counseling literature. The implications of socioeconomics and capitalism must also be broadened to include a global perspective. This is especially true when taking a closer look at the economics and the role that capitalism plays in developed as opposed to developing nations.

Last, from a feminist and social justice perspective, we must not forget the violence against women here in the United States and all over the world.

CONCLUSIONS

In this final chapter, I have attempted to summarize the telling of the cultural stories from these eight magnificent individuals. The implications for theory, practice, and continued qualitative research are by no means exhaustive; there are so many more. Although these counselors and I have made recommendations for multicultural counseling and the field of counseling and psychotherapy, these recommendations are not conclusive, final, or irrefutable, but rather come out of our professional and personal experiences of seeking mental health care.

These cultural stories represent the impressions and voices of counselors as clients and mental health professionals, who in most cases have had to struggle with the misfit of counseling to their cultural backgrounds. They shared how their personal and professional journeys forced them beyond racist and biased axiology and epistemologies; recounted their personal and professional experiences of discrimination, racism, and prejudice; and discussed their exposure to counselors with zero to little awareness, knowledge, or skills necessary to work with people from their ethnic, racial, and cultural backgrounds. They also shared their stories of how they have learned to tailor or find creative ways to make counseling work for them, in spite of training or exposure to theories and therapies that often did not work for clients from their ethnic and racial backgrounds.

Their cultural stories show their experiences of feeling disempowered, devalued, and invalidated as persons of color in and out of counseling. Yet their stories also tell how they have managed to maintain a profound faith in the art of helping, an unrelenting belief in the goodness of humankind, and a unified spiritual human connection to others who are culturally different from them. These counselors' stories show a strong conviction in, respect for, and celebration of our human differences, whether they be racial, ethnic, national, cultural, or tribal. Remarkably, 12 years later, they all still believe in counseling and the art of healing.

This is a story of how they have kept hope alive and managed to propel themselves beyond negative experiences and realities to self-growth, self-awareness, self-empowerment, and the internalization stage of racial identity development, with a silent commitment and fight to transform the counseling profession to meet the needs of not only people of color but also all people. They have been dignified warriors, loyal and true to the counseling profession but, most importantly, true to their convictions, their truths, their people, and themselves as people of color.

This book has allowed me the opportunity to participate in the richness of four different cultures, including my African American culture from two different perspectives. I have for more than 35 years considered myself a multicultural child of the world. Yet this book, via the sharing of Joshua and Shawn, Wai and Mai Li, Woodro and Lioma, and Angelica and Alexias over the last 12 years, and Yuchen more recently, has propelled me farther on my journey and taken me to heights and depths I never would have thought possible.

These healers, as Wai stated, are counselors who have "hearts with love and care." In his follow-up interview, he said that what is needed in the mental health field is to have mental health professionals do three things: to love, to appreciate others, and to humble ourselves. These folks have allowed me on this pilgrim's journey, as Mai Li so eloquently put it, "to walk with [them] for the short stretch." I will forever hold it sacred.

THE POWER OF FORGIVENESS

In essence, from a social justice counseling perspective, the mental health field has failed to take the lead in offering an apology (and possibly reparations) to the Native Americans, African Americans, Hispanics and Latinos, and Asian groups such as the Japanese, the Chinese, and any other group for the historical and systematic abuse they have suffered over the last 300 years, especially for its role in perpetuating this abuse.

For example, apologies should be offered for the atrocities and abuse of African Americans, Japanese Americans, Native Americans, and other groups of color such as slavery, concentration camps, the forced removal of American Indians, and the raping of cultures, dignities, and humanity that has been launched against women and people of color. And an apology is needed from the mental health profession for the revictimization of women and clients of color that has occurred in the mental health field by its professionals—those who are called to be healers of wounded souls.

Mental health professionals should know better. We know all about trauma, the deep emotional scars of sustained abuse. We know firsthand the devastating and long-term and secondary effects of both natural disasters such as hurricanes, tornados, and earthquakes and manmade ones such as wars, terror attacks, and holocausts—and the deep wounds left in the souls of people and countries as a result. We know all about the long-term effects of imprisonment and that incarceration of people doesn't rehabilitate them; rather, in too many cases, it creates people who are more violent and dangerous. We know that punishment doesn't work.

We know all about intergenerational themes and intergenerational trauma such as addictions, domestic violence, sexual assault, and even staying on government welfare. We know that intergenerational abuse of any kind interferes with not only the natural progression of individuals' personality development but also the mental health and development of communities and nations.

We have knowledge from not only holy books but also anecdotes, testimonials, and empirical data that prove the power of forgiveness and its healing abilities for persons who have been wronged. We also know that an apology is not necessary for the healing of the wronged person. But we do know that it is essential for reconciliation.

So the mental health field, armed with all this knowledge, and trained to know how important apologies and forgiveness are to healing and reconciliation, has not seriously examined its own role in healing the historical abuses and injustices against women and people of color. We have kept our hands clean even as African American men (in churches and temples) began apologizing to Black women for their role in the historical abuse that Black women suffered at their hands. We mental health professionals sat silent even when the legislatures of Alabama, New Jersey, Maryland, New York, North Carolina, and Virginia issued public apologies for slavery.

Forgiveness does not depend on the response of the offender. Slavery is over, and the Indian holocaust is over (though not the residual effects). The slave owners and Indian killers may not be alive, and people of color may be able to let go of feelings of revenge, punishment, and harm and become healthy. But what happens when the healer is the culprit?

Alternatively, according to Orathinkal, Vansteenwegen, and Burggraeve (2008), reconciliation depends on the response of the offender owning the offense. If the offender is willing to admit and own the offense, and communicate sorrow and repentance, then the offended can begin the difficult work of letting go of the desire for revenge, punishment, and harm to the offender. Reconciliation can begin.

Thus, in the name of social justice and all that is right for healing, reconciling, and mercy, I ask the question, "What is needed to engender hope and transform counseling to meet the needs of people of color?" I feel what is needed to begin the transformation process is both radical and revolutionary. A bit radical, but I believe that a public apology is a first, important step in that direction.

Radical as this may sound, let the healing begin with us, those of us in the mental health field. This means that in a public forum, each of the mental health disciplines (psychology, psychiatry, social work, and counseling) should first acknowledge its own offenses against people of color. And then the mental health associations should offer a public apology, just as the leaders of the American Medical Association made a public apology to Black doctors to formally acknowledge that the group's discriminatory practices may have contributed to the disparities in the U.S. health care system. All over the world, countries, states, and association are making public apologies for historical abuses. For example, the U.S. Senate and House of Representatives issued apologies for slavery and for the Jim Crow laws; the prime minister of Australia apologized to the orphans and child migrants abused in Australia; and, as mentioned, the states of Alabama, New Jersey, Maryland, New York, North Carolina, and Virginia issued a public apology for slavery.

Reconciliation begins with admitting a wrongdoing, coming clean. Therefore, the mental health field owes women and people of color a public apology for the historical abuse, sexism, racism, negligence, and exploitation (including misdiagnosis and unethical behavior) they suffered at the hands of mental health professionals.

Although forgiveness is necessary for the internal healing of communities of color, an apology can facilitate the racial healing and reconciliation of our society. It can also become a catalyst for the difficult process of repairing a trust relationship and restoring the trust of people of color in the mental health system. Perhaps it may even help groups of color confront the ghosts of their collective pasts together. At least, it's worth a try.

Now, here is the revolutionary part: Perhaps the mental health field could consider atonement, that is, retribution and reparations for the historical abuse of women and people of color in counseling. Thus, ethically, I believe that there is a moral responsibility to make amends. One possibility is to compensate the people and the descendants of those individuals who were victimized and harmed by mental health services. The issuance of an apology and reparations from the mental health field to women and people of color would indeed be, as said in Black church devotionals, "*In divine and decent order.*"

References

Akbar, N. (1979). African roots of Black personality. In W. Smith, K. Burlew, M. Mosley, & W. Whitney (Eds.), *Reflections on Black psychology* (pp. 79–87). Washington, DC: University Press of America.

Akbar, N. (1991). *Visions for Black men*. Nashville, TN: Winston-Derek.

Alford, K. (2003). Cultural themes in rites of passage: Voices of young African American males. *Journal of African American Studies, 7*(1), 3–26.

Allen, P. G. (1986). *The sacred hoop: Recovering the feminine in American Indian traditions*. Boston: Beacon Press.

American Counseling Association. (2005). *Code of ethics*. Retrieved from http://www.counseling.org

American Psychiatric Association. (1994). *Diagnostic and statistical manual of mental disorders* (4th ed.). Washington, DC: Author.

Aquino, K., Grover, S., Goldman, B., & Folger, R. (2003). When push doesn't come to shove: Interpersonal forgiveness in workplace relationships. *Journal of Management Inquiry, 12*(3), 209–216.

Arbona, C., Flores, C. L., & Novy, D. M. (1995). Cultural awareness and ethnic loyalty: Dimensions of cultural variability among Mexican American college students. *Journal of Counseling and Development, 7*, 610–614.

Arzubiaga, A. E., Artiles, A. J., King, K. A., & Harris-Murri, N. (2008). Beyond research on cultural minorities: Challenges and implications of research as situated cultural practice. *Exceptional Children, 74*(3), 309–327.

Asante, M. K. (2003). *Afrocentricity* (Rev. ed.). Trenton, NJ: Africa World Press.

Atkinson, D. R., Furlong, M. J., & Poston, W. C. (1986). Afro-American preferences for counselor characteristics. *Journal of Counseling Psychology, 33*, 326–330.

Atkinson, D. R., Morten, G., & Sue, D. W. (2003). *Counseling American minorities* (6th ed.). Dubuque, IA: William C. Brown.

Axelson, J. A. (1993). *Counseling and development in a multicultural society* (2nd ed.). Monterey, CA: Brooks/Cole.

Barham, L. S. (2001). Central Africa and the emergence of regional identity in the Middle Pleistocene. In L. S. Barham & K. Robson-Brown (Eds.), *Human roots: Africa and Asia in the Middle Pleistocene* (pp. 65–80). Bristol, UK: Western Academic & Specialist Press.

Baumgardner, R., & Richards, A. (2000). *Manifesta: Young women, feminism, and the future*. New York: Farrar, Straus and Giroux.

Bell, Y., Bouie, C., & Baldwin, J. (1990). Afrocentric cultural consciousness and African American male–female relationships. *Journal of Black Studies, 21*(2), 213–218.

Bem, S. L. (1974). The measurement of psychological androgyny. *Journal of Consulting and Clinical Psychology, 42*, 155–162.

Berkman, L. F., Berkman, C. S., Kasl, S., Freeman, D. H., Jr., Leo, L., Ostfeld, A. M., Cornoni-Huntley, J., & Brody, J. A. (1986). Depressive symptoms in relation to physical health and functioning in the elderly. *American Journal of Epidemiology, 124*, 372–388.

Bhungalia, L. (2001, Spring). *Native American women and violence*. National Organization for Women. Retrieved from http://www.now.org/nnt/spring-2001/nativeamerican.html

Bickerton, D. (2003). Symbol and structure: A comprehensive framework for language evolution. In M. H. Christiansen & S. Kirby (Eds.), *Language evolution* (pp. 77–93). Oxford: Oxford University Press.

Billingsley, A. (1968). *Black families in White America*. Englewood Cliffs, NJ: Prentice Hall.

Billingsley, A. (1993). *Climbing Jacob's ladder: The enduring legacy of African American families*. New York: Simon & Schuster.

Blue, R., & Naden, C. (1992). *Barbara Jordan: Politician (Black Americans of achievement)*. Hillside NJ: Chelsea House.

Boerwinkle, E., Schork, N. J., & Risch, N. J. (2005). Genetic structure, self-identified race ethnicity, and confounding in case-control association studies. *American Journal of Human Genetics, 76*, 268–275.

Bowie, J. V., Juon, H., Rodriguez, E. M., & Cho, J. (2007). Factors associated with over weight and obesity among Mexican Americans and Central Americans: Results from the 2001 California health interview survey. *Prevention of Chronic Disease, 4*, A10.

Branton, R. (2007). Latino attitudes toward various areas of public policy: The importance of acculturation. *Political Research Quarterly, 60*, 293–303.

Brayboy, B. M. (2006). Toward a tribal critical race theory in education. *Urban Review, 37*(5), 425–446.

Brooks, G. R., & Good, G. E. (2001). Introduction. In G. R. Brooks & G. E. Good (Eds.), *The new handbook of psychotherapy and counseling with men* (Vol. 1, pp. 3–21). San Francisco: Jossey-Bass.

Brown, C., Abe-Kim, J. S., & Barrio, C. (2003). Depression in ethnically diverse women: Implications for treatment in primary care settings. *Professional Psychology: Research and Practice, 34*, 10–19.

Brown, D. R., & Gary, L. E. (1985). Predictors of depressive symptoms among unemployed Black adults. *Journal of Sociology and Social Welfare, 12*(4), 736–754.

Brown, T. N. (2008). Race, racism, and mental health: Elaboration of critical race theory's contribution to the sociology of mental health. *Contemporary Justice Review, 11*, 53–62.

Bryson, S., & Cody, J. (1973). Relationship of race and level of understanding between counselor and client. *Journal of Counseling Psychology, 20*(6), 495–498.

Bureau of Justice Statistics. (2003). *The sourcebook of criminal justice statistics*. Washington, DC: Author.

Burrell, L., & Rayder, N. F. (1971). Black and White students' attitudes toward White counselors. *Journal of Negro Education, 40*, 48–52.

Butterfield, F. (2002, August 28). Study finds big increase in Black men as inmates since 1980. *New York Times, 151*, p. A14.

Cabezas, A. Y., & Kawaguchi, G. (1988). Empirical evidence for continuing Asian American income inequality: The human capital model and labor market segmentation. In G. Y. Okihiro, S. Hune, A. A. Hansen, & J. M. Liu (Eds.), *Reflections on shattered windows: Promises and prospects for Asian American studies* (pp. 144–164). Pullman: Washington State University Press.

Caldwell, L. D., & White, J. L. (2001). African-centered therapeutic and counseling interventions for African American males. In G. R. Brooks & G. E. Good (Eds.), *The new handbook of psychotherapy and counseling with men: A comprehensive guide to settings, problems, and treatment approaches* (pp. 737–753). San Francisco: Jossey-Bass.

Campbell, J. (2004). Helping women understand their risk in situations of intimate partner violence. *Journal of Interpersonal Violence, 19*(12), 1464–1477.

Carnes, J. (1995). *Us and them: A history of intolerance in America*. Montgomery, AL: Southern Poverty Law Center.

Cattaneo, L., & Goodman, L. (2005). Risk factors for reabuse in intimate partner violence: A cross-disciplinary critical review. *Trauma, Violence & Abuse, 6*(2), 141–175.

Centers for Disease Control and Prevention (2005). *HIV/AIDS Surveillance Report, 2004, 16*, 1–46. Atlanta: U.S. Department of Health and Human Services.

Chan, S. (1989). Beyond the affirmative action: Empowering Asian American faculty. *Change, 21*(6), 48–51.

Chapleski, E. E., Lichtenberg, P. A., Dwyer, J. W., Youngblade, L. M., & Tsai, P. F. (1997). Morbidity and comorbidity among Great Lakes American Indians: Predictors of functional ability. *Gerontologist, 37,* 588–597.

Chase, P. G., & Dibble, H. L. (1990). On the emergence of modern humans. *Current Anthropology, 31*(1), 58–59.

Chatters, L., Taylor, R. J., & Neighbors, H. W. (1989). Size of informal helper network mobilized during a serious personal problem among Black Americans. *Journal of Marriage and the Family, 51*(3), 667–676.

Chen, P., & White, H. (2004). Gender differences in adolescent and young adult predictors of later intimate partner violence. *Violence Against Women, 10*(11), 1283–1301.

Cimbolic, P. (1972). Counselor race and experience effects on Black clients. *Journal of Consulting and Clinical Psychology, 39,* 228–332.

Claudio, E. (1998). Hispanic Americans and philanthropy. *National Society of Fund Raising Executives Journal, 23*(2), 14–16.

Coates, D. L. (1987). Gender differences in the structure and support characteristics of Black adolescents' social network. *Sex Roles, 17*(11/12), 667–687.

Constantine, M. G. (2001). Predictors of observer ratings of multicultural counseling competencies in Black, Latino, and White American trainees. *Journal of Counseling Psychology, 48,* 456–462.

Cooke, M., & Kipnis, D. (1986). Influence tactics in psychotherapy. *Journal of Consulting and Clinical Psychology, 54,* 22–26.

Correa-de-Araujo, R. (2004). A wake-up call to advance women's health. *Women's Health Issues, 14,* 31–34.

Coyle, C.T., & Enright, R.D. (1997). Forgiveness intervention with postabortion men. *Journal of Consulting and Clinical Psychology, 65,* 1042–1046.

Cross, W. E. (1987). A two-factor theory of Black identity: Implications for the study of identity development in minority children. In J. S. Phinney & M. J. Rotherman (Eds.), *Children's ethnic socialization: Pluralism and development* (pp. 312–333). New York: Jossey-Bass.

Cross, W. E. (1991). *Shades of black: Diversity in African American identity*. Philadelphia: Temple University Press.

Crow Dog, M., & Erdoes, R. (1990). *Lakota woman*. New York: Feminist Press.

Curyto, K. J., Chapleski, E. E., Lichtenberg, P. A., Hodges, E., Kaczynski, R., & Sobeck, J. (1998). Prevalence and prediction of depression in American Indian elderly. *Clinical Gerontologist, 18,* 19–37.

D'Andrea, M., & Daniels, J. (1997, April). *The promises and challenges of multicultural supervision*. Paper presented at the World Convention American Counseling Association, Orlando, FL.

D'Andrea, M., & Heckman, E. F. (2008). A 40-year review of multicultural counseling outcome research: Outlining a future research agenda for the multicultural counseling movement. *Journal of Counseling and Development, 86,* 383–384.

Das, A. K. (1995). Rethinking multicultural counseling: Implications for counselor education. *Journal of Counseling and Development, 74,* 49–51.

Davis, A. (2000). The color of violence against women. Keynote address at the Color of Violence conference in Santa Cruz. *Colorlines, 3*(3). Retrieved from http://www.hartford-hwp.com/archives/45a/582.html

Dews, E. (1995). *This fine place so far from home: Voices of academics from the working class*. Philadelphia: Temple University Press.

Dornin, R., Mattingly, D., Phelan, M., & Walsh, S. (2006). *Suspect: Church fires started as "joke": Three Birmingham college students arrested, charged*. CNN Law Center. Retrieved from http://www.cnn.com/2006/LAW/03/08/alabama.churches/index.html

DuBois, W. E. B. (1996). *The souls of Black folk*. New York: Penguin. (Original work published in 1903)

Edwards, J. R., Jr. (2001). *Public charge doctrine: A fundamental principle of American immigration policy*. Washington, DC: Center for Immigration Studies.

Eisner, E. (1991). *The enlightened eye: Qualitative inquiry and the enhancement of educational practice*. New York: Macmillan.

Evans-Campbell, T. (2008). Historical trauma in American Indian/Native Alaska communities: A multilevel framework for exploring impacts on individuals, families, and communities. *Journal of Interpersonal Violence, 23*, 316–338.

Evans-Campbell, T., & Walters, K. L. (2006). Indigenist practice competencies in child welfare practice: A decolonization framework to address family violence and substance abuse among First Nations peoples. In R. Fong, R. McRoy, & C. Ortiz Hendricks (Eds.), *Intersecting child welfare, substance abuse, and family violence: Culturally competent approaches* (pp. 266–290). Washington, DC: Council on Social Work Education Press.

Fagundes, N. J. R., Ray, N., Beaumont, M., Neuenschwander, S., Salzano, F. M., Bonatto, S. L., et al. (2007). Statistical evaluation of alternative models of human evolution. *Proceedings of the National Academy of Sciences of the USA, 104*, 17614–17619.

Faludi, S. (1991). *Backlash: The undeclared war against American women*. New York: Crown.

Field, C. A., & Caetano, R. (2003). Longitudinal model predicting partner violence among White, Black, and Hispanic couples in the United States. *Alcoholism: Clinical and Experimental Research, 27*(9), 1451–1458.

Fong, M. L., & Borders, L. D. (1985). Effect of sex role orientation and gender on counseling skills training. *Journal of Counseling Psychology, 32*, 104–110.

Friedsam, D., Haug, G., & Rust, M. (2003). Tribal benefits counseling program: Expanding health care opportunities for tribal members. *American Journal of Public Health, 93*(10), 1634–1636.

Gandhi, M. (n.d.). BrainyQuote.com. Retrieved October 27, 2010, from BrainyQuote. com Web site. http://www.brainyquote.com/quotes/quotes/m/mohandasga130962.html

Garrett, M. T. (1995). Between two worlds: Cultural discontinuity in the dropout of Native American youth. *The School Counselor, 42*(3), 186–195.

Garrett, M. W., & Myers, J. E. (1996). The rule of opposites: A paradigm for counseling Native American Indians. *Journal of Multicultural Counseling and Development, 24*, 89–104.

Glodava, M. & Onizuka, R. (1994). *Mail-order brides: Women for Sale*. Fort Collins, Colorado: Alaken, Inc.

Goel, M. S., McCarty, E. P., Phillips, R. S., & Wee, C. C. (2004). Obesity among U.S. immigrant subgroups by duration of residence. *Journal of the American Medical Association, 292*, 2860–2867.

Gould, S. J. (1981). *The mismeasure of man*. New York: Norton.

Grady, D., Chaput, L., & Kristof, M. (2003). Diagnosis and treatment of coronary heart disease in women: Systematic reviews of evidence on selected topics: Summary (Evidence Report Technology Assessment 81, AHRQ Publication No. 03-0037). Rockville, MD: Agency for Healthcare Research and Quality.

Graff, G. (1992). *Beyond the culture wars: How teaching the conflicts can revitalize American education*. New York: Norton.

Greeley, A. T., Garcia, V. L., Kessler, B. L., & Gilchrest, G. (1992). Training effective multicultural group counselors: Issues for a group training course. *The Journal for Specialists in Group Work, 17*(4), 196–209.

Grier, W. H., & Cobbs, P. M. (1968). *Black rage*. New York: Basic.

Grine, F. E., Bailey, R. M., Harvati, K., Nathan, R. P., Morris, A. G., Henderson, G. M., et al. (2007). Late Pleistocene human skull from Hofmeyr, South Africa and modern human origins. *Science, 315*, 226–229.

Guralnik, D. B. (Ed.). (1976). *Webster's new world dictionary* (2nd ed.). New York: Simon & Schuster.

Gwynn, R. C., McQuistion, H. L., McVeigh, K. H., Garg, R. K., Frieden, T. R., & Thorpe, L. E. (2008). Prevalence, diagnosis, and treatment of depression and generalized anxiety disorder in a diverse urban community. *Psychiatric Services*, 59(6), 641–647.

Hall, G. C. N., Teten, A. L., DeGarmo, D. S., Sue, S., & Stephens, K. A. (2005). Ethnicity, culture, and sexual aggression: Risk and protective factors. *Journal of Consulting and Clinical Psychology*, 73, 830–840.

Harper, F. D. (1994). Afrinesians of the Americas: A new concept of ethnic identity. *Journal of Multicultural Counseling and Development*, 22, 3–6.

Heckler M. M. (1985). *Report of the secretary's task force on Black and minority health*. Washington: U.S. Department of Health and Human Services.

Heilbrun, A. B. (1986). Androgyny as type and androgyny as behavior: Implications for gender schema in males and females. *Social Roles, 14*, 123–139.

Heinrich, R. K., Corbin, J. L., & Thomas, K. R. (1990). Counseling Native Americans. *Journal of Counseling and Development*, 69, 128–133.

Helms, J. E. (1984). Toward a theoretical explanation of the effects of race on counseling: A Black and White model. *The Counseling Psychologist, 12*, 153–164.

Helms, J. E. (Ed.). (1990). *Black and White racial identity: Theory, research, and practice*. New York: Greenwood Press.

Helms, J. E. (1995). An update of Helms's White and people of color racial identity models. In J.G. Ponterotto, J. M. Casas, L. A. Suzuki, & C. M. Alexander (Eds.), *Handbook of multicultural counseling* (pp. 181–198). Thousand Oaks, CA: Sage.

Heppner, P. P., & Heppner, M. J. (2008). The gender role conflict literature: Fruits of sustained commitment. *Counseling Psychologist*, 36, 455–461.

Herring, R. D. (1996). Synergetic counseling and Native American Indian students. *Journal of Counseling and Development*, 74, 542–547.

Herrnstein, R., & Murray, C. (1994). *The bell curve*. New York: Free Press.

Hickson, J., & Mokhobo, D. (1992). Combating AIDS in Africa: Cultural barriers to effective prevention and treatment. *Journal of Multicultural Counseling*, 20, 11, 22.

Hilliard, A. G. (1976). *Alternatives to IQ testing: An approach to the identification of gifted "minority" children* (Report No. PS 009 639, ERIC Document Reproduction Service No. ED 147 009). Sacramento: California Department of Education, Special Education Division.

Hindin, M., & Adair, L. (2002). Who's at risk? Factors associated with intimate partner violence in the Philippines. *Social Science & Medicine*, 55(8), 1385–1399.

Hoch, P. (1979). *White hero, Black beast: Racism, sexism, and the mask of masculinity*. London: Pluto.

Hodgin, D. (1991). "Mail-order" brides marry pain to get green cards. *Washington Times*, (April 16): E1.

hooks, b. (1989). *Talking back: Thinking feminist, thinking Black*. Boston: South End Press.

hooks, b. (1991). *Rock my soul: Black people and self-esteem*. Boston, MA: South End Press.

Horsman, R. (1999). The origins of Oneida removal to Wisconsin, 1815–1822. In L. M. Hauptman & L. G. McLester III (Eds.), *The Oneida Indian journey*. Madison: University of Wisconsin Press.

Huff, R. M., & Kline, M. (1999). *Promoting health in multicultural populations: A handbook for practitioners*. Thousand Oaks, CA: Sage.

Hunter, A. G., & Davis, J. E. (1992). Constructing gender: An exploration of Afro-American men's conceptualization of manhood. *Gender and Society*, 6(3), 464–479.

Idowu, A. I. (1992). The Oshun festival: An African traditional religious healing process. *Counseling and Values*, 36, 192–200.

Indian Child Welfare Act (ICWA). (1978). 25 U.S.C. §§ 1901–1963.

Institute of Medicine (2002). *Unequal treatment: Confronting racial and ethical disparities in health care.* Washington, DC: National Academies Press.

Institute of Medicine (2004). *Insuring America's health: Principles and recommendations.* Washington: National Academies Press.

Irwin, J., Schiraldi, V., & Ziedenberg, J. (2000). America's one million nonviolent prisoners. *Social Justice, 27,* 135–147.

Ivey, A. E., Ivey, M. B., & Simek-Morgan, L. (1993). *Counseling and psychotherapy: A multicultural perspective* (3rd ed.). Boston: Allyn & Bacon.

Jackson, G. C., & Kirschner, S. A. (1973). Racial self-designation and preference for a counselor. *Journal of Counseling Psychology, 20,* (6), 560–564.

Jackson, J. J. (1981). *But where are the men? The Black scholar,* 30 et passim.

Jasinski, J. L., & Dietz, T. L. (2004). Domestic violence and stalking among older adults: An assessment of risk markers. *Journal of Elder Abuse and Neglect, 15*(1), 3–18.

Johnson, C. R. (1990). *Middle passages.* New York: Atheneum.

Joshi, K. Y. (2006). *New roots in America's sacred ground: Religion, race, and ethnicity in Indian America.* Piscataway, NJ: Rutgers University Press.

Jost, J. T., Pelham, B. W., Sheldon, O., & Sullivan, B. N. (2003). Social inequality and the reduction of ideological dissonance on behalf of the system: Evidence of enhanced system justification among the disadvantaged. *European Journal of Social Psychology, 33,* 13–36.

Kakar, S. (1982). *Shamans, mystics, and doctors: A psychological inquiry into India and healing traditions.* New York: Knopf.

Katz, W. L. (1986). *Black Indians: A hidden heritage.* New York: Athenaeum.

King, M. L. (1964). Dr. Martin Luther King, Jr.: The quest for peace and justice. Nobelprize. org. Retrieved from http://nobelprize.org/nobel_prizes/peace/laureates/1964/king-lecture.html

King, M. L. (1968). *Dr. Martin Luther King, Jr.: I have a dream.* In *Annals of America* (Vol. 18, p. 156). Chicago: Encyclopedia Britannica.

Kluckhohn C., & Kroeberg A. L. (1952). *Culture: A critical review of concepts and definitions.* New York: Vintage.

Kochhar, R. (2006). *Latino labor report 2006: Strong gains in employment.* Washington, DC: Pew Hispanic Center. Retrieved October 20, 2008, from http://pewhispanic.org/files/reports/70.pdf.

Kogawa, J. (1981). *Obasan.* Toronto: Penguin.

Kogawa, J. (1994). *Obasan.* New York: Anchor.

Koo, G. (2001). Asian American ticket to the American dream. *Chinese American Forum, 16*(3), 23–26.

Kramer, B. J. (1991). Education and American Indians: The experience of the Ute Indian tribe. In M. A. Gibson & J. U. Ogbu (Eds.), *Minority status and schooling: A comparative study of immigrant and involuntary minorities* (pp. 287–308). New York: Garland Publishing.

Ku, L., & Matani, S. (2001). Left out: Immigrants' access to health care and insurance. *Health Affairs, 20,* 247–256.

Kunjufu, J. (1982). *Countering the conspiracy to destroy Black boys* (Vol. 1). Chicago: Afro-American.

Kunjufu, J. (1985). *Countering the conspiracy to destroy Black boys* (Vol. 2). Chicago: African American Images.

Kunjufu, J. (1987). *Countering the conspiracy to destroy Black boys* (Vol. 3). Chicago: African American Images.

Lambert, M. (2007). Gunpowder and lead. On Crazy ex-girlfriend [CD]. Sony Records.

Lazur, R. F., & Majors, R. (1995). Men of color: Ethnocultural variations of male gender role strain. In R. F. Levant & W. S. Pollack (Eds.), *A new psychology of men* (pp. 337–358). New York: Basic.

Lee, H. (1960). *To kill a mockingbird*. Philadelphia: Lippincott.

Lee, I. & Kelly, E. W. (1996). Individualistic and collective group counseling: Effects with Korean clients. *Journal of Multicultural Counseling and Development, 24,* 254–266.

Lee, S. M. (1998). Asian Americans: Diverse and growing. *Population Bulletin, 53*(2). Retrieved from www.prb.org/source/53.2asianamerican.pdf

Lee, Y-T., Vue, S., Seklecki, R., & Ma, Y. (2007). How did Asian Americans respond to negative stereotypes and hate crimes? *American Behavioral Scientist, 51*(2), 271–293.

Legends of America. (2003–2010). *Native American legends: Great words from great Americans*. Retrieved from http://www.legendsofamerica.com/na-quotes.html

Legters, L. (1988). The American genocide. *Policy Studies Journal, 16*(4), 768–777.

Lerner, G. (Ed.). (1972). *Black women in White America*. New York: Vintage.

Levy, J. E., & Ross, F., Jr. (2007). *Cesar Chavez: Autobiography of La Causa*. Minneapolis, MN: University of Minnesota Press.

Liang, C. T. H., Alvarez, A. N., Juan, L. P., & Liang, M. X. (2007). The role of coping in the relationship between perceived racism and racism-related stress for Asian Americans: Gender differences. *Journal of Counseling Psychology, 54,* 132–141.

Lin, K. M. (1983). Hwa-byung: A Korean culture-bound syndrome? *American Journal of Psychiatry, 140,* 105–107.

Long, J. C., & Kittles, R. A. (2003). Human genetic variation and the nonexistence of human races. *Human Biology, 75*(4), 449–471. Retrieved from http://muse.jhu.edu/journals/human_biology/v075/75.4long.pdf

Makinde, O. (1974). The indigenous Yoruba Babalawo model: Implications for counseling in West Africa. *West African Journal of Education, 18,* 319–327.

Manica, A., Amos, W., Balloux, F., & Hanihara, T. (2007). The effect of ancient population bottlenecks on human phenotypic variation. *Nature, 448*(7151), 346–348.

Mannix, D. P., & Cowley, M. (1962). *Black cargoes: A history of the Atlantic slave trade, 1518–1865*. New York: Viking Press.

Manso, S. M. (1992). In C. Barresi & D. E. Stull (Eds.), *Ethnicity and long-term care* (pp. 130–143). New York: Springer.

Manson, S. M., Ackerson, L. M., Dick, R. W., Baron, A. E., & Fleming, C. M. (1990). Depressive symptoms among American Indian adolescents: Psychometric characteristics on the Center for Epidemiologic Studies Depression Scale (CES-D). *Psychological Assessment, 2,* 231–237.

Manson, S. M., Shore, J. H., & Bloom, J. D. (1985). In A. Kleinman & B. Good (Eds.), *Culture and depression* (pp. 331–368). Berkeley, CA: University of California Press.

Marbley, A. F. (2005). African American women's feelings of alienation from third-wave feminism: A conversation with my sisters. *Western Journal of Black Studies, 29,* 605–614.

McAdoo, H. (1981). Factors to stability in upward mobile black families. In H. McAdoo (Ed.). *Black families*. Beverly Hills, CA: Harper and Row Press.

McAdoo, H. P. (2002). *Black children: Social, educational, and parental environments* (2nd ed.). Thousand Oaks, CA: Sage.

McBrearty, S., & Brooks, A. S. (2000). The revolution that wasn't: A new interpretation of the origin of modern human behavior. *Journal of Human Evolution, 39,* 453–563.

McDougall, I., Brown, F. H., & Fleagle, J. G. (2005). Stratigraphic placement and age of modern humans from Kibish, Ethiopia. *Nature, 433,* 733–736.

McGill, D. W. (1992). The cultural story in multicultural family therapy: Families in society. *The Journal of Contemporary Human Services, 73*(6), 339–349.

McWhirter, E. H. (1994). *Counseling for empowerment*. Alexandria, VA: American Counseling Association Press.

Medicine. (2001). *Crossing the quality chasm: A health system for the 21st century*. Washington, DC: National Academy Press.

Mindell, R., de Haymes, M. V., & Francisco, D. (2003). A culturally responsive practice model for urban Indian child welfare services. *Child Welfare Journal, 82*(2), 201–217.

Mio, J. S., & Iwamasa, G. (1993). To do or not to do: That is the question for White cross-cultural researchers. *Counseling Psychologist, 21*, 197–212.

Narayan, U. (1995). Male-order brides: Immigrant women, domestic violence, and immigration law. *Hypatia, 10*:1 (Winter): 104–120.

National Association of Latino Elected & Appointed Officials (NALEO), Community Investment Network. Retrieved from http://www.communityinvestmentnetwork.org/nc/single-news-item-states/article/national-association-of-latino-elected-appointed-officials-naleo/?tx_ttnews%5BbackPid%5D=1242&cHash=b312bc4e71

National Institute of Mental Health. (1995). *Mental illness in America: The national institute of mental health agenda*. Rockville, MD: Author.

Native Hawaiian Government Act, H.R. 2314, 111th Cong. (2009).

Nelson, M. L., & Holloway, E. L. (1990). Relation of gender to power and involvement in supervision. *Journal of Counseling Psychology, 37*, 473–481.

Nixon, S. J., Kayo, R., Jones-Saumty, D., Philips, M., & Tivis, R. (2007). Strength modeling: The role of data in defining needs and response for American Indian substance users. *Substance Use & Misuse, 42*, 693–704.

No Child Left Behind Act. (2001). 20 U.S.C. § 6301.

Nunez, A. E., & Robertson, C. (2003). Multicultural considerations in women's health. *Medical Clinics of North America, 87*(5), 939–954.

Orathinkal, J., Vansteenwegen, A., & Burggraeve, R. (2008). Are demographics important for forgiveness? *The Family Journal, 16*, 20–27.

Parham, T. A. (1993). To do or not to do: White researchers conducting multicultural counseling research: Can their efforts be "mo better"? *Counseling Psychologist, 21*, 250–256.

Parham, T. A. (2002). *Counseling persons of African descent: Raising the bar of practitioners' competence*. Thousand Oaks, CA: Sage.

Parham, T. A., & Caldwell, L. (2006). Dual relationships revisited: An African centered perspective. In B. Herlihy & G. Corey (Eds.), *Boundary issues in counseling: Multiple roles and relationships* (2nd ed.). Alexandria, VA: American Counseling Association Press.

Parham, T. A., & Helms, J. E. (1981). The influence of Black students' racial identity attitudes on preferences for counselor's race. *Journal of Counseling Psychology, 28*, 250–257.

Parham, T. A., & McDavis, R. J. (1983). Black men, an endangered species: Who's really pulling the trigger? *Journal of Counseling and Development, 66*, 24–27.

Parham, T. A., White, J., & Ajamu, A. (2000). *The psychology of Blacks: An African centered perspective*. Upper Saddle River, NJ: Prentice Hall.

Patton, M. Q. (1990). *Qualitative evaluation and research methods*. Newbury Park, CA: Sage.

Patton, M. Q. (2002). *Qualitative evaluation and research methods* (2nd ed.). Thousand Oaks, CA: Sage.

Pedersen, P. (1988). *A handbook for developing multicultural awareness*. Alexandria, VA: American Association for Counseling and Development.

Pedersen, P. (1990). The multicultural perspective as a fourth force in counseling. *Journal of Mental Health Counseling, 12*, 93–95.

Pedersen, P. (1991). Multiculturalism as a generic approach to counseling: *Journal of Counseling and Development, 70*, 6–12.

Pedersen, P. (1997). *Culture-centered counseling interventions: Striving for accuracy.* Thousand Oaks, CA: Sage.

Pilling, A. R. (1997). Various kinds of two-spirit people: Gender variance and homosexuality in Native American communities. In S. Jacobs, W. Thomas, & S. Lang (Eds.), *Two-spirit people: Native American gender identity, sexuality, and spirituality.* Chicago: University of Chicago Press.

Pollack, W. S., & Levant, R. F. (Eds.). (1998). *New psychotherapy for men.* New York: Wiley.

Ponterotto, J. G., Casas, J. M., Suzuki, L. A., & Alexander, C. M. (2010). *Handbook of multicultural counseling* (3rd ed.). Thousand Oaks, CA: Sage.

Population Reference Bureau. (1999). America's racial and ethnic minorities. *Population Bulletin, 54*(3). Retrieved from http://www.prb.org/Source/54.3AmerRacialEthnicMinor.pdf

Poston, W. S. C., Craine, M., & Atkinson, D. R. (1991). Counselor dissimilarity confrontation, client cultural mistrust, and willingness to self-disclose. *Journal of Multicultural Counseling and Development, 19,* 65–73.

Ramirez, R.L. (1993). *What it means to be a man: Reflections on Puerto Rican masculinity.* New Jersey: Rutgers University Press.

Random House unabridged dictionary (2nd ed.). (1993). New York: Random House.

Rogers, M. R., & Molina, L. (2006). Exemplary efforts in psychology to recruit and retain graduate students of color. *American Psychologist, 61,* 143–156.

Rogler, L. H., Malgady, R. G., & Rodriguez, O. (1989). *Hispanics and mental health: A framework for research.* Malabar, FL: Krieger.

Rollock, D. A., Westman, J. S., & Johnson, C. (1992). A Black student support group on a predominantly White university campus: Issues for counselors and therapists. *The Journal for Specialists in Group Work, 17*(4), 243–252.

Rose, C. (Executive Producer). (2008, March 21). *The Charlie Rose show* [Television broadcast]. New York: Public Broadcasting System.

Rosenberg, N. A., Pritchard, J. K., Weber, J. L., Cann, H. M., & Kidd, K. K. (2002). Genetic structure of human populations. *Science, 298,* 2381–2385.

Rubin, H. J., & Rubin, I. S. (1995). *Qualitative interviewing: The art of hearing data.* Thousand Oaks, CA: Sage.

Sandhu, D. S., & Brown, S. P. (1996). Empowering ethnically and racially diverse clients through prejudice reduction: Suggestions and strategies for counselors. *Journal of Multicultural Counseling and Development, 24,* 202–217.

Scheurich, J. J., & Young, M. D. (1997). Coloring epistemologies: Are our research epistemologies racially biased? *Educational Researcher, 26,* 4–16.

Sedlacek, W. E. (1994). Issues in advancing diversity through assessment. *Journal of Counseling and Development, 72,* 549–553.

Seger, B., & the Silver Bullet Band. (1980). Against the wind. On *Against the wind* [CD]. Hollywood, CA: Capital Records.

Senier, S. (2003). *Voices of American Indian assimilation and resistance* (Red River Books ed.). Norman: University of Oklahoma Press.

Sodowsky, G. R., & Johnson, P. (1994). World views: Culturally learned assumptions and values. In *Multicultural counseling in the schools: A practical handbook* (pp. 59–79). Boston: Allyn & Bacon.

Solomon, R., & Solomon, J. (1993). *Up the university: Re-creating higher education in America.* Reading, MA: Addison-Wesley.

Somervell, P. D., Beals, J., Kinzie, J. D., Leung, P., Boehnlein, J., Matsunaga, D., & Manson, S. M. (1993). Use of the CES-D in an American Indian village. *Culture, Medicine and Psychiatry, 16,* 503–517.

Staples, R. (1984). Racial ideology and intellectual racism: Blacks in academia. *Black Scholar, 15*(2), 2–17.

Staples, R. (1994). *The Black family: Essays and studies* (5th ed.). Belmont, CA: Wadsworth.

Stranges, R. J., & Riccio, A. C. (1970). Counselee preferences for counselors: Some implications for counselor education. *Counselor Education and Supervision, 10*, 39–45.

Strauss, A., & Corbin, J. (1990). *Basics of qualitative research*. Newbury Park, CA: Sage.

Sue, D. (2007). Racial microaggressions in everyday life: Implications for clinical practice. *American Psychologist 62*, 271–286.

Sue, D. W., Arredondo, P., & McDavis, R. J. (1992). Multicultural counseling competencies and standards: A call to the profession. *Journal of Counseling and Development, 70*, 477–486.

Sue, D. W., Ivey, M. B., & Pedersen, P. B. (1996). *A theory of multicultural counseling and therapy*. Pacific Grove, CA: Brooks/Cole.

Sue, D. W., & Sue, D. (1990). *Counseling the culturally different: Theory and practice* (2nd ed.). New York: Wiley.

Sue, D. W., & Sue, D. (2007). *Counseling the culturally different: Theory and practice* (5th ed.). New York: Wiley.

Sue, S., & Zane, N. (1987). The role of culture and cultural techniques in psychotherapy: A critique and reformation. *American Psychologist, 42*(1), 37–45.

Sue, S., & Zane, N. (1990). Predictors of utilization intent of counseling among Chinese and White students: A test of the proximal-distal model. *Journal of Counseling Psychology, 42*(1), 37–45.

Suzuki, B. H. (2002). Revisiting the model minority stereotype: Implications for student affairs practice and higher education. In M. K. McEwen, C. M. Kodama, M. K. McEwen, A. N. Alvarez, S. Lee, & C. T. Liang (Eds.), *New directions for student services* (Vol. 97, pp. 21–32). San Francisco: Jossey-Bass.

Takao Ozawa v. United States, 260 U.S. 178 (1922).

Tang, J. (1993). The career attainment of Caucasian and Asian engineers. *The Sociological Quarterly, 34*(3), 467–496.

Thompson Sanders, V. L., Bazile, A., & Akbar, M. (2004). African Americans' perceptions of psychotherapy and psychotherapists. *Professional Psychology, Research and Practice, 35,*19–26.

Thornton, R. (1987). *American Indian holocaust and survival: A population history since 1492*. Norman, OK: University of Oklahoma Press.

Torres-Rivera, E., Phan, L. T., Garrett, M. T., & D'Andrea, M. (2005). Integrating Che Guevara, Don Pedro Albizú Campos, and Paulo Freire in the revolution of counseling: Re-visioning social justice when counseling Latino clients. *Radical Psychology Journal*. Retrieved from http://www.radpsynet.org/journal/vol4-1/che.html

Torres-Rivera, E., Wilbur, M. P., Phan, L. T., Maddux, C. D., & Roberts-Wilbur, J. (2004). Counseling Latinos with substance abuse problems. *Journal of Addictions and Offender Counseling, 25*, 26–42.

Tsai, J. L., Ying, Y., & Lee, P. A. (2001). Cultural predictors of self-esteem: A study of Chinese American female and male young adults. *Cultural Diversity & Ethnic Minority Psychology, 7*(3), 284.

Turner, W. H. (1977). Myths and stereotypes: The African man in America. In D. Wilkinson & R. Taylor (Eds.), *The Black male in America*. Chicago: Nelson-Hall.

Underhill, R. M. (1939). *Social organization of the Papago Indians*. New York: Columbia University Press.

United States v. Bhagat Singh Thind, 261 U.S. 204 (1923).

U.S. Bureau of Indian Affairs. (1988). *American Indians today*. Washington, DC: Author.

U.S. Census Bureau. (1990). *Census '90*. Retrieved from http://www.census.gov/main/www/cen1990.html

U.S. Census Bureau. (1992). *Population projections of the United States, by age, sex, race, and Hispanic origin: 1993–2050* (Series P25-1104). Washington, DC: Government Printing Office.

U.S. Census Bureau. (1996). *National survey of homeless assistance providers and clients.* Washington, DC: Government Printing Office.

U.S. Census Bureau. (2000a). *United States Census 2000.* Retrieved from http://www.census.gov/main/www/cen2000.html

U.S. Census Bureau. (2000b). *Projections of the resident population by race, Hispanic origin, and nativity: Middle series, 2001 to 2005.* Washington, DC: Government Printing Office.

U.S. Census Bureau. (2001a). *Profiles of general demographic characteristics: 2000 census of population and housing, United States.* Retrieved from http://www.census.gov/prod/cen2000/dp1/2kh00.pdf

U.S. Census Bureau. (2001b). *The Asian and Pacific Islander population in the United States: March 2000 (update)* (PPL-146). Retrieved from http://www.census.gov/population/www/socdemo/race/api.html

U.S. Census Bureau. (2002). *The American Indian and Alaska Native population: 2000* (Census 2000 Brief, C2KBR/01-15). Washington, DC: Government Printing Office.

U.S. Census Bureau. (2006). *Social and economic characteristics of the Hispanic population.* Retrieved from http://www.allcountries.org/uscensus/45_social_and_economic_characteristics_of_the.html

U.S. Census Bureau. (2008a). *Statistical abstract of the United States: The national data book, 2002.* Naperville, IL: Hoovers.

U.S. Census Bureau. (2008b). *Trends in the Black population: 2000–2050.* Retrieved 11/10/10 from http://www.census.gov/population/www/socdemo/race/Black-US.pdf.

U.S. Department of Health and Human Services (USDHHS). (1999). *Mental health: A report of the surgeon general.* Washington, DC: Government Printing Office.

U.S. Department of Health and Human Services (USDHHS). (2001). *Mental health: Culture, race, and ethnicity—a supplement to mental health: A report of the surgeon general.* Rockville, MD: Substance Abuse and Mental Health Services Administration, Center for Mental Health Services. Retrieved from http://www.surgeongeneral.gov/library/mentalhealth/cre/

Usher, C. H. (1989). Recognizing cultural bias in counseling theory and practice: The case of Rogers. *Journal of Multicultural Counseling and Development, 17,* 73–83.

Vasquez, H., & Magraw, S. (2005). Building relationships across privilege: Becoming an ally in the therapeutic relationship. In M. P. Mirkin, K. L. Suyemoto, & B. F. Okun (Eds.), *Psychotherapy with women: Exploring diverse contexts and identities* (pp. 64–83). New York: Guilford Press.

Vontress, C. E. (1988). An existential approach in cross-cultural counseling. *Journal of Multicultural Counseling and Development, 16,* 73–83.

Vontress, C. E. (1991). Traditional healing in Africa: Implications for cross-cultural counseling. *Journal of Counseling and Development, 70,* 242–249.

Wade, P., & Bernstein, B. L. (1991). Culture sensitivity training and counselor's race: Effects on Black female clients' perceptions and attrition. *Journal of Counseling Psychology, 38,* 9–15.

Watts, I. (2002). Ochre in the Middle Stone Age of southern Africa: Ritualized display or hide preservative? *South African Archaeological Bulletin, 57,* 64–74.

Weisman, C. S., & Henderson, J. T. (2001). Managed care and women's health: Access, preventive services, and satisfaction. *Women's Health Issues, 11*(3), 201–215.

White, T. D., Asfaw, B., Degusta, D., Gilbert, H., Richards, G. D., Suwa, G., et al. (2003). Pleistocene *Homo sapiens* from Middle Awash, Ethiopia. *Nature, 423,* 742–747.

Witherspoon, D. J., Wooding, S., Rogers, A. R., Marchani, E. E., Watkins, W. S., Batzer, M. A., et al. (2007). Genetic similarities within and between human populations. *Genetics, 176*(1), 351–359.

Witvliet, C. V. O., Ludwig, T. E., & van der Laan, K. L. (2001). Granting forgiveness or harboring grudges: Implications for emotion, physiology, and health. *Psychological Science, 121,* 117–123.

Wolma, B. B. (Ed.). (1989). *Dictionary of behavioral sciences* (2nd ed.). San Diego, CA: Academic Press.

Wurz, S., le Roux, N. J., Gardner, S., & Deacon, H. J. (2003). Discriminating between the end products of the earlier Middle Stone Age sub-stages at Klasies River using biplot methodology. *Journal of Archaeological Science, 30,* 1107–1126.

Yu, A., & Gregg, C. H. (1993). Asians in groups: More than a matter of cultural awareness. *The Journal for Specialists in Group Work, 18*(2), 86–92.

Yu, T. (2006). Challenging the politics of the "Model Minority" stereotype: A case of educational equality. *Equity and Excellence in Education, 39,* 325–333.

Zhang, W. (1994). American counseling in the mind of a Chinese counselor. *Journal of Multicultural Counseling and Development, 74,* 575–581.

Index